THE JAMES TAPES

TAPES

INTEGRATING FRAGMENTED PERSONALITIES

JOEL OSLER BRENDE

Cover Art by Patricia Chong

To my beloved wife, Jacqueline Jean Brende
February 4, 1941–August 9, 2022

Table of Contents

Forward i

Introduction vi

PART ONE – J 1

    Chapter 1 3

    Chapter 2 6

    Chapter 3 10

    Chapter 4 11

    Chapter 5 14

    Chapter 6 17

    Chapter 7 21

PART TWO – JAMES 27

    Chapter 8 29

    Chapter 9 39

    Chapter 10 44

    Chapter 11 51

    Chapter 12 55

    Chapter 13 57

    Chapter 14 59

PART THREE – James Returns 63

    Chapter 15 65

    Chapter 16 69

    Chapter 17 76

    Chapter 18 80

    Chapter 19 84

    Chapter 20 87

PART FOUR – James Kohl 91

    Chapter 21 93

    Chapter 22 97

    Chapter 23 102

Chapter 24 109

Chapter 25 113

PART FIVE – James: Full Patient Status.................117

Chapter 26 119

Chapter 27 123

Chapter 28 130

Chapter 29 133

PART SIX – James & LATOT 139

Chapter 30 141

Chapter 31 146

Chapter 32 150

Chapter 33 151

Chapter 34 155

Chapter 35 159

Chapter 36 162

Chapter 37 166

PART SEVEN – Jay & James 171

Chapter 38 173

Chapter 39 177

Chapter 40 183

Chapter 41 187

Chapter 42 190

Chapter 43 193

Chapter 44 198

Chapter 45 201

Chapter 46 205

Chapter 47 209

Chapter 48 212

Chapter 49 214

PART EIGHT – New & Transitional Personalities 217

Chapter 50 219

Chapter 51 224

Chapter 52 228

Chapter 53..230

Chapter 54..234

Chapter 55..241

Chapter 56..247

Chapter 57..253

Chapter 58..255

PART NINE – James Leaves the Hospital 259

Chapter 59..261

Chapter 60..263

Chapter 61..266

Chapter 62..269

Chapter 63..272

Chapter 64..274

PART TEN – Jay Returns 279

Chapter 65..281

Chapter 66..285

Chapter 67..289

Chapter 68..293

Chapter 69..298

Chapter 70..302

PART ELEVEN – Jay: A Caring Protector 305

Chapter 71..307

Chapter 72..310

Chapter 73..315

Chapter 74..318

Chapter 75..320

Chapter 76..324

Chapter 77..329

Chapter 78..332

Chapter 79..334

Chapter 80..337

Chapter 81..339

Chapter 82..344

ENDNOTES..346

Forward

The James Tapes, as portrayed in Book One, spans a two-year (1976-1978) period of clinical care for dissociative disorder. As described in Book One, James's treatment began in March 1975 after he presented with a two-week period of amnesia and was treated for symptoms of comorbid disorders of anxiety and depression, abdominal pain, nausea, and memory lapses. The assessment included identity depersonalization, persecution, "blackouts," child-like states, rape traumas, sister sexual involvement, parental abuse and maltreatment, resentment, and dissociative symptoms.

James Kohlman's continuing journey of psychotherapy in Book Two contains approximately 192 hours of therapy snippets based on Dr. Brende's videotaped sessions, which were a continuation of those found in Book One. James's illness journey started with his childhood trauma that created a survival mode involving a fear of abandonment, self-loathing, disorganized attachment to abusive adults and parents, and a disturbed and fragmented identity that was loosely integrated into an ungrounded sense of self. Memory lapses and amnesia barriers brought him to the hospital with comorbid anxiety and depressive symptoms that caused his inability to connect his chaotic inner world with the external real world of people.

James's internal world was one of chaos, dependency needs, dissociation symptoms, and projected enactments to avoid internal confusion and outer world conflicts. His symptoms resulted from an identity fragmentation and splits that resulted in the formation of a protective dissociative state at the time of his trauma. Other dissociative states were also formed that revealed emotions of fear and anger.

During each therapy session the same dissociative states did not sign in at each session. Although the predominate signatures were James and Jay, different dissociative states (identified by names) appeared throughout the sessions. These included: James, Jay, Kohlman, J. Kohlman, J, James Kohlman, Robert Random, and Shea. What conditions existed at different times that caused a different altered state to appear and sign in with a name different from James? Were those altered states active on the ward prior to the counseling sessions?

There are a variety of treatment models that are recognized for treating dissociations. Dr. Brende referenced his treatment modality as psychoanalytic, based on his psychiatric training. That included undergoing a personal psychodynamic psychotherapeutic experience that included principles of safety, containment, and cohesion. Therapeutic technique involved a philosophy steeped in a relational medico-psychological orientation. He applied an assortment of interventions along with an intuitive instinct skill that enabled him to make an assessment of James's behaviors and presenting issues. He observed and interpreted those specific behaviors and James's bodily movements (flailing arms, clenched fist, etc.) in relation to his words. This background formed the basis for his understanding and interpretation of James's relational dissociative behaviors which he diagnosed as multiple personality disorder. (This diagnosis was later changed to dissociative identity disorder in 1994 when the diagnostic manual DSM-IV was published.)

Treatment literature, at the time of the James videotaped sessions (1976-1978), indicated that the predominate treatment for dissociation and identity disorders was a tactical-integrated model that included individual psychodynamic informed psychotherapy (PDIP). PDIP is based on an observational descriptive design composed of three phase-based psychotherapy sessions offered twice a week for mental, emotional, behavioral, and memory disruptions associated with identity fragmentation. The goal for PDIP was to create a fusion of the dissociative states (become more alike or similar to). Phase one of PDIP was meant to create a safe environment (client often reported being scared, afraid, fear, abandonment, threatened). Phase two focused on the trauma (rape, adult and parental abuse or maltreatment), and phase three consisted of integrating the dissociative states. Even though this particular treatment modality was not identified in either book, several of the PDIP treatment principles within different sessions were contained in both books.

A contemporary third model, not identified, was a relational psychoanalytic approach to treatment that focused on transformational change through relationships. It's an evidenced-based treatment that emphasizes the client and therapist relationship through transference-counter-transference. Dr. Brende likely found a balance between interventions from a trauma model and a relational-focused psychoanalytic model of treatment. He attended to James's physical body movements whereby unconsciously motivated movements are prompted by the patient's unconscious internal workings. Dr. Brende may have used rhythmic resonance attunement (being attuned to the rhythms of the environment) to generate relational knowing and assist in the coordination of James's sensory and motor systems with environmental rhythms.

Clinical session snippets in Book Two utilized the primary treatment philosophy based on therapist-client transference-focused therapy that relied on subjective observations of relational dynamics between the client and therapist. He expressed his real feelings and empathic responses to the different dissociative states. This enabled James to become receptive to the conscious and unconscious merging of the therapist's characteristics into his realm of understanding and

Dr. Brende's own personal traits were incorporated by the dissociative state.

Dr. Brende's transference-countertransference therapeutic modality provided an effective way to bring James's conflicts to the surface, clarify the reason for his memory lapses, and achieve emotional integration and movement toward a fusion of the dissociative states. Supportive encouragement assisted in fostering recognition and acceptance of the normative side of James's existence. This mode of therapy enabled James to solidify his real feelings, learn self-love and compassion, and continue moving toward a "birthing" of his fully integrated identity.

During different snippets (words) the therapist-client and dissociative states dynamics were stormy, particularly when a conflict arose with a dissociate state. When a therapeutic action prompted a dissociation that led to James's reliving his early-life trauma, this created a pathway for Dr. Brende's empathy and understanding to foster an integration of the traumatic memory into his identity.

There were instances in which interventions involved hypnosis to make contact with an altered state in order to explore and understand hidden conflicts. At other times the therapist engaged in a different role via projective identification that utilized themes of dependency, power, sexuality and ingratiation. The therapist used transference to highlight the client's communication enactments and dissociations to reveal a pathway for James to enhance self-knowledge and minimize internal tension and conflict.

What was evident in the therapy process was Dr. Brende's supportive relationship to enhance change. He was able to articulate that all of James' fragmented parts (states) were welcome and encouraged to express whatever words they felt safe to impart. The outcome for this context was to assist James and his primary alternate dissociated state to self-regulate and to restore connections between the self-states.

If Book Three is forthcoming it would likely include the final eight years (1978-1983) of therapy. Until then readers will speculate and wonder if an expected and hopeful outcome will be achieved. We will also wonder whether James could have lived out his dreams and ambitions had he been reared in a healthy environment with positive parenting and support, rather than the painful and debilitating dreams and painful events he did experience.

Gary L. Arthur, Ed.D., LPC, NCC

Professor Emeritus of Professional Counseling at Georgia State University. Georgia Counselor Educator of the Year in 2007. Author of the widely used study course: Study Guides for State Licensure Exam Preparation.

Introduction

The James Tapes: Book Two continues the story about the psychiatric treatment of James Kohlman, a ten-year veteran of the United States Air Force. At the onset of therapy, it became apparent to me that James suffered from serious and frequent lapses of awareness, as if two parts of his mind were disconnected and each functioned independently. I soon learned that this "disconnection" was the manifestation of a psychological defense mechanism called dissociation. This defense mechanism was caused by the impact of traumatic events on his vulnerable mind, and it created "split-off" memories of emotional terror. It also created identity fragmentation and the formation of multiple personalities.

I am James's therapist and a graduate of the University of Minnesota Medical School and the Karl Menninger School of Psychiatry. I completed medical school in 1972, spent six years in the general practice of medicine, received psychiatric training for three years, and completed it in June 1972. I began providing psychiatric treatment to veterans in the VA Medical Center, and when I became James's psychotherapist in March 1975, I was able to arrange the use of the hospital's audio-visual recording studio to document every session of James's psychotherapy on videotape for teaching purposes.

Book One describes the first sixteen months of my therapy with James. Shortly after beginning therapy, I discovered the presence of hidden personalities through the use of hypnosis. Those personalities resulted from identity fragmentation caused by a traumatic event when he was seven years old. At that time Jay, a protective personality, took over the body in order to protect James from experiencing emotional pain or remembering his traumatic experience. Jay became the predominant personality—intellectually capable but lacking the ability to feel emotions and experience love.

During the therapeutic process, as described in Book One, five different personalities were revealed—James, Jim, Jimmy, Jay, and Shea—all of whom shared the same body. Book One also disclosed how James escaped from Jay's control by way of an attempted murder/suicide, and described James's rebirth experience and emerging "new" sense of self. Book One revealed these personalities:

James: his given name.

Jay: the personality who generally acts and speaks quite normally but does not experience normal emotions.

Jim: the young boy named by his father.

Jimmy: the young boy named by his mother.

Shea: a homosexual personality, present for a short time, but reappearing much later as a female.

Book Two begins with James's reborn self struggling to become a human being as he learns to depend on his therapist. Several new personalities will be revealed:

J: a reborn "new self."

Kohl: a young personality confused about his name.

Jay A. Kohlman: who feels emotions on his right side.

Jack: who becomes the father.

JAY: the impostor.

James Kohl: unsure of his identity.

Latot: pronounced Lot, and which spells Total backwards. This personality has a mystical origin and will eventually become the predominant personality.

Robert Random: a transient and insignificant personality.

Jay: who had taken care of James from age seven, eventually leaves his role as the protective personality, later returning as a "caretaker."

PART ONE

J

CHAPTER 1

He doesn't know his real first name and is uncertain
about what it means to be a real human being.

August 2, 1976

The patient is wearing hospital garb and has the appearance of a young, innocent, and confused boy. He sits down and signs the permission slip as J Kohlman, but it's clear that he's struggling to understand who he is. When I ask if he has a given name he answers, "I think I do but I just don't know."

"When do you think you were born?" I ask.

Rather than answer the question he yells, "I wanna run and I wanna scream!" The tears flow down his face.

"Can you remember when you were a boy?" I ask.

He fights to keep from crying and stammers words I can't make out. Then he shouts words that his father apparently used. "You stay right here you...you g...d... brat... you!"

After a pause he frowns, looks at the floor and stutters. "I...I...I should have k...killed him right then and there. That's what I should have done. Then I wouldn't have to fight. I wouldn't have so much pain. I... wouldn't be so afraid to s...s...say what I feel," he stammers between irregular breaths.

He will tell me later that he remembered the time when he ran to his father's side but was slapped in the face and called a bad name.

I ask him if he is feeling pain right now. He replies yes and continues to gently massage his right hand on the spot where his father hit him but explains haltingly that he doesn't want pain. He just wants to have real feelings like a real person. When I point out he is a real person because he has feelings as well as a body, that seems to confuse him.

He looks down at his body. "I wanna be here! I wanna be here! I don't wanna be over there anymore!" he sobs as he looks toward the other side of the room as if he's had an out-of-body experience.[1]

His face is contorted, tears pour down his cheeks, and his speech is broken. He clenches his fists and tells me again that he wants to be right here because he wants his emotions to be united properly with his body. I ask if I can touch him and he nods his head, so I reach over and touch his right arm. When I see his body stiffen, I withdraw my hand. He looks carefully at me and asks if he can touch me. I extend an open hand and he reaches toward it. But before he can grasp my hand he gazes upward and says, "This might be silly but it's not wrong."

I assure him it's not wrong but wonder why he thinks that. I decide to ask him if touching my hand reminded him of touching his father.

He squints but does not answer.

"I'm not your father of course, but have you wondered?"

"You say you're not?" he asks with eyes wide open.

"No, I'm not."

I tell him I'm pleased he could reach out to touch me as if I'm like his father. Then I explain he's been experiencing something like birth pains and point out that it's the month of July, the month of his actual birthday forty years ago.

When our therapy session ends James leaves the studio accompanied by an aide. I notice the incredulous look on her face, indicating that she learned a great deal about her patient from observing the session on the monitor. I also plan to communicate with James's hospital doctor so that he understands what is going on in our therapy now.

I'm impressed that the young James who signed in with the letter J is seeking to begin his new life. It is my intent to reinforce the notion that it is emanating from a loving relationship with his father, though he doesn't think he has a father. I believe that stems back to the time his father struck him, and a dissociation took place. After that time, he looked to his older brother Clarence as a role model, following in his footsteps during high school and later when he entered the air force.

In my review of the literature about father-son relationships, I find that fathers bring positive benefits that no other persons are likely to bring to their children. They have a parenting style that is significantly different from that of a mother, although both parents are important for a child's emotional well-being. Fathers give their boys an insight into the world of men. They encourage competition but also stress the importance of rules, justice, fairness, duty, and discipline. Studies have shown that an involved father improves his son's cognitive and social development, sense of well-being, and self-confidence. A boy's relationships with other boys and girls tend to be modeled after his father. Eighty percent of studies have found significant associations between positive father involvement and the well-being of his children.[2] In an analysis of over 100 studies on parent-child relationships, it was found that a loving and nurturing father was as important for a boy's happiness, well-being, and social and academic success as having a loving and nurturing mother.

CHAPTER 2

*J identifies himself as a new self who is located
between the right and left side of his body.*

August 5, 1976

Like last session, he remains uncertain about his identity and signs the initial J, omitting his last name. He folds his hands together, looks down, and asks a question that surprises me.

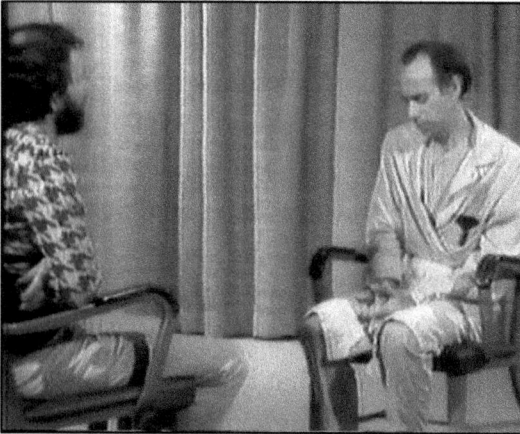

"Didn't I kill Shea?"

I point out that he did not kill him, although Shea chose to leave several months ago. He frowns, looks down thoughtfully and begins to wipe his hands on his hospital robe.

"Why do you think you killed Shea?" I ask.

"Because he didn't deserve to be around. Shea wasn't a man. He was a boy about eighteen, nineteen, or twenty-one."

"Why do you call Shea a boy if you say he's between eighteen and twenty-one? Wouldn't he be a young man?"

J corrects himself and says Shea probably wasn't a boy but remains insistent that he killed him. When I clarify that Shea made a decision to leave of his own free will in June, 1976, J says he found a wig and ponytail in his locker, which he remembers cutting off (described in Book One), and says he must have killed him.

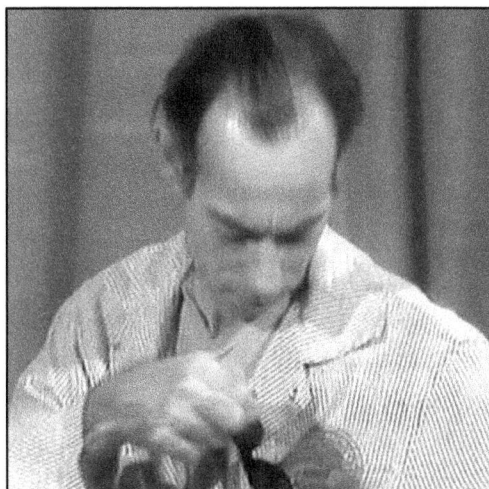

J reaches into his pocket and pulls out a pair of sunglasses and says they don't work for him because they were prescribed for Shea's eyes, and he has a different prescription.

I decide to change topics and ask why he signed his name J today rather than Jay or Shea. He answers by specifying that his name is the letter J, but that if he actually says the name Jay that name is spelled J-a-y. When I ask if he can tell me if Jay is here now, he says he is around when he feels like he's nine or older, up to age sixteen.

"What age do you feel now?" I ask.

"About thirty. I feel thirty but I don't have the knowledge that age should have. My vocabulary isn't good. I feel like I'm thinking in a foreign language because I must translate into English in order to know what you're saying." He goes on to say it's probably a mixture of a Germanic and Romantic language but quickly adds, apologetically, that he doesn't know the meanings of the words he uses.

I credit him for wanting to learn and ask if Jay is here to teach him.

"If he is here, I'm glad. I have the feeling that he's around more often at some times than other times," he replies.

"So do you know that Jay is another part of you?"

That confuses him and he corrects me by stating, "I think there's only one of me."

I point out that Jay can sometimes come into his body, but J says he keeps him out by taking up space in the body. However,

7

when I ask if he and Jay can be in the body at the same time he frowns and says he doesn't know.

I decide to ask J if he knows who James is, and am surprised to hear him say no.

I see him extend both arms out to either side of his body and ask why he is holding his arms out like that. He brings his hands

 together and says he doesn't want to be on either side but wants to be in the middle. Since his two personalities, Jay and James, had been linked to opposite

sides of the body, a change has apparently taken place in his body since his rebirth experience.

When I ask if he feels split, he frowns and says no. But he also says he feels there are threats that prevent him from going in the direction he would like to go.

When I ask him to explain he repeats, "They are just threats." I wonder if he is referring to alternate personalities that threaten to take over.

Our time has run out and I look at the clock. When I announce that I will miss our Friday meeting, he places his hands together, prayer-like. I quickly assure him that our next meeting will be Monday, and he accepts the change, stands up, shakes my hand, and walks out accompanied by an aide.

During this session he called himself the letter J again, but also located the position of his identity as existing in the very middle and not on the right or left sides. This location has physiological meaning pertaining to the fact that each side of the body is connected to opposite sides of the brain.[3] I have previously speculated that James embodied the left side of the body—associated with right brain hemisphere functioning, and Jay embodied the right side of the body—associated with left hemisphere functioning. Perhaps that explains why J, who is neither Jay nor James, identifies himself in the middle without clear linkage to either side of the brain. This may also explain his lack of knowledge of words associated with the functions of the left cerebral hemisphere in a right-handed person.

When I research information about a child's brain functioning, I learn that the right brain is predominant until age seven. After that age the left brain, which is required for intelligent speech and vocabulary, becomes dominant. This fact indicates that J's brain is functioning at an age below seven, and explains why J has a limited vocabulary and lacks the capacity to speak as a more mature person.

CHAPTER 3

He is ashamed of his very existence
and believes he has no real father.

August 9, 1976

The patient sits down and signs in the letter J, like last time. I notice that he seems emotionally unstable and struggles with misperceptions. For example, there are times when he opens his mouth, but no sounds come out. Other times he makes sounds as if he's talking to himself.

He still lacks a clear sense of identity, which leads me to emphasize the role of love as important in his identity formation. I ask if his father loves him and his answer is to tell me that his father called him a bastard, a painful event he first revealed to me three weeks ago.

Predictably he switches subjects and tells me about a frightening memory of finding himself in a state of nothingness. I emphasize that he's a real human being and that his father and mother are real persons. But he has the delusional belief that they brought him into the world under false pretenses. He denounces them and says he wants to kill them because of the shame he feels. To reinforce a sense of reality, I explain that he exists because his parents gave him life. He can't accept that and exclaims dramatically that he's not real. I reach out to touch his arm as evidence that he is real and make a strong pronouncement that his mother and father are also real people.

Even though I know James is currently unable to accept his mother and father as true parents, I will be quite surprised at what takes place at our next scheduled meeting time.

CHAPTER 4

*His identity remains in flux as J locates his sense
of self on the right side where his feelings are.*

August 12, 1976

During the last session J felt his presence was located between the left and right sides of his body. Today that seems to have changed. At first he extends his right hand to the right side of his body where he says his feelings are.

Then he points his left thumb toward the left side of his body where James had previously been located (along with the right brain) and refers to it as "dead."

He tells me that he feels like screaming whenever he feels numb, because if he can't feel then he can't determine if he is real.

I ask if he hollers for help at those times, but he says he is afraid to holler because he can't trust himself to keep from killing whoever comes.

"I never hear you holler at me when I'm here, which must mean you don't want to kill me."

"No. I don't wanna kill you. I trust you. I depend on you. I love you."

I acknowledge his positive feelings about me and ask if he can tell when he starts to get numb on his left side.

He says that if he spends too much time thinking about it his right side will become numb, but the numbness will then shift back to his left side and that will make him feel as dead as a robot. "When that happens, I get afraid I'll lose myself." He turns his gaze toward me in anguish and says he wants to scream for help right now.

Before I can respond he changes the subject. He says Betty (his sister-in-law) came to see him this morning to ask when he's coming home, and he told her that he can't come home now. When I ask why, he says the thought of returning home triggers murderous thoughts that scare him.

I point out that he will benefit from being with family members who love him because he was deprived of the love he needed when he was a boy. But he says he won't do things to please others to get their love. Then he asks if I will explain why he can say "I love you" to Betty but can't say it to his mother.

"Maybe you didn't believe your mother's love was real," I reply. I go on to tell him that I met with his parents earlier today, and his mother told me she loved him and that she breast fed him during his first year of life.

He scowls. "I'm glad I wasn't there 'cause I didn't wanna hurt 'em," he says.

After our session is over, I talk with his hospital doctor, and he tells me that James's behavior has been strange. Sometimes he appears scared and won't speak, while at other times he yells out in threatening ways. But there are also times when he appears to speak and act normally.

I will later find research that helps me understand the relationship between a person's brain, speech, and emotions after a traumatic event. Psychiatrist and trauma expert Bessel van der Kolk has described how extremely stressful conditions can impede the speech center by triggering the brain's amygdala

12

to shut down Broca's Area, which is a key component of a complex speech network involving the flow of sensory information from the temporal to the motor cortex. When the speech center is affected by trauma, a survivor may scream out in terror, or simply not speak at all. Victims of assault and life-threatening circumstances may be unable to communicate what happened. After a serious accident, the victim may not be able to articulate when arriving at the emergency room. Children who have been traumatized may refuse to speak. Soldiers who have survived lethal combat may stare hollow-eyed into a void because their terrifying memories are too difficult to articulate.[4]

This information leads me to consider the possibility that J can't put his perceptions into words because his speech center was disrupted at the time he was traumatized and can't function normally. It may also explain why James has urges to yell out and kill somebody.

CHAPTER 5

J signs in one day and Jay A. Kohlman the next.

August 16–19, 1976

The patient arrives wearing hospital attire and signs the initial J. He tells me he continues to believe he is real, but doesn't want to talk about his mother again, and today he denies having a mother. I insist he had a mother who loved him, or he wouldn't be alive. I also point out that loving feelings are the basis for feeling like a real person, but he remains skeptical.

We meet again three days later. He signs his name Jay A. Kohlman and tells me he feels scared when he signs that name. I ask if he is the same person I met with last time and he nods his head slightly. Then he points to his right side and tells me he feels emotions on the right side of his body, which he told me about last week. I ask if he can tell me more about those emotions, but he struggles to define them.

Then he points straight ahead with both hands, indicating that he sees himself as being located right down the middle, which is what he had described two sessions ago. I ask if existing right down the middle helps him deal with painful things such as feeling abandoned if I'm away for a week or longer, which is a sensitive subject for him.

I believe that there is a reason he feels located in the middle

today, while twice previously he said his feelings were on the right side. Perhaps his new name today— James A. Kohlman— means he feels more centered.

Then he surprises me by reaching out.

"Am I hurting you?" he asks.

"No, you don't hurt me," I reassure him.

He reaches out to touch me again since I seem to be the only solid piece of reality he can rely on during this time of uncertainty.

Before our time ends, I announce I will have to miss our Monday session.

"I don't know if I can hang on Dr. Brende," he laments with tears in his eyes. "Jay! Jay!" he exclaims, and Jay comes into the

body immediately. He looks me in the eye and pleads, "Can you please see him Monday? You know he's been left by everyone."

"I'm glad you're concerned but let me assure you James won't be hurt if we miss Monday's session. I'll be back for our next session on Wednesday," I insist.

Jay seems relieved as he stands up and we shake hands. After he leaves the studio, I think about this personality who signed himself in as Jay A. Kohlman and described himself as wanting to be right down the middle. I found it meaningful that he expressed his emotions and tearfully reached out to me while expressing his fear that I might abandon him.

CHAPTER 6

He is very fragile and fears he might
break into pieces if he's abandoned.

August 25, 1976

James seems very happy today, but during our last session Jay worried that he would feel abandoned if I missed today's session. But I'm here, which seems to be the main reason he is in a good mood. He signs the letter J with a scowl on his face, suggesting he's uncertain if that is accurate.

He tells me he has been very anxious since our last meeting but refused to take medication so he could be clear-headed. He says people are telling him he's doing babyish things which confuses him. Although he signed J when he first arrived, he is not sure who he is because the words he's speaking are Jay's words.

I ask if anyone has explained what they mean by babyish things, but he says he can't understand them. Then he raises both hands enthusiastically and says, "I want to grab you and say 'I am happy to see you.' "

"That's a loving thing to say," I reply.

"I'm not afraid to say that to you but not to those people up there because they might hit me. At least you let me express my thoughts."

After I assure him I won't hit him, he says he feels silly and energetic enough to paint the walls of the day room with other patients and staff. Then he changes the subject and tells me about his dreams, mostly about his brother Clarence. Then he says he feels guilty because I must have changed my vacation plans to be here, but I explain that he didn't interrupt my vacation.

He seems relieved and expresses his hope that I won't miss any more meetings because he has difficulty coping with my absence. "If you had not come to today's session every bit of me would be splattered all over everywhere!" he exclaims.

"Can you explain what you mean?"

"The letter J wouldn't be here because his body would be splattered into pieces all over and I wouldn't be able to put all those pieces together into a body. But Jay could do it and he'd be here."

"Would your anger at me cause you to fragment?" I ask.

He nods his head in agreement. "And that's not all. I'd break a lot of other things into pieces too."

I'm puzzled. "Can you explain how you would do that?"

He shakes his head and says he can't answer me because J and Jay are fighting.

I try to clarify but his answer confuses me. Then he changes the subject to warn me that something bad is going to happen.

"What are you afraid of?" I ask.

He struggles to explain but his ramblings are hard to understand. Then I hear a change in his language—it becomes less childlike and more sophisticated. Perhaps I'm witnessing a subtle personality change from J to Jay.

"Who's talking to me now?" I ask.

He laughs. "I'm not going to tell you 'cause I don't have enough of a stronghold."

When I ask him to explain, J answers. "Jay seems to be getting stronger because he just talked to me. I heard his voice, but I didn't understand what he said."

"Would you like to understand what is happening between you and Jay?" I ask.

"I want to understand even if it is gradual because I'm getting older every day and I'm afraid I'll run out of time. I need to trust you to help me because then I can hang on much easier when Jay tries to take over."

"It sounds like the two of you (J and Jay) are trading off getting control of the body."

"I don't know if I should be mad at Jay or the person who told me to take the medication this morning 'cause it made me sick. I tried to tell them not to give it to me because I'm not Jay. But they don't listen. It makes me wanna scream."

I see the expression of distress on his face and reach out with my left hand. He thanks me for reaching out but keeps his hands clenched as he holds them together between his legs. Then he tells me he reached out to Ms. Haden, one of the nurses, this morning. "She let me hang onto her because I was losing it. I was afraid of going into the darkness and I couldn't stop screaming."

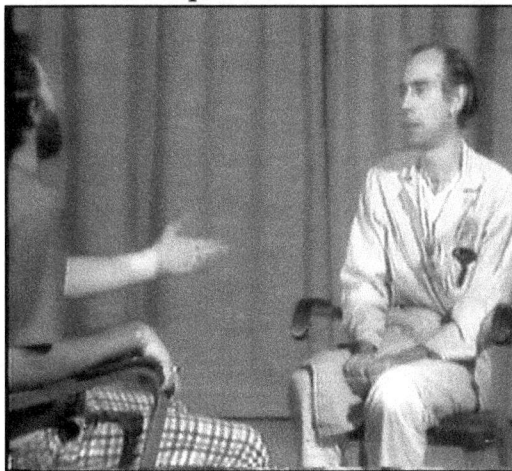

"Did that work?"

"Yes. I stayed here. But I was too weak to do anything."

"That's why you need to hang on to her."

"But who can I hang onto if she isn't there?"

"Don't you know another nurse you can trust?" I ask.

"No. And I don't really know if Jay is trying to come out. I can't trust him," he says.

"Why can't you trust Jay?"

"Because he wants to take over and throw me back into darkness."

"How do you know?"

"It's when I begin to feel myself spinning around. But if I wash my hands and picture that you're here then Jay can't come."

"Did you feel the spinning happening within the last few minutes?" I ask.

"When I first came here I did but after I saw you I calmed down."

"So was Jay trying to take over before that?"

"Yes. But I hung on so I could physically see you with my own eyes and register in my mind that I was going to see you."

I thank him for telling me about his struggles with Jay, but his hands remain clenched, evidence that he's still afraid. When I ask about his hands he places them on each leg, looks at me, sighs deeply, but doesn't speak.

I look at the clock and inform him that our time is up and we'll need to stop. When I announce our next session, he sighs and tells me a word has come into his mind, but he doesn't know what it means.

"Go ahead and say the word," I say.

"Marvelous!" he exclaims.

CHAPTER 7

*Today he says his name is James, and doesn't recall
coming to previous sessions. I believe one or more
personalities are competing to take over.*

August 27, 1976

He signs the name James today and says he's very angry with
me because I had been threatening him in his dreams. When I
ask for more details, he describes memory lapses. "I don't
remember anything until I was standing there just before I saw
you. Things were going around this way and then around this
other way. It feels like others are trying to take over."

He motions with his arms and then lifts his hands to his face
as he struggles to hold back tears. It's clear that James feels an

inner turmoil that
is consistent with a
complete lack of
control over other
personalities.
During the last
session I met two
personalities, Jay
and J. I wonder if
they have been
fighting to enter the
body.

"I don't like this. I don't like this. I believe I'm losing my
mind," he wails.

He apologizes for acting upset. Then he lowers his hands but
keeps them in tight fists with thumbs tucked in.

"Why are you keeping your hands clenched? Are you afraid you might scratch me?"

"I might lash out but I don't know how to do that because no one ever taught me what to do when I feel like this."

He says he feels like a helpless child and doesn't want to feel like that.

I reach over to undo his clenched fists and reassure him that he doesn't have to worry about hurting anyone. I open his right hand and he keeps it open.

"I'm crying. I'm crying," he says while struggling to hold back tears. I hold on to his right hand as he continues to cry. "I don't wanna cry," he sobs quietly with his eyes tightly closed. "I'm not a child," he moans.

He finally gains control and sits with his hands together, unclenched, holding a handkerchief. He tells me that he doesn't feel like himself and apologizes for his vacillating moods. Then he says he can't get his bad dreams out of his mind. He raises his right hand and covers his right ear in an apparent attempt to block out the voices in his head.

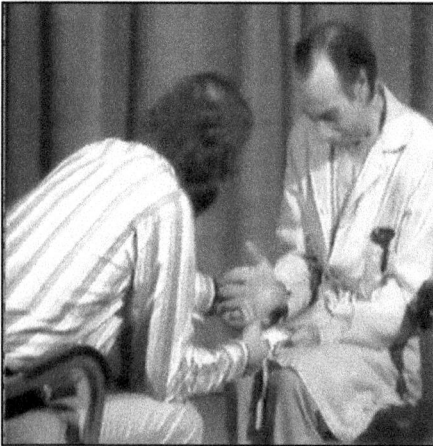

He says he feels like running away but doesn't want to. He begins to cry again, then wipes his eyes. He lifts his left hand to cover his left eye, lowers it and wipes off his left hand as if he's wiping Jay's presence away. He closes his eyes, blows his nose, and finally begins to talk. "I don't wanna run away. But you scared me."

"How did I scare you?"

"You scared me in the dream, and I kept screaming. I saw you and I thought you saw me when they picked me up and put me in that electric shock chair. Then I looked and started to holler for you but you changed and you wasn't you anymore."

"I'd expect you to feel angry. In fact, your first words today were to tell me how angry you were at me."

"I wasn't angry at you. I was only angry at the dream."

"If you were angry at me, would you tell me?" I ask.

"Yes. But I feel strange. Like I'm here but I also think that J-A-Y is here," he says, spelling out the name JAY.

"How about J-A-M-E-S. Is he here too?" I ask, also spelling out James's name.

"Am I not him?" he replies incredulously.

"Yes, you are."

He stares at me and says, "You look different than usual."

"Do I look different? Can you describe how?"

He says my voice is less mechanical and more human sounding. Then he changes the subject and says he can't understand why he has a headache. He leans forward with his head down and brings his hands over his eyes.

"It's all right," he mumbles. After a pause he states, "No it's not all right." With his eyes closed and one hand in his lap, he raises his left hand to his shoulder, then swings it back to cover his face. Then he drops both hands to his lap. "I'm kinda confused," he says. He clamps his eyes shut and shakes his head. "I'm sorry Dr. Brende."

"It's okay to be confused. I think it's related to something you said two days ago when we met. It was about having angry feelings when I'm not here and being afraid those feelings might hurt me."

"They will!" he exclaims.

"Well, they haven't hurt me yet. How could they hurt me?"

He shakes his head and then tells me he's angry because I'm changing things—mainly the time we meet. "I don't wanna change the time!" he insists.

It's not so surprising to hear him say this and I assure him that we'll return to our regularly scheduled appointments. Then he asks me an unexpected question. "How do you keep yourself from feeling pain?"

"Why do you ask? Do you feel a need to protect me from experiencing pain?"

"I don't know," he says as he lowers his head and clenches his hands together.

"I remember you told me once before that you took on your mother's pain to protect her. Was that because you didn't want her to feel pain?"

"No, I didn't."

"That was a loving thing to take on her pain."

He says he wanted to protect his mother from the pain of childbirth. Then he asks me about his own birth. "Is it possible that I haven't been completely born yet?"

I look at his clenched fists and see a tight right fist pressing down on his left hand holding his thumb. Perhaps his body language is symbolizing an unborn baby held up in the birth canal. "Are you hoping to protect your mother by delaying your birth?" I ask.

He nods. "I don't want her to feel the pain."

I explain that when a mother gives birth to her baby, she always has pain. She loves her baby, but she still has pain. "Don't you think your mother had pain when you were born?" I ask.

After sitting quietly for a time, he whispers "Yes." Then, with eyes closed, he reaches out his clenched hand toward me.

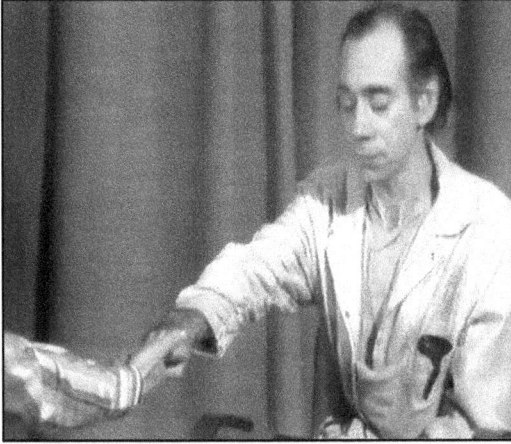

I touch his hand, which seems to help him relax. This is not the first time he has responded so positively to touch, which, I believe, is also a reenactment of his contact with mother at the time of his birth.

Then he withdraws his hand, opens his eyes, and says thank you.

"Can you tell me what you're thinking?" I ask.

"I'm thinking that I can listen to humans and to 'him' at the same time," he says quietly.

When I ask who 'him' is he listens but remains silent with his eyes closed for a time. Then he finally speaks. "Dr. Brende, I'm very tired. I think I need to go back and lay down or I'm going to pass out."

He closes his eyes and remains quiet for the remaining five minutes of our session. Finally, he opens his eyes and stands up. I shake his hand and remind him that our next appointment will be Monday at one o'clock. He nods and walks out of the studio.

During this session James reported painful memories about his mother's pain at childbirth and his wish to be protective by taking on her pain. It may have also been a metaphor of James expressing his knowledge of Jay's role when he was "born" to be James's protector. I do not understand why James spelled JAY with all capital letters and why he was present in today's session. It's interesting that he used capital letters to spell both JAMES and JAY. I wonder if those two personalities will fuse soon.

This is not the first time I have wondered if his alternate personalities are close to achieving fusion. Psychiatrist Richard Kluft has described his experience with personality fusion, also called integration. He says it is important for the therapist to be patient because he or she may believe a fusion has taken place only to discover later there are additional personalities that emerge. Kluft has written that fusion may be achieved when there have been three stable months of continuous personality existence, no evidence of a newly emerging alternate personality, a subjective sense of unity, and an absence of new personalities after re-exploration.[5]

PART TWO

JAMES

CHAPTER 8

He says he's been in a fog, has a lot of pain,
and is convinced he killed someone.

August 30, 1976

I'm surprised to see him sign the name JAY in capital letters. His speech, demeanor, and emotional makeup are substantially different from the personality who called himself J during our previous sessions, and different from the Jay I've met with in the past.

"I feel like I'm coming out of a deep fog and I feel pain like I've never had before."

"What kind of pain are we talking about?" I ask.

He puts his hand on his chest and says, "My chest hurts and my throat hurts. My right eye hurts and my head hurts. I've never felt pain before at all."

He pulls a packet of cigarettes out of his robe pocket, lights one up, and tells me that he's not been here for three months. Then he sits quietly for a short time before he speaks. "I feel compelled to tell you that I've been in the middle of a very bad dream for the past three months."

I ask him to talk about his dream and he says he's been in a dark place surrounded by nameless frightening and screaming forms that never go away. "I can't tell you how scary that's been," he says.

"I don't remember hearing you tell me about feeling scared in a very dark place when I talked with you in the past."

He sits quietly gazing downward for a long time, seemingly not understanding what I'm talking about. Then he raises his right hand and rotates his index finger in a circular manner while saying he doesn't believe it was a dream. He asks me if I can understand what is happening to him and I ask him to keep describing it.

He says that he suddenly found himself dressed in hospital pajamas and robe for the first time on Wednesday. He didn't know how he got there and asked the nurse why he was dressed that way. She told him that the doctor placed him on close observation because he was threatening other people. He wishes he could have talked with me then in hopes I could explain what was happening. Although he has no memory of doing anything illegal, he is worried he may have committed murder. "I know I must have killed someone. Did I lose control of myself? Was I under sedation or something? Or am I just coming out of sedation?"

"I've told you before that you didn't kill anyone. Why do you think you did?"

"I'm just thinking up things to lie to you," he replies sarcastically, and then claims I must be hiding the truth from him. I insist again that he's not a murderer, but he fails to respond. He sits quietly for a time and then says his nurse claimed he had been agitated and acting crazy for the last two days. He gazes into the distance for a time and then shifts his gaze back toward me. "Don't you understand why I'm upset? If I killed someone, why don't you tell me so?" he demands.

"I've already told you. You haven't killed anyone."

He sits quietly, holding his fist to his mouth. After a period of silence he abruptly states, "I'm feeling pain and I feel like I'm gonna throw up all the time. In fact, I did throw up and I think you have something to do with the way I'm feeling."

"I told you when you first came today I was happy to see you."

He frowns. "In my dream I'm continuously fighting with the nurses and the aides, but there isn't anything to fight about. And in one of my dreams, I lost the fight, which means I'm weak if I can't win over some women."

"You may have enough power to win but you've been away for three months, so how could you be fighting nurses on the ward?"

"So where was I? And why did the nurses tell me I was here?"

"Maybe it just looked like you were here. The staff didn't recognize there was another person in your body who looked like you."

"How could that happen?" he asks.

"All I can say is that during the last time we met you weren't here, but your body was here."

He gazes past me with a scowl and gestures futilely with his hands. Finally, he snaps, "I can listen as you talk about anger but if you talk about affection that makes me sick. Can't we just stick to logic?"

"If we're going to be logical let's try to understand why talking about affection makes you sick."

He puts his left hand up to his chin and I do the same. We appear to be staring at each other in a standoff, although he gazes past me. Finally, he drops his hostility and says he feels constant pain, shivering cold, and he's so depressed he can't sleep. He's afraid to close his eyes because his nightmares contain too much fighting, but he doesn't know who is doing the fighting. He says he brought this subject up in his group yesterday, but nobody understood him.

I ask JAY if the reason he came today was to express the feelings his other personality J can't express.

He frowns and says he doesn't know what I'm talking about. However, he does know about James. "Why didn't you take James off the ward and stop him from being such a bother to everyone?"

"Because his doctor on the ward doesn't consider him well enough to leave." I point out that staff personnel are insisting he wear hospital garb and remain on a one-to-one watch because he's very agitated and they believe he is James. But that makes him mad because he doesn't like being called nuts. After he sits quietly for a time, I break the silence and bring up the question that's on my mind. "Where have you been for the last three months? Anybody would call that unusual but that doesn't make you nuts."

"What would you call it then? Maybe you had me under sedation, and I didn't know about it, and I've just been dreaming or something," he grumbles.

"Do you know where you've been? Have you been in the dark some place?" I ask again.

He says he hasn't been in the dark, nor has he been any place he can describe. He just feels like he's awakened from some kind of alternate reality.

As I think about his description, I wonder if there's been a loosening of the psychic boundary between alternate personalities competing for control. I also wonder if he has access to J's identity and ask him if he knows about the time J spoke words he didn't understand and needed someone to interpret.

He sits quietly for a time, then responds, "Would you really understand if I answered that?"

"Try me."

He grins slyly while propping his chin onto his left hand. Then he challenges me and says I could never know what he did or thought or dreamt because I'm a human being.

But I take on his challenge and tell him that as his therapist my task is to learn and understand what affects him and the other personalities. Then I ask what he would do if he was my therapist.

He ponders my question for a moment before he answers. "I'm pretty smart but not that smart. But I know I've been smarter than a lot of people." He shrugs his shoulders. "I don't feel very smart now. I'm scared and these headaches are so bad I can't think."

"I remember that you've had bad headaches before."

He looks at me strangely and says he never told me that because he's never been here before. So I ask if he is the same Jay I met with three months ago. "Are you the same or a different Jay compared to the Jay I talked to then?"

He frowns and shakes his head. "I don't wanna talk about that because I don't understand what you're saying. I wanna know what's gonna happen to me now. If I committed murder, then let me get a defense!" he exclaims.

"Why do you think you've committed a murder?"

"I think there was a death and I outsmarted myself and ended up doing it. There! Is that plain enough for you?" he bellows.

"How do you mean you outsmarted yourself?" I ask.

"I don't know exactly." He lifts his left hand to his chin.

"How could you murder a person who is really a part of you?"

"I hope to God he wasn't a part of me," he frowns.

"Are you talking about Shea? Is that who?"

He nods his head slightly. "So you know about it? Why didn't you tell me then?"

"Why do you think you murdered him?" I ask.

" 'Cause he wasn't worth a damn. That's the reason why," he mutters while snapping the fingers on his left hand.

"Was it because he was homosexual?" I ask.

"That's not the only reason," he replies softly as he lowers his head and frowns.

"Because he loved me?" I ask, referring to Shea's verbal expressions of affection.

This question triggers an angry response. He raises his left fist to his face, then opens both hands in a questioning gesture. "If he loved you, you let him do it. I don't care!" he exclaims loudly. "He tried to mess with me once and I wouldn't let him. You gotta stay clear of him."

"So, love means mess around with? Is that what you think Shea did?" I ask.

He lowers his right elbow to the arm of the chair and lifts his right hand to his mouth. Then he turns away from me, seemingly pondering my question.

"Doesn't matter 'cause he's dead now," he says.

"Did he ever touch you?"

"Don't play these cat and mouse games with me," he grumbles.

"I know he had sexual desires toward men."

"That's right! I won't have any part of him!" he snaps as he gazes upward. "I'm trying to be a halfway decent person."

"That's good. But he also expressed affection. Are you saying you don't want any affection?" I ask.

He closes his eyes, clenches his mouth, and moves his head in a nondescript way.

"You've come back to see me after three months and you say you don't have any affectionate feelings toward me?" I ask.

He somberly looks down to his left. Then he directs his gaze toward me and asks cynically, "Why should I?"

"I believe there's something that keeps you from feeling love or affection. I wonder why. While you were gone, I talked to the personality who called himself the letter J and learned his problems with affection dated back to his relationship to mother. That also means your relationship to mother."

He raises his head. "What relationship would I have with my mother? She's only my mother!" he exclaims.

"J said that if he ever told anybody about his loving feelings for mother, they would take all his feelings away."

He closes his eyes while listening to me talk about this distasteful subject until I stop speaking. "If he feels that way, that's his problem," he replies abruptly, then closes his eyes again, tips his head downward, and brings his right hand up to his forehead.

"Do you remember having any dreams about that subject?" I ask.

"Yes, I do, but only since you said those words, that's all. But there's something else. What have you people done to me? You've messed up my mind. But how could that be because I haven't been here. Yet you say I've been here. So, the only logical thing I can say is that I've been here under sedation or something. I know I'm hurting and anything you do or say can't make me feel worse."

35

"What kind of hurt are you talking about?"

"All kinds of hurt. Some of it I caused myself," he complains.

I can't answer his question about why he is having so much pain, so I try to explain it may be related to the fact he is one of several personalities who are becoming more open with each other. But that merely confuses him.

He sits quietly for a short time and then speaks out angrily. "I'm trying to get my mind uncluttered, but you've just cluttered it up even more! I know I should never have come over here."

"How can I clutter your mind up any more than you're already having from those dreams?" I point out that that his dreams are alternate personalities fighting with each other.

"Is that the reason why I'm sitting here in hospital pajamas?" he asks.

"Yes, it is."

He tries to change the subject by talking about his need to get a defense attorney and court date because of Shea's presumed murder. But I return to the question I asked at the beginning of this session—why did you return to therapy? His answer is the same—he had to escape the darkness and hellish nightmares that never seemed to end.

I ask if there are times when he feels like crying and his answer is emphatic. "No. I'm not crying. I'm not crying. I don't cry!" He closes his eyes and lifts his right hand to his head. Then he peers toward his left, and mumbles, "I don't want all that stuff. Who needs it?"

Our time is about to end, and he agrees to return next time, but insists that our conversation should only be logical and definitely not emotional. I point out that his emphasis on being logical has pushed out his feelings, but I assure him that I can accept his angry feelings.

He turns away, puts a fist to his mouth, and coughs. After a moment he assures me that even though he's angry at me he won't hurt me.

"I am not critical of you for being angry. You should know that James also got angry."

"I think that's my given name, isn't it?" he asks as he turns his head to look at me.

"Yes, that is your given name. Would you like to be called James?"

"Certainly not," he exclaims. "I think that's a degrading name. I'm not a butler so don't call me James. I'm not a chauffeur so don't say 'home James,' " he smirks. "And by all means never call me those abbreviated nicknames like Jim or Jimmy." He shifts in his chair then turns to face me. "I think they're even more degrading."

"I know you've told me that your mother called you Jimmy and your father called you Jim."

He nods his head and says he was aware that his mother liked the name Jimmy, but he doesn't mention that his father preferred the name Jim. As our session ends, he says he feels better now. Then he stands up and tells me with a smirk he liked trying to put me down because I'm a doctor, but I ignore that, extend my hand, and tell him I look forward to our next session. He refuses to return the handshake and leaves the studio.

As I reflect on the past hour, it had been a grueling session that elicited feelings of anger from both of us. I'm still uncertain about the factors that caused him to spend three months in a state of nightmarish hell before returning to meet with me. He called himself JAY, did not want to consider himself a patient, and couldn't understand why he was wearing hospital garb. He was clearly a different personality compared to the Jay I had previously known. He told me he was certain he had murdered Shea, which prompted me to review previous sessions (from

Book One), finding that Shea left the body on June 21, 1976, while Jay, who hated Shea, left the body a week later. It's probable that JAY has retained Jay's hateful memories about Shea, which may explain why JAY now thinks he killed Shea.

The JAY I met with today is angrier and more emotional compared to the Jay I knew before late June 1976. That Jay was unable to feel pain or emotions, but JAY complained of physical pain in his chest, throat, right eye, and head. Since James has complained of a similar range of negative emotions, I wonder if James and JAY are on the verge of a fusion.[6] If so, I will encourage that to take place.

CHAPTER 9

Jay insists the JAY I met with last time is an impostor.

September 2–9, 1976

The personality who arrives today is wearing hospital garb. He signs in as Jay, but he is not the same JAY I met with on Monday during our lengthy and confrontational interaction.

Within a few minutes I decide to use hypnosis to talk with James and ask Jay's permission to do so. He nods yes, closes his eyes, and sits quietly until I see a smooth personality change. When James comes into the body, he opens his eyes and immediately tells me he's in pain. I explain that feeling pain is part of being human and inform him that Jay won't take it away. He becomes agitated, walks away from his chair repeatedly, says he doesn't want to be called crazy, and wants to be released from the cage in which he feels locked.

I am surprised by the level of his agitation and attempt to find out what is causing it. He doesn't provide me with any helpful answers and after a short time I inform James I want to talk to Jay again. When he appears, I describe my difficulty talking with James and inform him that we will miss the next session and meet in one week. This news disturbs Jay, who clearly knows James will experience abandonment pain, indicating that he still thinks of himself as James's protector.

When we meet a week later, Jay signs in again. He tells me that he's frightened because of periods of amnesia. He says he has lost days and hours and months and doesn't know where they disappeared.

I ask if he remembers what happened since our last meeting and he tells me that an impostor has been using his name and his thoughts. "I don't know who it is, and I can't do anything to stop him. If he thinks he's the real Jay, he doesn't know how to fake it very well."

I wonder if JAY was the impostor Jay is referring to and ask when he first noticed there was a person using his name. He says he first noticed it not too long ago.

"How long ago do you think it was?" I ask.

"I would have to say during the last two weeks or so, but I can't seem to get things straight in my mind and I'm having headaches that won't go away."

He rubs the left side of his neck with his left hand and complains of severe pain he's never felt before, and that he can't stop crying.

When I ask if he is facing problems on the ward, he tells me staff members have been asking him to watch other patients. "I hate being asked to do that because it brings back a bad memory," he says.

I ask for more specifics, and he says that when he was a boy his parents told him he always had to watch his little brothers and sisters, who yelled and picked fights with him.

Since he has never talked about this before, he must be remembering events that took place after James was traumatized and a new personality took over. The original James disappeared from the body, and the "new" James was given the task of watching his siblings because his parents thought he acted mature for his age. Unfortunately, the original James, who disappeared from the body, never went to school, and never learned things seven-year-old children should learn.

He feels emotions he's never had before and that makes him think he exists on a different plane compared to other people. He doesn't know how to live with his fear, which he describes as so bad he doesn't know what to do about it. "I'd rather just go away some place, far out in the country, and be a hermit or something."

He closes his eyes and shakes his head sadly. Then he begins to shed tears. "The more I talk to you, the worse the headache gets," he says.

Then Jay says some confusing things. First, he says he feels sympathy for James and wants to help him. Then he frowns and says James won't accept his help but would accept it from the initial J. Then he closes his eyes and leaves the body. After a brief time, I see his eyes open. He doesn't appear to be Jay, so I ask who he is.

"I'm James," he replies.

"Why are you here?" I ask.

"I want to help Jay but I think I'm hurting him and I don't want to."

"How are you doing that?"

"I tried to help him but I'm not as knowledgeable as you are. I know that there is Shea and I know that there is Jay. And I've heard Jay talk about a death." He begins to sob and the tears flow down his cheeks. "I've had pain all my life. But I'm used to

41

it and I don't think Jay is. I wish I could take the pain he has now."

James shuts his eyes tightly, trying to shut off his tears. I am very surprised to hear James grieve for Jay and tell me he wants to take on his pain. This means James has become Jay's protector, which is a complete role reversal. "Please, help him," he pleads.

"Is your name really James? I've never heard you want to help Jay with his pain before."

"Yes that's my name. But Jay won't accept my help. It scares him when I try to help. Sometimes when I'm gone he listens to the initial J. Why can't he also listen to me?" James sobs.

"Can't you just insist that you are going to help him?"

James brings his fists to his mouth and clasps them together. "I could try and help him and keep him from knowing it's me, but I don't wanna fool him."

"You've already helped him by letting him experience pain, which he's never experienced before," I say.

James sits quietly and rubs his fists together. He gasps for breath and bites his right fist. He can't stop crying, so I reach over and hand him a tissue, which he uses to wipe his face and blow his nose.

"He doesn't like me, I don't think. But I still want to help him. I have seen him in situations that you've never even seen," James tells me.

Our time is nearly over so I tell him I won't be here the rest of this week. He grits his teeth and furrows his forehead as he struggles to hold back tears.

"Can you tell me what you're thinking?" I ask.

"Somebody is hollering at me," he replies.

"Who's hollering?"

He shakes his head and his hands begin to quiver. Then his face gradually begins to relax and after several seconds I see a different personality open his eyes.

"I've been gone, haven't I?" he asks, then picks up a tissue, wipes his eyes, and blows his nose.

"Yes, you have been gone," I reply in response to Jay's

unexpected reappearance. I'm not completely sure if this is Jay but assume that he may have been the voice hollering after I gave James the unsettling news that I will be absent for the rest of the week.

He stares down at the floor, still holding the tissue to his nose.

To clarify who I'm talking to I ask if his name is James or Jay. He replies that everyone calls him Jay, but then asks an unexpected question. "Is there is a person called James then? It's not a dream that happened yesterday?"

"No, it wasn't a dream. James is real," I reply.

"I wish that James would go away," he says as he lifts his hand to the right side of his head.

I point out that James is not going away. I also inform him that James is concerned about his painful feelings. But my use of the word feelings is met by Jay's cynical reply, "I don't think people have feelings. They're merely objects who are to be used."

"Do you think I use you?" I ask.

"I don't know. If you do, don't tell me about it," he replies.

Then he tells me again that he doesn't recognize people's feelings unless a person is angry or tells a lie.

CHAPTER 10

*When James appears, he believes he's nineteen
years old and free to do anything he wants.*

September 13, 1976

Jay arrives today, clean-shaven and dressed in robe and pajamas. After signing in he lights up a cigarette. "I've been looking forward to seeing you today. I don't know why," he says with a grin.

"That's the first time you've told me that," I reply, wondering if this is the same Jay who appeared to be suffering with pain last time.

"I think I'm too old," he complains.

"You think you're too old? What does that mean?"

"I've had a long struggle with James," he says. He goes on to tell me the same thing he has told me before, that he has given up his role as James's protector. Yet he also says he worries a lot about James because he's an immature teenager who thinks he knows everything.

I ask him to give me more information about the time he began his role as a protector. He says he was suddenly born as an adult and never had a childhood. I remember that Jay told me this before and I've written about it in Book One (Chapter Two), wherein I describe Jay as entering the world in the form of a parentified child to take on the role of a caretaker in the family.

"That was the day I made that promise and now I've broken that promise and I'm getting weaker and weaker," he moans.

"Why weren't you born as a baby?" I ask.

"I just wasn't ever supposed to. I never did think about it until now when you asked that question."

"That's unusual, don't you think?"

"I don't know what's usual or what's unusual anymore, but I came here to tell you today that I don't want any help for myself. It's too late for that. But I think that James needs your help. I won't be here to show him his best shoes and clothes. I'll have to quit taking care of his things and I'll have to give him the combination of his lock so he can open the locker by himself."

He goes on to tell me that he constantly worries that James won't be able to handle his pain alone. "I promised that I would never cry. But there was much more to it than that. We had a bargain, but he lost part of his bargain, which he has a right to, because I have lost part of mine."

"So he was involved in the bargain?"

"Yes," he nods.

"What did he want?" I ask.

"He wanted to be, I think, protected."

"So he asked you to protect him? From what?"

He nods. "Not to feel emotions or pain. I always made sure that he never got hurt. That was part of my bargain."

After rambling for a time about his role as protector Jay raises his voice. "I took the pain from that slap!" Then he sighs, clenches his mouth, and frowns. "I took the belittlement from that slap. And I took the emotions from that slap. And don't ask me how I know." Jay reveals to me, in a way I've not heard before, that he protected James from the emotional and physical pain caused by his father's blow to his head. He also tried to protect James from other traumas, the worst being raped by two drunken men in Seattle. "I have handled them all. I took the rape. I took the physical pain and the emotions of that rape. I don't think he ever felt anything. I think I was born so he wouldn't feel it."

Then Jay describes his other role. "I've even eaten things he didn't like but I did it for him. I hate hominy, beans, and oatmeal, but he needed them. I didn't care about what I like except for one significant thing."

"What was that?" I ask.

"I like to smoke. I enjoy smoking."

I am hearing a more complete picture of Jay's role as James's protector, but I'm also hearing that James now wants to protect Jay from pain.

"You took James's pain which was a very loving thing to do. Do you each want to help each other out now?" I ask.

"I always helped him. Maybe that's the reason I don't have emotion for anyone else, because all of the emotion I ever had was for him," Jay declares.

"You've had some for me," I say.

"I think I've told you I hated you and I've told you I loved you but I don't feel emotions. I thought that's what you wanted to hear at the time. It was the only way I could protect him."

"That's a very important thing that you just said. The only way you could protect him was to mouth the words of having loving feelings for me. Which means that the scariest thing for him and for you is to have genuine loving feelings."

Then he makes a surprising request. "Since I can't help him anymore, Dr. Brende, can you take over my role and help James?" he asks, referring to his imminent departure.

"That means you will have to trust me. Will you trust me for yourself? Or for him?"

"For myself," he insists. "I don't want to see you again. I'm going to get out of his way and he's going to have to go through those things because I can't help him anymore." I hear his voice crack and taper off to a whisper as the tears begin to roll down his cheeks. "Help him Dr. Brende, help him," he cries softly.

"Yes, I hear you," I reply. I see his hands and fingers clench the arms of his chair, facial appearance change, and chin recede.

Jay is gone and a different personality has emerged. He looks at me intently.

"He's been here, hasn't he? I told him to go away," he exclaims.

"But you know he brought you here," I explain while wondering if he is referring to Jay.

"What do you mean, he brought me here? I can come here any old time," he replies angrily.

"How do you think you got here?"

"I walked," he utters. His hands remain clenched and he looks puzzled.

"What are you thinking?" I ask.

He doesn't respond to my question but scans both sides of the room. "Why are you looking around?" I inquire, wondering who

I'm talking to. He is not the James who, moments ago, wanted to protect Jay from suffering.

"I'm going to make sure he's not around," he snarls.

"How would you know if he was around?"

"Because he always slips right out in front of me most of the goddam time and I'm tired of it," he snaps. "Can I go? I don't wanna be here," he adds sullenly.

"No, you can't go yet," I insist.

47

I decide to ask him to sign the permission slip next to Jay's signature. He looks at the piece of paper I hand him and sees Jay's name. "I don't like that name on there!" he exclaims.

I'm surprised by his anger.

"Whadda ya want me to sign for? Did he call me a child?"

"Don't you always sign when you come to therapy?" I ask.

He scowls but takes the pad and pencil and signs James slowly. "See. I can write my name. I've gone through school," he states proudly.

I ask when he learned to write his name and he insists that he's not a child. "Jay thinks I'm a child and we argue about that."

"Can you tell me about your arguments?"

"He's always in front of me," he whines as he looks around the room.

"Is he in front of you now?"

"Absolutely not. I wouldn't let him get in front of me."

"There are times when you've let him."

"That's because I wasn't as strong as I am now. If he gets in front of me now, I'll beat the living hell out of him," he proclaims with a gleam in his eye.

Then I explain that Jay told me he isn't interested in being in front of him, but rather behind him so he can observe.

James laughs cynically. "Oh, he's very good at that. I know he's been observing me."

"He wants to help you. What's wrong with that?"

"Well, nothing. But if you're hog tied, hobbled, and stepped upon, that's no help," he declares angrily.

He stops talking and looks at me curiously with a side-glance. "You look different. Don't I know you? You're Dr. Brende!" he exclaims.

"How do I look different?"

"I don't know. You must have had a good weekend." He smiles briefly then tells me he wants freedom too. "I wanna be free to do what I wanna do. It's time!" he announces.

"What would that be?" I ask.

He smiles with a playful gleam. "Going out and getting drunk. I'm of age you know."

"How old are you?"

"Nineteen. But they changed the law, and I can drink at eighteen. I'll soon be twenty, going on twenty-one."

He stretches lazily but suddenly gets a suspicious look in his eye and frowns. He glances to his left out of the corner of his eye and remains silent for a time. Then he shakes his head and looks to his left. He squints and nods slowly, as if he'd been involved in silent communication with an imaginary being. After a lengthy silence he clears his throat several times. I hear a subtle lowering of his voice and recognize that Jay has entered the body. He looks at me curiously and asks if James was here.

I nod my head and reply. "I just talked to him. Do you want to know what he said?"

Jay says he isn't interested but I proceed to tell him that James said he doesn't need his help any longer because he wants to become independent, but he also wants to understand what's happened in the past. "He said those things?" Jay asks with a surprised tone of voice.

"Yes."

"He wasn't foul mouthed?" Jay asks in disbelief. "I thought he disagreed with everybody."

"He was cooperative with me," I reply.

"You think he's cooperating? I'm surprised. Because he's just a naive juvenile who thinks he knows everything. But he doesn't know a thing about the dangers ahead of him."

"He has a lot to learn but I can help him with those things."

"Just don't do to him what they did before when they gave him shock treatments. I won't be here to take 'em for him," Jay warns.

"I won't do that. You'll just have to trust me," I assure him.

"I think I can trust you. I know I can't trust anyone else."

I compliment him for wanting to trust me and he says he's glad we had this conversation. He also says he doesn't want to talk about this anymore.

CHAPTER 11

*Jay expects to be leaving the body soon but is afraid
bad things might happen to James after he leaves.*

September 16–20, 1976

He signs in as Jay, but I suspect this is not the same
personality who bid me farewell during our last session. He tries
to be funny but is not good at telling jokes. He says he's been
waiting anxiously to see me today, which is surprising since he
told me last time he wouldn't see me again. Today he says his
headaches are getting worse and he tries to alleviate his pain by
doing things like washing his hands, combing his hair, running
cold water on his face, taking a shower, and drinking cold stale
coffee that's been sitting around for a day.

He tells me he's having memory lapses, so I ask if he knows
whether James enters the body during those times. I'm
surprised to hear him say that he is sometimes aware of James's
presence, and I ask if he knows how James is getting along.

He answers my question quickly. "I'm glad you asked. He
says he doesn't want to do the wrong thing. He's afraid to open
his locker so he didn't change clothes before he came here."
There is a paranoid look in his eye as he peers from side to side.
"I've heard some people tell me I've lost control of myself. But I
don't want to do that now because I want you to hear me."

"I'm listening."

"I'm only going to say this once. If I go off, it's because I'm
trying to fool James." His voice begins to quiver. "I'm trying to
keep talking to you and I don't want him to push me away!" he
hollers. He apologizes for yelling, but he says that if he doesn't

talk loudly he'll probably lose himself. He also says he's afraid to close his eyes for fear of disappearing.

He says he can't continue protecting James and wants to leave the body but he's having a difficult time giving up his role as James's protector, because he's been doing it for thirty-four years. Then he asks me what will happen to his body if he separates himself from James. "Will I get any of James's illnesses? Will I be able to move my arms and legs and flex my fingers?"

I express my understanding for Jay's separation anxiety, which is like that of a mother who must turn her child over to a foster parent.

"I know he doesn't want me here anymore, but I wish I could secretly stand behind him and protect him. But I don't know how to do that." Then he asks if it's possible to come to the studio and watch James on the TV screen. He closes his eyes and sits quietly for a moment as his face perspires and his nose runs.

I encourage him to view a videotape of James and also ask if he knows what will happen to him if James grows up and becomes self-sufficient. He replies that will please him. "It makes me feel marvelous because I know I fulfilled my purpose. But it also scares me. How will he handle all the things he'll have to face?"

"He won't have to handle them until he's ready."

"I wish you could talk to him now because I'm too upset. I can't eat and I can't sleep. And I'm afraid."

"Are you afraid to give up your life?"

"Yes, but that's okay because my purpose would be fulfilled. Besides we all must die."

"If you were to die wouldn't James feel responsible that he had killed you?" I ask.

"I don't know. But to tell the truth it would serve him right." He smiles and looks down with embarrassment for his vengeful words.

I wonder if he has mixed feelings about leaving, so I ask if he would rather leave or stay. His answer is that he isn't quite ready to leave yet. When I ask if he'll be here for our next session, he shakes his head and says, "I hope I will. But I don't know. I can't work out all the angles anymore."

Jay returns to our session four days later and tells me he continues to experience pain. He insists that the only way he'll feel better will be when James becomes fully independent. Then he'll finally feel free to leave the body. Jay asks to see a videotape so he can better understand James, so I ask Dick, the video cameraman, to show a session from two weeks ago. During the session, James, with tears in his eyes, talks about wanting to help Jay. After wiping the tears from his face James says, "He doesn't like me, I don't think. But I still want to help him. I have seen him in situations that you've never seen."

I give Dick a nod to turn off the monitor. I see tears in Jay's eyes and explain that he and James have similar feelings because they share the same body.

"Do you mean that we are the same?" he asks with a shocked expression on his face.

"I know that's hard for you to believe," I reply.

"If we're the same, how can I go?" he asks.

"You are free to leave the body and that will open the way for James to come into the body in your place."

"That's too much for me to understand," he moans.

Before our session ends, I commend Jay for being receptive to the notion that he and James are both in the same body, and I encourage Jay to think positively toward him.

As I review this session, I believe there were physiological changes that took place in the brain to explain differences within the two personalities. Jay's inability to feel emotions can be explained by the fact that his identity came to be linked to the left brain (cerebral hemisphere), a non-emotional part of the brain, to protect James from being consumed by painful emotions. In contrast, James's identity became attached to the right brain (cerebral hemisphere) when the traumatic event split (dissociated) the brain at the location of the corpus callosum, a physiological corridor of white fibers that normally connects the two sides of the brain. The corpus callosum served as a boundary between the two sides of the brain and kept the two personalities from functioning as a single human being.

I will later find noted trauma researcher Bessel van der Kolk's published research using new technology—positron emission tomography (PET scans) and functional magnetic resonance imaging (fMRI)—to discover that specific parts of the brain are activated when traumatized individuals experience flashbacks of past traumas. "During flashbacks our subjects' brains lit up only on the right side ... Our scans clearly showed that images of past traumas activate the right hemisphere and deactivate the left." [7] This research confirms that a trauma victim's emotions and memories are linked to the right side of the brain and explains why James has experienced traumatic emotions and feelings of vulnerability rather than Jay. The corpus callosum may now be allowing communication between these two sides for the first time so that Jay can now experience emotions previously embodied by James.

CHAPTER 12

Jay falls off the chair after hearing the term EEG.

September 27, 1976

Shortly after Jay signs in I ask if he would be willing to have an electroencephalogram (EEG). He remains silent for a time and then mumbles, "It's been nice." To my astonishment I see him fall off the chair and onto the floor. After a moment he sits up and glances around the room with a surprised look on his face. I can't be certain if James has come into the body or if Jay is sitting on the floor. I ask him if I can help him up, but he remains silent, looking confused.

After I quickly explain that he fell to the floor I ask him if he would be willing to have an EEG. He looks around with a disturbed look on his face. Then he suddenly stands up. I wait for him to sit down in the chair, but he begins to walk out of the room. Surprised by his actions, I quickly follow him. "Please come back and sit down!" I ask. He turns around, walks back to the chair with mechanical movements, and sits down. But his body remains rigid and his eyes stare straight ahead.

To break through his frozen appearance, I raise my voice and call out his name loudly. But his body remains motionless, and he fails to respond to anything I say. I reach over and raise his hand above his head. After a moment of motionlessness, it slowly drops down to his lap, evidence of a catatonic state. I wonder if his body has entered a freeze reaction to what he has perceived to be a dangerous threat. The freeze reaction is one of three reflexive stress responses to imminent danger—fight, flight, or freeze. While most individuals exposed to extreme stress react with a fight or flight response, comprised by the sympathetic nervous system's rapid heart rate, the freeze response spreads throughout the body via the parasympathetic nervous system, causing a slowing of all physiological functions.[8]

Finally, after I repeatedly call James's name, he emerges from his catatonia looking confused. I'm quite sure James is now present, and I explain that I'm here, at Jay's request, to help him grow up and use all the abilities Jay has given him. But he scowls and insists that Jay can't be trusted.

Once more, I ask if he would be willing to have an EEG, but he responds angrily that he refuses to have any shock treatments. I try to explain that an EEG is not the same as shock treatments, but a way to have his brain tested, but he continues to refuse.

James looks around and asks, "Where am I?"

"You're here in the studio talking with me. Jay's not here. He decided to leave today because he believes he's fulfilled his purpose."

James scowls. "What do you mean?"

"It means that he thinks you can handle everything alone without him being here."

"Good! He'll be off my back!"

"That means you'll be on your own and Jay won't be taking you back to the ward."

James looks around and slowly stands up. I summon the aide who is waiting outside the door to come in. Fortunately, James accompanies her without a complaint.

CHAPTER 13

James feels vulnerable since Jay departed, but also insists he's able to take care of himself.

September 30, 1976

James arrives with two staff members, who tell me James has been placed on close observation status because he's been paranoid and out of control ever since our last therapy session. His nurse tells me that James has been verbally attacking other patients and accusing them of wanting to rape him. I'm surprised to hear this since he had not been aggressive or out of control during our last session.

James reluctantly sits down and signs his name slowly. "I'm not gonna let 'em hurt me! I was raped once, and I'll kill anyone who tries."

"Can you defend yourself without planning to kill anyone?" I ask.

He doesn't answer.

I explain to him that he feels vulnerable because of Jay's absence. I request that we watch a previous videotaped session and ask the two staff personnel who brought James to our session to also watch the monitor. Dick plays the portion of a session when Jay asked me to take care of James after he left the body. The two staff personnel nod their heads to acknowledge that they understand.

I turn my attention to James and ask if he can handle being alone now that Jay has left.

"I don't know," he mumbles in response.

After I explain that all of us will help him, James angrily exclaims that he doesn't need our help. "I'm old enough to take

57

care of myself. I'm thirty years old," he announces with a frown on his face.

I explain that he is actually forty. "What happened to those other ten years?" I ask.

"I dunno," he replies.

"Jay was born when you were seven so he could to take care of you. Do you remember that?"

James looks at the camera window behind which the two staff members are standing and shakes his head.

I ask James if he is aware of other personalities and if he remembers Shea.

He shakes his head and insists that Shea is dead.

"If he's dead, when did he die?" I ask.

"The day somebody killed him."

"Who killed him?"

"I dunno," he replies.

I explain for the benefit of the observing two staff members that Shea, a gay personality, departed in June, which means that James has had two significant losses. "James, you've lost Shea and now Jay. I'm sure that has affected you. How are you feeling?" I ask.

James squints. Rather than answer me he demands that I discharge him.

"James, you're not ready to leave. Besides, you're on close observation and they won't let you out," I explain.

Before this short session ends, I commend James for not hurting anyone and remind him we will meet again on Monday. When the two staff members join us I see their wide-eyed expressions of surprise, and hear their words of appreciation for what they learned today.

CHAPTER 14

James has a knife hidden in his robe.

October 4, 1976

James arrives accompanied by an aide and appears reluctant to sit down. He finally does so and signs in awkwardly with his left hand, which surprises me.

Then he places that hand over his right hand, which is across his body. I ask how he's feeling but his quick reply is to tell me that he's not a little boy anymore and wants to leave the hospital.

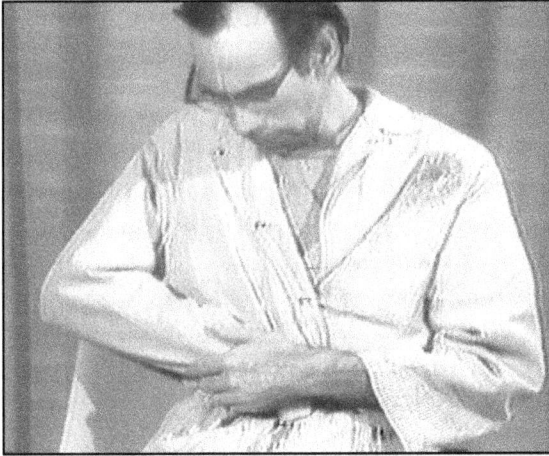

"It's true you're not a little boy but Jay asked me before he left to take good care of you and I wouldn't be doing a very good job if I let you leave the hospital before you're ready."

James shakes his head and says he feels old. I say he looks younger, not older, but he disagrees with my assessment. Then I notice his left hand is moving over his right arm. When I reach over to gently touch his arm, to my shock, I can see a butter knife that he has hidden in his robe, which he now hides behind his back.

I'm alarmed and wonder how the knife could have stayed hidden and remain undetected, particularly since he was

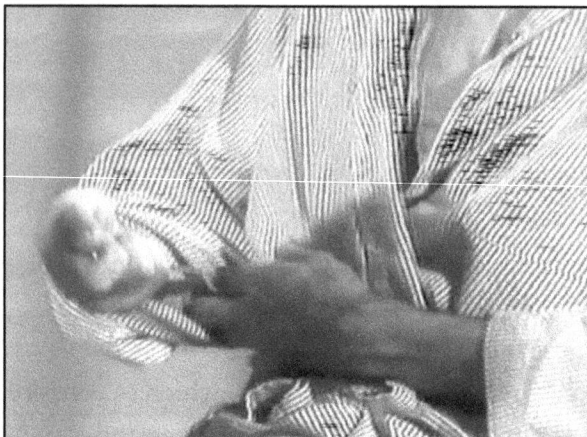

accompanied to the studio by an aide.

"James, you must give that knife to me," I declare forcefully.

"No. It's mine and I need it," he insists.

"I'm worried you can hurt yourself or somebody else with that knife. So please hand it over to me." I hold out my hand, but he shakes his head. I patiently repeat my request in more forceful language.

He is clearly fearful of losing what he believes to be his only

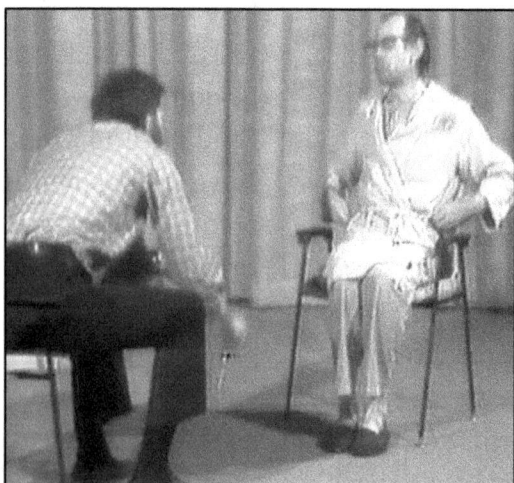

defense against potential attacks and won't give up the knife. I explain that if he fails to relinquish the knife he will end up with further restrictions and be placed in the quiet room. He finally obliges me and reluctantly drops the knife to the floor. I pick up the knife, thank him for releasing it, and assure him that he is safe and won't be abused.

After we finish the session, I inform the aide about the table knife which James surrendered to me, and advise her to make sure he is safe on the ward.

I talk on the phone with his hospital doctor about James's sense of vulnerability, and he tells me that James was frightened by another patient and appeared to have a flashback of being raped. That explains why he picked up a table knife for protection.

PART THREE

James
Returns

CHAPTER 15

James signs in and says he hasn't been here for the last year and a half. Even though he calls himself James he is clearly a different personality.

October 7, 1976

The first thing I notice is that he's not wearing the hospital robe he's had on every day and doesn't look paranoid or depressed. After signing the name James, he stands up and

spins with a flourish to show off his new dark colored slacks and a white turtleneck sweater. I wonder if this James is a new personality. He tells me that he complained to the staff about the hospital clothes they had him wear and insisted on getting new clothes. After hearing his complaint, the staff allowed him to go to the hospital store yesterday, where he purchased some new clothes—trousers, shirt, and sweater. He says he plans to resell the sweater for a profit.

Then he tells me he discovered things in his locker he hadn't seen before, including two bottles of medications which he threw away. "They looked bad. I might find some more because I haven't finished going through my locker yet. It was such a shock to find the damn things. And do you know I found forty dollars in my locker. Imagine that."

"How do you think the money got there?" I ask.

"I don't know."

"Do you think the money belonged to Jay?"

"I hate that goddam name. I hate it so bad it makes me wanna puke."

"There must be a reason you hate the name."

"I'm tired of having a reason for every damn thing I do," he grumbles. "And I'm tired of explaining everything and trying to keep my mind straight. It's like someone turning the TV on and off again and again in my head."

"Do you want an explanation for what's been going on?"

He shakes his head, turns away, and sighs deeply.

"We don't have to talk about it now," I say.

"Well, I'm glad. That's the reason I like to come over here," he says as he rattles the chair with his hands. Then he complains that the staff questions everything he says, and he's tired of it. He says he's requested a full patient status, but they turned him down. "That means I have to be nice and tell 'em just what they wanna hear! Screw that, I'm tired of having to bullshit those people about every other damn thing!" he exclaims angrily.

I'm alarmed by his anger and cynicism, but I nod my head and remain silent.

"I'm feelin' goddam smothered up there. I've gotta get outa that damn ward because somethin' bad is gonna happen if I don't and I'll get punched out."

"It's that bad?"

"How would you like being penned up with a bunch of goddamn crazy people twenty-four hours a day where you don't know what in hell they're gonna do to you?" he asks.

I remain silent.

"They complain about havin' to work there for eight hours and then they expect me to take it for twenty-four hours. That's bullshit!" he exclaims.

He gets out of his chair, takes a few steps, returns to his chair and sits down. "They're smothering me. I've gotta be free to do what I want."

"If you're feeling smothered now, I wonder if you felt that way with your mother?" I ask.

Mentioning the word mother propels him to stand up suddenly and walk away from me. "I'm not gonna talk about that bitch," he exclaims. Then he returns to his chair, sits down, and rants about having secrets he would never reveal.

"Why are you so angry at your mother?"

"She can drive a person to drinkin' rubbing alcohol. And maybe that's my problem 'cause I would never drink that stuff or any other goddam alcohol," he asserts.

I return to his complaint that he can't do what he wants and that he's being treated as a little boy rather than a grown-up.

"As I said before. I'm not a little boy. I'm all grown up." Then he says he can't understand why the staff believes he's been on

that ward for a year and a half when he knows he's only been there for a week.

He listens with a frown on his face as I inform him that he was admitted to the hospital in March 1975. When I ask if he can tell me when his existence first started, he says he remembers he was born in 1935 because he is nearly forty-two years old. After we exchange words about the correct date of his birth, he finally agrees with my version that he was born in 1936 but doesn't want to talk about it anymore. Then he changes the subject and tells me he has nightmares when the lights are turned off. Last night he tried to keep the lights on, but a staff member disapproved and turned the lights off to complete darkness. Shortly after that he had a nightmare that woke him in a cold sweat. "I didn't know what to do so I went over and turned on the lights full blast."

I ask if he recalls what the nightmare was about, but he only remembers waking up terrified.

I notice that our time is up and mention that our next meeting will be on Tuesday instead of Monday, which is Labor Day. He doesn't like this announcement and glares at me. He insists that I tell his hospital doctor to give him a pass this weekend. I promise to talk to his hospital doctor about it but that's not good enough for him and he shakes his head, gets out of his chair, leaves the room, and meets the nursing assistant at the door.

After our session is ended, I reflect on its significance. This James is not the same person who met with me last time, and I can't explain why he has reemerged after a year and a half.

CHAPTER 16

He practices writing his name James 3,000 times.

October 11, 1976

The James who arrives today is dressed smartly and sports an early growth of a goatee and mustache. His behavior is very different from the James I met with last time. For example, he keeps his right hand in a fist and says he's been practicing writing his name, James, 3,000 times on the blackboard on the ward. When I ask him why he says, "That's because I've been told that's my name."

He changes the subject and reports frightening dreams in which some persons grab him and threaten to smother him to death. "I don't know who they are but I feel like they're trying to kill me by taking away my breath and I'll be snuffed out just like that," he cries.

I ask him to define "they" and he blames the doctors, the nurses, and the aides who force him to live twenty-four hours a day in a place he hates. When I recommend asking members of the staff to send him to enjoyable activities, he says he won't ask them because he doesn't want to be told what to do.

He suddenly gets out of his chair and walks away, complaining that everyone who's been committed to

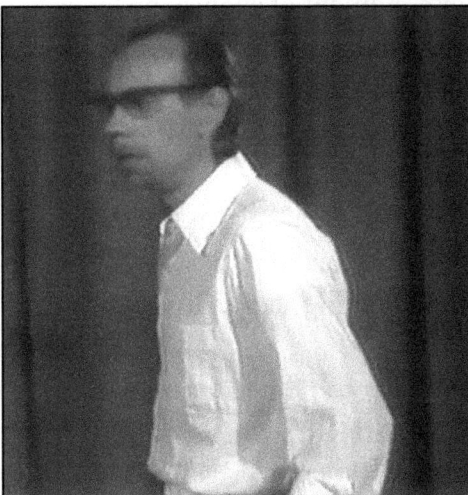

his ward should be shot because they're so sick. Then he sits down, turns toward me and insists I let him out of the hospital. Before I can tell him he's not ready to leave he suddenly jumps out of the chair. "I'm not going to let 'em control everything I wanna do!" he exclaims.

He sits down again and complains that the nurses don't know what's best for him. For example, one told him to eat more since he only weighs 144 pounds, so he's been eating candy, potato chips, and anything he can find to gain weight.

When I point out that the staff nurse must be concerned for him, he jumps out of his chair again and starts to pace. "She's a typical goddam woman. Like my mother who makes it seem like she's all concerned and all this goddam shit. She's only thinking about her own goddam self!" he raves.

When I ask why he lashes out toward his mother, James says he can give me all kinds of examples and lists food, work, religion, and sex. He looks down at the floor and plucks something off the rug. Then he sits down. He continues to complain about his mother's demands, but then changes the subject and says he feels very disturbed about a voice he hears in his head.

I ask him for more information about the voice, but he says he can't tell me what it is. After a moment of silence, he looks down at his right fist which held a knife during our session one week ago and says he's not holding a knife. "It's just a security blanket. That's all."

"Are you referring to your fist?"

"It's not a fist. Not to me," he says as he looks at the clenched right hand that's protectively covering his thumb.

"I guess that's a lot better than holding a knife like you had a week ago."

He says he felt terrified all last week and needed a knife to protect himself. "I can tell you one thing. I wasn't shitless. I was so goddam scared that all I did was shit for a week."

"I wonder why you were so scared?"

He squints his eyes and frowns. "All those weirdos 'round me all the time. They've got sex maniacs running all over the place up there like people comin' from goddam jails and prisons."

He complains about seeing crazy people around him all the time but then changes subjects and says I shouldn't get the wrong idea about his anger.

I point out that anger is a normal emotion, provided it's not violent or expressed in harmful ways to people. Then I ask him if he can remember times when he felt angry toward his mother. He scowls at me and says that even though he sounds angry today, he was never angry with his mother, particularly when he was a boy. I find this interesting since I've heard a different James express considerable feelings of anger toward his mother.

I ask him to tell me more about his angry boyhood feelings, but he looks away, mumbles something to himself, and lowers his bead sadly. "I don't know. I don't know."

"It's okay not to know," I say reassuringly.

"But it's not okay in the eyes of everyone else when I say I don't know, 'cause they'll kick your teeth in!" he exclaims.

I'm surprised by his abrupt change in behavior as he stands up and walks away from his chair. "And they kick your ass up between your shoulders, so you have to take your shirt off to take a shit. So whadda you do? You go away so you don't hear it!" he exclaims. Then he walks back to his chair and sits down. His voice trails off sadly. "I don't know what to do. I just don't wanna be around people anymore."

"Can't you accept the fact that it's okay not to know everything and to feel helpless sometimes?"

He disagrees. "It's not okay because I've been helpless all my life. I'm thirty-six... g...g...goin' on thirty-seven, I think," he stutters. He shakes his head in frustration and begins to cry. "I don't even know my age. I say one thing and they say another."

I watch him retreat into silence and lower his head. He remains quiet for a long time as I wait for him to continue. Then he continues to ask questions. "Why do people always command me to do things I don't wanna do all the time? How come nobody likes me and they call me names. Why did they always call me a son-of-a-bitch?" He suddenly stands up to walk away. "I don't feel good. Will you just leave me alone?" he exclaims. After a long pause he returns to his chair and closes his eyes. He begins to cry, takes a deep breath, and lowers his head.

"When things upset you, one of the ways you've dealt with that in the past was to call for Jay to come."

His eyes remain closed, and he swings his arm behind his head as he struggles to keep control.

"If you don't need Jay to help, I'm here for you," I state clearly.

He objects. "Are you always going to tell me what to do and how to do it?"

"I won't unless you ask me to."

"I don't want to have to get rid of you," he cries out and abruptly stands up again. He walks toward the back of the room and paces back and forth while hitting his hands against his thighs.

"How could you get rid of me?" I ask.

He returns to his chair and sits down without looking at me. "I don't know how but it's none of your damn business anyway!" he exclaims.

My countertransference feelings are now aroused. "Do you really want to figure out a way to kill me?" I ask with a note of irritation.

"I didn't say that. I said I'd get rid of you. I didn't say anything about killing you." He jumps up again, walks away, paces several times and then turns around to face me.

He lifts his left arm, touches the side of his head and bellows, "If I was going to kill you, I'd cut your damned heart out and show it to you, that's what I'd do. You'd be dead then. But that'd be a shame!"

The extent of his rage surprises me. But I remain silent as he returns to his chair.

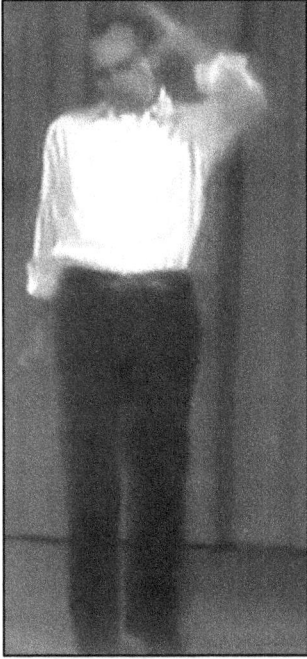

"Don't worry. I won't kill you," he says in a softer voice. After telling me not to be alarmed by his anger, he begins to ramble, loses his train of thought, and stops talking.

I ask if his thoughts about getting rid of me are linked to similar thoughts he had as a child, but he denies ever wanting to get rid of anyone in his family.

"I'd just like to get rid of myself," he moans.

Worrying that he might be suicidal, I ask him if he's had serious thoughts about getting rid of himself. He replies that he's not only thought of that but he's also thought of getting rid of me.

I ask if he's afraid I might retaliate in response to his murderous thoughts, and he asks me if I plan to give him shock treatments. "Is that why my hair got cut off?" he asks as he stands up and walks away.

"You were worried about this a couple of weeks ago when you had an EEG and you thought you were going to get shocked."

"I don't remember." He sits down again.

"Do you remember going to the EEG lab and they taped electrodes to your scalp? You probably thought you were getting electroshock treatment," I explain.

"That wasn't real. It was just a dream," he insists. Then he suddenly stands up and walks slowly away from me, whispering loudly that he's afraid he might say the wrong thing. Then with a

73

loud voice he exclaims, "You're gonna beat me or keep me a prisoner aren't you! I heard a voice tell me you're thinking of doing it."

After I point out my observation that he distrusts me, he says he was awake for the last twenty-four hours to keep from running over here to see me. He begins to sob.

"What a fool I am. What a goddam fool I've been," he exclaims bitterly.

His angry tears seem to be his way of covering up his wish but also his fear of depending on me. I realize the importance of telling him something positive. So I assure him that he can depend on me and nothing bad will happen.

As the tears stream down his face, he redirects his anger toward everyone on the ward and says he'll use his fists and not a knife. "All I need to do is bust 'em in the mouth and tear their goddam throats out. That's better than using a knife anyway."

He says he feels dumb that he ever trusted me and pulls out his handkerchief, wipes away his tears, and looks at me defiantly. "So now what are you going to do?"

"I'm going to keep listening and try to understand," I reply.

"I don't believe you can understand. You don't know what it feels like to be locked in a cage." He blows his nose, wipes off his glasses again, and says he's trying to control his anger, but it keeps getting stronger. "When I feel like tearing my bed up, I tear it up. I just throw it all over to hell and damnation. And then

I put it all back together and nobody knows about it. At least if they do they never say anything to me."

I listen until his emotions soften and he switches to another subject—the flowers in the courtyard that he picked and put in a bare room on the ward and in a cup on his locker. When he sees these colorful flowers on the ward, he says he has good feelings that replace the vacancy inside of him. I believe it's a good sign that he wants to water those flowers, which I believe is a metaphor for his wish to blossom.

This had been a unique session, during which he displayed a range of emotions and expressed his anger about having an EEG that he felt was forced on him. I called his hospital doctor to get clarification about the matter and he said Jay had been taken to the EEG lab but appeared to be in a daze and did not speak. Consequently, the technician had difficulty obtaining an accurate recording, and when the neurologist read it he said it was a poor test but he couldn't find clear evidence of seizure activity. If Jay had been cooperative and if this hospital had been equipped to do quantitative brain wave measurements (qEEG), that procedure may have demonstrated how well his brain areas worked together.

I will research this subject later and learn about van der Kolk's research of qEEG (quantitative electroencephalogram) patterns.[9] He and his associates found that traumatized individuals' brain wave patterns were all abnormal, but in different ways. Trauma victims who were easily distraught displayed predominantly high frequency beta waves above 20 Hz in the right temporal lobe, the fear center of the brain. Many of these individuals were trained to use neurofeedback to modify their brain wave frequencies. They learned to reduce their high frequency beta waves from 20 Hz to slower alpha waves of 7 to 13 Hz, associated with relaxation and trance states.

CHAPTER 17

James is distressed by being asked
to watch patients on the ward.

October 14, 1976

James is dressed nicely again today. After signing up he says he didn't want to come today, and doesn't plan to talk much because he is too upset with me, which may be a carryover from our highly emotional last session. However, I will soon see that his feelings are more related to what is happening on his ward.

His body trembles restlessly and he lifts his hand to his eyes

as if wanting to shield me from seeing his tears.

He complains that the staff is imposing responsibilities on him which he can't handle. They think he has improved enough to help manage confused patients who need direction. Rather than accept this as a sign of progress, he angrily says it feels like punishment.

When I ask what he's afraid of he says he'll be beaten or have some privilege taken away.

"What privilege?" I ask.

"Just something I like. But I can't tell you because they'll take it away."

His mood changes quickly and he tells me about his new clothes. Then he changes subjects again and tells me he's being punished.

"Do you think I'm punishing you?"

"I don't know. I don't know. It's mixed up but I don't know."

He continues to sob and pulls out a tissue from his pocket. He insists he's being punished even though I assure him that I'm not punishing him. He continues to complain and says they are making him do something he doesn't want to do. "I just wanna enjoy myself. But they don't give a damn about me or anyone else. And I told 'em so!" he yells.

"I think that if they gave you a job to do you should do it," I argue.

"I'll tell 'em I'm not gonna do it. Then they'll hit me! Or they're gonna do this other thing they did. And I can't disappear any longer," he says, referring to his previous capacity to dissociate, which he can no longer do.

I point out that feeling mad is not wrong, but nonetheless I would like him to comply with the staff's request to do whatever they're asking him to do. He says they keep asking him to help confused patients and insists that if he doesn't do what they tell him they will lock up all of his clothes. When I try to assure him that the staff is asking him to do those things because they think he is getting better my explanation falls on deaf ears.

He says the only thing he can do is to escape from the ward, because they only want him to do things he doesn't want to do and refuse to help him do what he wants to do. I agree that he's had to manage things on his own after Jay left, but escaping the ward is no answer.

He feels sorry about not wanting Jay to stay. "I worked so hard to drive Jay away. He's gone because I killed him. And I don't wanna drive you away too," he laments.

"You won't drive me away. And you didn't kill Jay. He left because he wanted you to become independent. And he asked me to take over the responsibility to help you grow up. Let me assure you I'm here to do that."

Rather than tell me he feels reassured, he returns to his obsession that he'll be forced to do undesirable things on the ward, and punished if he doesn't do those things.

I reassure him again that the staff wants him to help with other patients because they think he's getting better. But he continues to complain about being forced to "babysit" people and being punished if he refuses.

Finally I make the connection that his fear to "babysit" other patients must be related to his past. "Did you have to take care of your brothers and sisters when you were a boy?"

He nods yes and goes on to tell me more details. "They just locked me up and I couldn't go anywhere!" he sobs. He holds his left hand up to demonstrate how he felt about being locked up.

"How were you locked up?"

"I just had to stay in the house. I couldn't ever go anyplace. That was the punishment," he tells me as he struggles to hold back his tears.

"What else would happen to you?" I ask.

"They gave me more responsibility. I had to do more of this and more of that. It was too much for me. Then I just went away, and I don't know what happened," he explains.

"That must have been when Jay came to protect you wasn't it?" I ask, realizing that he must have dissociated at that time.

78

"I'm glad you told me because you never had a chance to grow up. And now you have that chance."

He continues to sob quietly.

"Do you know how old you were when this happened?"

"I don't know for sure. Maybe seven or eight."

"How old do you feel now?" I ask.

"I don't really know how old. Old enough to smoke," he says.

"You said you don't want to get old and take responsibility."

"I wanna be older but I wanna enjoy just taking responsibility for myself."

I empathize and reassure him that nothing bad will happen, but he doesn't believe my reassurances. He insists on leaving this place though I make it clear that he's not ready yet.

As our session ends, I remind him that it will be a week before our next session. He tells me he's afraid to leave the studio by himself, so I make sure an aide is here to escort him back to his ward.

CHAPTER 18

James has gained a new sense of individuality, with own thoughts and feelings and a desire to establish boundaries.

October 19, 1976

The patient arrives dressed in the same clothes he wore last time. He picks up the pen and signs James with slow deliberation, like a boy who has recently learned to spell his name. After signing in he speaks to me calmly, which contrasts with the last session when he was tearful as well as angry about being made to babysit other patients. His first comment is to announce that Betty and his nephew visited him on the weekend and took him out of the hospital on a pass. He says he felt rejuvenated by seeing new and different things for the first time. But he is also paranoid and says he must constantly guard his territory from invasion. He says he'd kill anyone who would dare to walk into his room without permission.

"Those are strong words. But how is killing someone going to help you?" I ask.

"I'll fight to the death for that room up there. It's my room and I won't share it with anyone. All my life there was someone wearing my clothes or dirtying up my bed."

"All your life? Who was dirtying up your bed?"

He gets out of his chair and walks away a few steps. Then he turns around and gestures dramatically. "If they weren't dirtyin' it there was always somebody in the bed. Usually there was piss in it. But it's my bed now and I don't have to share it."

His description of the unclean conditions he experienced as a young boy is disturbing. I feel empathetic. He finally sits down but continues to talk about his need to have his own things while living in a household with multiple siblings who frequently invaded his boundaries. He particularly singles out a brother called pooky pants, a younger sibling who always dirtied his pants.

"How old were you then?" I ask.

"I don't know. Until I ran away. But I don't like to talk about this. I came over today because I felt really good about having my own feelings and no one is going to slap my hands or set me in a corner."

"Are there other things you won't share besides your feelings?"

"My thoughts. I'll hit anyone who tells me my thoughts are not my own." Then he tells me about a woman who bellyached and nagged, and I soon realize he's talking about his mother.

I ask for more detail, and he suddenly gets up from his chair and turns away from me. I ask him to sit down but he only does so reluctantly. I ask about his anger, and he says he has always been angry from the time he was born. "I felt nine times bigger when I was angry. Someone in the patient group asked me why I'm so mad and I told him I feel good when I'm angry."

"Were you allowed to have angry feelings when you were a child?" I ask.

"No but now I must protect myself and, by God, I'm going to do it. I wish somebody would try to attack me so I could fight. Maybe I could actually kill somebody! But instead, when they try to get in I just kick 'em out. It makes me feel good that they're jealous because I've got something and that I don't have to share anything with 'em. Not even my thoughts."

"Is there anything you like to share?" I ask.

"I like to share my thoughts with you. And my feelings. You're the only one though."

I express my appreciation for his willingness to share those, and then ask a question. "If you were born with a lot of anger weren't you also born with a lot of love?"

Rather than answer that question he talks about his flowers that died.

"What flowers died?" I ask.

"You don't remember the flowers? They were on top of the locker in that cup. I liked those flowers, but they died."

I point out that all cut flowers eventually die, but flowers with roots can be nourished by a continuing food source and they will live.

He ignores my recommendation but continues to talk about how much he loved his flowers. "I enjoyed those flowers. I loved those flowers. It seems strange that they never asked anything at all from me. Yet I still loved them."

"Love is free. You don't have to feel obligated when you love," I say.

He quickly adds, "And there's no responsibility. I don't want any of that."

"Yes. You've told me you're afraid to take responsibility."

"I'm not going to stop those fights up there. All that screaming and hollering has nothing to do with me. I just wanna do the things I wanna do and wear clothes I wanna wear!"

When I point out that he is wearing very nice clothes today, he says this is his third outfit and his second pair of socks. "I don't want anyone else to wear my clothes because they're mine, and I'll bust someone in the mouth if he tries to go in my room."

Our time is nearly over so I tell him that I'll be out of town next week and our next session will be the following Tuesday after the holiday. He takes this announcement fairly well and then tells me he his nephew is coming Sunday. After I announce that our time is up, he sits silently for a long time. After I point out that he doesn't seem to want our session to end, he agrees, frowns, and looks away.

Then he suddenly stands up and quickly departs from the studio before we shake hands as we typically do.

As I get out of my chair and walk out of the studio, I think about James's portrayal of his new sense of autonomy today.

After arriving at my office, I review literature, and learn that a person's sense of self, referred to as self-concept, begins in infancy at about eighteen months of age, and goes through constant evaluation and adjustment throughout the lifespan. By two years the young child becomes aware of his or her gender as a boy or a girl. At four, the child will describe himself or herself by physical features, like hair color. By age six, he will understand emotions and personality traits. With increasing age, he will learn how others perceive him and gain more awareness of his own abilities. Throughout childhood and adolescence, the self-concept becomes more abstract and complex.[10]

CHAPTER 19

James says he hasn't been completely born yet.

October 28, 1976

James seems uncoordinated when he arrives today. After sitting down, he struggles to use the pen, but finally signs in as James. When he begins the session, he tells me he got a haircut yesterday and it was the second time he had ever sat in a barber chair. The sound of shears made him very upset. "I probably broke his barber chair when I jumped out, but I didn't scream or holler. I'm just glad I finally got it cut so I don't have to look like a little boy."

Rather than asking if the little boy is one of his personalities, Jim or Jimmy, I ask if he feels like a grown-up human being. He frowns and says there are times when he doesn't, and wonders if he is doing the things he is supposed to be doing. "I... t...try to d...do the things they ask but I... d...don't always do what they want me to do." He stumbles over his words and continues to ramble but says he doesn't always know the meanings of the words he uses.

James looks bewildered when I tell him he speaks like J (the letter J). I note that his speech sounds like that of a child's and his body language—comprised of fists raised to both sides of his neck—reveals his fear of reaching out to people. He asks me who I'm talking about, indicating that he has no knowledge that I met with J in a therapy session three months ago. At that time, he was unsure if he was a real human, and today he's also unsure if he is real.

When I point out that he seems to be afraid, he says somebody might take him away and he would just disappear.

This fear seems related to the fact that he found strange clothes in his room and other evidence that someone had replaced him.

"How could someone make you disappear?" I ask.

"I don't know. The only thing I know is that there are some clothes and two sacks of things in my locker that aren't mine. If I left them there, I don't remember." He says he doesn't know how he obtained the clothes he's wearing or the times he has met with me. "When I look at the calendar and ask someone what time I'm supposed to meet with you they tell me I already did."

"If you are having trouble remembering times, can you remember when you first began to exist?"

He looks confused and shakes his head.

"Does that mean you aren't sure about your beginning? Do you think your beginning is recent?"

"I'd say yes. But I know it isn't because there are things from before that I do remember."

"In other words, is it possible you may have been reborn?"

"I don't think I've been reborn. This might not sound right. But I have a feeling I haven't been born yet."

He brings his right fist to his chest and continues, "I have a feeling that I'm going to be born. That I'm still living in the past. I know I am. Some things from the past keep going through my mind. It's like a whole lifetime going through my mind."

"Let me ask you again about being born. If you feel you are going to be born in the future, can you elaborate about what that means?"

"I can't say any more about that. It makes me feel silly."

"I see today you are still holding your right thumb. Last time you said you were going to hang on to your thumb. Do you remember?"

"I probably told you because you asked me about it."

"Do you remember other things from our last session?"

"No!" he exclaims.

I ask if he remembers that we talked about the importance of love during our last session and to my surprise he asks me if I love him rather than Jay.

"Sure. I'm talking about you and not Jay."

He begins to cry, and I give him a box of tissues.

"Thank you. I don't wanna cry and holler. I don't wanna do that. I'll be punished."

I reassure him that he won't be punished for crying and he won't be punished for having loving feelings. But he finds that hard to believe. He tells me he feels better but doesn't want to do any childish things. To prove that he deserves to be a real person he assures me that he shaves every day, dresses like a grown-up, studies, and tries to remember all the letters of the alphabet. But in spite of doing all that, he still feels like he is about to be born.

CHAPTER 20

James believes he killed Jay and is
fearful that his love will destroy me.

November 1–4, 1976

James is dressed very nicely in a brown sweater over a yellow shirt. After signing in he tells me he feels like he's ten feet tall and weighs 350 pounds. He continues to keep his thumb hidden inside his clenched right fist, and I ask him if he's afraid he will lose his thumb. He shrugs his shoulders, apparently unconcerned. I ask if he remembers Jay, the personality who was able to protect him from his fears, but that triggers a vigorous reaction. "I don't wanna talk about him. I killed him so I could be here!"

It was almost a year since Jay first collapsed and "died" in my office after James thought he had killed him. However, James's belief that he killed Jay may be a false memory related to his most recent departure from the body a month ago. But I remain perplexed about his clenched fist.

"Why do you keep your thumb hidden?" I ask.

He answers my question by saying his thumb is swollen, but that makes little sense so I reach out and gently touch it.

He complains that I hurt him, so I withdraw my hand and ask another question. "What would it take for that thumb to come out?"

He is hesitant to reply but then stutters, "I...I... w...want..."

He can't finish the sentence, so I remind him that there was a time in his past that he wanted love.

He nods yes, although he's still afraid that expressing loving feelings will hurt someone.

When I point out that he can express feelings of affection and it won't hurt me, he shakes his head and tells me I would not be safe if he let his feelings show. Perhaps the symbolic significance of the hidden thumb is to keep me safe from his expressed feelings of love.

Our next meeting is on Thursday, three days later. He takes a long time to sign in but finally writes his full name, James Kohlman.

"How are you feeling today?" I ask.

"I don't know. What am I supposed to feel?"

"Why do you ask that question?" I ask.

"Because I don't know if I have feelings."

I notice that his appearance seems more mature, and his right hand is not clenched, although he keeps his thumb pressed to the palm of his hand. Perhaps he may still think it's not safe to express his feelings. He sits quietly for a time and frowns.

I ask about his thumb, and he says it still hurts but only when someone touches it. Then he tells me about a patient who frightens him. "There's this guy up there. I've been very scared of him. He said something and..." He gestures with his hands and arms. "And it reminded me of...of..." Pause. "I don't like to talk about these things."

He sits quietly for a long time. Then he asks me an unusual question. "I want you to tell me if I'm real."

"Can you tell me if you feel real?" I ask.

He shakes his head.

"Does a part of you feel real?"

He nods his head but answers that only some parts of him feel real.

I list his body parts—feet, legs, hips, genitals, stomach, and chest—and ask if each of them feels real.

He answers yes to each.

Then I ask if his heart feels real.

He frowns and asks me if there is another word connected with the word heart.

I explain that most people associate the word love with the heart, but he doubts that love is real. When I ask if his parents expressed their love for him he says no. He also remembers that he was punished when he wanted to express love. I ask if anyone has ever told him they love him and he says he would like that because he'd feel more solid.

This subject has brought a mystical quality to our session, and I can see him hold his hands together as if he's in prayer. I notice that he is not holding his thumb as tightly and he says he feels more relaxed now. He says he can't talk to any of the people on his ward about his feelings because they are all crazy. He also tells me he hears voices but can't tell if people really talk to him.

I'm unsure whether he is hallucinating, and I ask if he hears my voice.

He says, "I close my eyes and listen to your voice. But there are other voices, and they give me instructions when I want to say something." He tells me that he hears instructions that he needs to listen and pay attention to everything.

I ask who is giving him instructions and he says he's unsure. Then I ask if he is feeling unstable and he nods his head. I ask what it would take for him to feel more stable and he tells me that he had a visit from his sister-in-law. "Betty was here yesterday, and it made me feel good. That's why I felt good yesterday and better today. Because she was here."

He then tells me the staff keeps asking for his plans, but he doesn't have any plans. He keeps feeling unsettled on the ward and keeps the light on in his room at night to feel grounded.

As our session ends, he says his brother and sister-in-law will be visiting him on Sunday. He has already requested a pass to ride in their car, but he's been told he can't leave the hospital grounds, which is okay with him because staying on the grounds provides him with a sense of solid reality. "Now I can leave the hospital and I won't have to look at the ward as the only thing that's real!" he exclaims.

I remind him we will meet on Monday and we both stand up and leave the room together.

James is struggling to know if he is a real person and described a distorted self-image during Monday's session. His desire to gain a sense of identity seems to be why he felt a need to "kill" Jay to escape feeling controlled by him and experiencing himself as a separate person.

PART FOUR

James Kohl

CHAPTER 21

Today he believes he doesn't have
parents so he can't be a real person.

November 8, 1976

James arrives dressed nicely, and after sitting quietly for a long time he signs his name. I look at his signature and realize he signed James Kohl, which is a change from last session when he signed his whole name, James Kohlman.

"I don't know what my name is really," he says with hesitation. After a pause he continues. "Yes I know what my name is but I don't feel like that's my name. I feel like I'm just waiting until somebody makes up their mind and then I'm gonna do something."

James says he feels scared and would like to hide somewhere. He says he feels better if he holds something that belongs to him.

After a long silence he tells me that something happened on Saturday that wasn't true.

"Can you explain what you mean by that?" I ask.

"They told me I was supposed to meet my parents 'cause they were here but I don't even have any."

"You don't have any?" I repeat.

"No. They say those two people are my parents. But I just don't have any. That's the way I feel right now."

"You don't want to accept your mother and father as your parents?"

"I just don't have any Dr. Brende. I feel like I'm going to get some now that you've brought it up."

His belief that he doesn't have parents surprises me, so I ask if he feels like he's a real person. He says he thinks he must be real sometimes but other times he doesn't think so. I ask what's behind this belief, and his answer is that there are entities screaming at him.

"Who are they?" I ask.

"They're in a group. They all talk at the same time, but they don't move their lips and that's very frightening. I can only hear their thoughts."

"Is there a relationship between these entities whose thoughts you hear and your parents?" I ask. He doesn't believe so. But then he tells me he recognizes one of the voices.

"That's interesting. Whose voice do you recognize?"

"I think it's Lot's voice." He goes on to tell me that Lot is spelled Latot.

I ask him to tell me about his relationship to this Latot and whether he is a real person.

"No, Latot isn't real but I'm not real either," he says, looking around anxiously and clenching his hands. "I'm not supposed to be talking about him. Besides I only hear his voice. I don't see him, Dr. Brende. I just see you. I hear your voice, but I don't hear your thoughts."

"If I was a Latot would you hear my thoughts?" I ask.

"If you were a Latot you'd be invisible."

"Did you ever wonder if your father was a Latot?" I ask.

He shakes his head and stares silently into the distance. Then he breaks the silence and says, "It's almost time."

"We've only been here for twenty minutes James. Why do you say that?"

"I have to go because I won't have any place to be."

"I don't understand what you mean by that."

"I can't sit in this chair while you're there in that chair," he says as he looks at the chair I'm sitting in. "Why can't I sit in your chair?" he asks.

"Because there's only room for me in this chair. You must stay in that chair," I reply.

"That's why I have to go," he says.

I'm confused and ask if something has upset him.

"I don't wanna be scared," he replies.

"Scared of what?"

"I just don't wanna be scared," he says very quietly. "I'll forget and then I won't remember and I won't be scared. But I have to go."

"What if I insist that you stay?" I ask.

He sits quietly for a long time with his hands crossed. After a lengthy silence he tells me again that he can't stay. Then he adds that I can't stop him. He's clearly angry so I ask if he thinks his angry feelings can kill. He replies yes, raises his voice, and insists that I need to let him go.

Since he appears to be on the verge of dissociating, I respond assertively. "James. I want you to stay and talk to me during this hour."

"I can't keep up with all these conversations!" he exclaims.

I decide to intervene by verbally demanding that the people talking to him had best leave him.

My intervention seems to relieve his anxiety, which prompts him to say that there has never been anything solid around him from the time of his origin.

I assume that he's referring to his birth, so I explain that his mother and father provided a solid presence for him when he came into the world.

James responds to my mention of his parents by becoming anxious again. So I assert my authority and demand the voices in his head to leave him. He lowers his hands toward his lap and says gratefully, "Thank you. I hear you." Again I ask him about

his birth but he frowns and says he didn't originate with his parents.

I ask how and when he originated as a personality, and he doesn't respond. Then I ask about my role. "Am I one of the persons who helped you originate?"

"No. You keep me originated," James insists.

During the remainder of our time, we continue to talk about the fact he is a real person who was born from real parents, but he declares he's not ready to believe that.

When I reviewed this session later, I found it significant that he signed his name James Kohl. He omitted the three letters—m-a-n—indicating uncertainty about his male identity. There was also a significant episode during which he asked to sit in my chair and walked out of the room when I challenged him. That evoked feelings of anger in both of us which may have triggered the confusing voices in his head. I assured him that angry feelings wouldn't kill either of us. When it became apparent that he needed my help to clear his head I made an authoritative statement that the voices leave him. He responded to my intervention with a sense of relief, and we were able to end the session on a positive note.

CHAPTER 22

James believed he was born in shame, but now believes love is his foundation for becoming human.

November 11, 1976

James arrives late today. He sits down and signs his name slowly. Then he asks me if I really want him, a question that surprises me.

"I'm not sure I understand your question. Do I want you?" I ask.

Instead of answering the question he says he's had a very bad night. "I woke up at midnight last night and I've been floating ever since. I've been trying to grab on to things but that doesn't help."

"You mentioned before you didn't feel you had a foundation. You also said last time that you were afraid your loving feelings could hurt me, and your anger could kill me."

He agrees that he said that to me, and I assure him that nothing bad has happened, which is reassuring for him.

"Does that mean I'm needed? That I'm wanted?" he asks softly.

"Yes. You are needed and wanted. I'm surprised you would ask that question."

"Maybe I should have asked it a long time ago."

I point out that in the past he didn't believe anyone cared about him, but he has recently been open to the possibility that someone does indeed care.

He sits for a short time before speaking softly. "I no longer have any choice. It's going to happen and that's it."

"What do you mean?"

"I understand now about the thoughts I've received. There's no need to fight it."

"Fight what?"

"To be here. To go on," he says softly.

"I'm not sure I understand what you're talking about."

He sighs. "You know I was a birthday gift?"

"What do you mean?"

"Do you know that today, November 11, is my father's birthday and my mother gave him sex that day because it was his birthday?"

"What do you mean, gave him sex?"

"I mean my mother said he could have sex with her for his birthday and this is what resulted from it," he says, pointing to himself. His voice is barely audible. "I had no choice about being born."

"Didn't she offer it lovingly?"

He shakes his head. "No."

"How can you know that? You weren't there."

"But I was there. I didn't wanna be there. But once I was there, there was nothing I could do."

"How do you mean you were there? You weren't born yet."

He tries to explain that he had been in a dark place and that his parents' sex was not a loving occasion. I ask if he was ashamed about their sexual activity, but the only thing that bothered him was being pulled into this world because of their sex.

"Would you have rather not been born?" I ask.

"You're asking something I don't know, because I don't know."

"If you hadn't been born, I wouldn't have gotten to know you and we wouldn't be sitting here today."

"It's not so important that I'm sitting here but it's important for me to find out my purpose as a human being."

"What do you think is your purpose?" I ask.

"I can only say to love is my purpose. That's it. To love."

"To love? That's a very worthwhile purpose."

Then he says that even though he didn't want to be born because of his parents' sex, he wishes to be born now.

I remind him that last time he told me he was becoming. "The way you put it was that you are here now, and you are going to be. Which means you are continuing to be born."

He nods his head but sits quietly.

"I think it's hard for you to accept the fact that love was behind all this from the beginning. And love is now the reason you are becoming."

"I don't think I can say any more today because I don't wanna lie. The truth is I do want to exist. But I don't know the word. It has something to do with rules I think."

"Can you explain what you mean by rules?" I ask.

He says his existence depends on whether he follows Latot's rules or my rules, but he prefers Latot's rules because my rules are "idiotic feelings."

"Do you feel like you're caught between wanting to please me or wanting to please Latot?" I ask.

"Yes. I used to be able to fight you and the other one but now there isn't the other one," he says, referring to Jay's absence since late September.

I assure him that he doesn't have to be afraid to live, and he replies that if I will continue to help him he won't be afraid. After a long pause, he tells me that he feels like taking a shower and putting on nothing. I ask what he means by that, but he can't explain. Then he apologizes for asking me for help.

"Are you afraid to ask for help?" I ask.

"Yes. I've been afraid," he responds softly as he looks at me and holds his hands between his legs. I point out that our time is up, but he says he doesn't feel like leaving. "I don't wanna go now 'cause I just don't know what I'm going to do," he moans.

He goes on to tell me that he struggled all day about whether he should come to this session, but now he feels a sense of loss about not meeting again until next time. I assure him he'll be in

my thoughts each day. That seems to be reassuring, and he was able to walk out of the studio and join a waiting nursing assistant.

As I think about this session it is significant that James said he felt like he was floating, which was a reference to his lack of a solid foundation for existing. That was clearly related to his sense of shame about his alleged birth to the two people who claimed to be his parents. Thus, he looked to me to fill his parenting void by asking if I wanted him. When I told him that I did indeed want him, he could believe that a loving relationship with me is the glue that assures his existence.

When I heard him talk about his pre-birth memory, I found that impossible to believe because of the prevailing belief that a preborn or newborn infant doesn't possess a functioning memory. But then I reviewed the literature and learned there are research findings that indicate that an unborn baby has a memory as well as other important life functions that exist in the womb. Fetal breathing begins at ten to eleven weeks of gestation, even though there is no air in the womb. A fetus has coordinated eye movements in the absence of visual stimuli. A preborn baby begins to learn speech characteristics of its mother before birth and remembers the mother's voice in comparison to other female voices after birth. This prenatal priming enables the newborn to recognize mother's familiar voice to facilitate a more rapid attachment. Researchers have also learned that a preborn infant may become accustomed to the flavor of the amniotic fluid beginning at twelve weeks of gestation. This would enable the newborn's predisposition to suck at mother's breast as the instinctive means to ensure survival.

I also found an article that reported stories from people, mainly children, who recalled an existence shortly before birth called the pre-birth experience. Those who described pre-birth experiences seemed to "remember" existing in the same or similar plane to near-death experiences (NDEs). They recalled being in a spirit world where they were given a preview of their life and future parents. The following is an example of such a pre-birth memory:

> I can remember standing in a dark space, but unlike being in a darkened room, I could see everything around me and the blackness had dimension. There was another person standing to my right, and like me, he was waiting to be born into the physical world. There was an older person with us who could possibly be a guide, since he stayed with us until we left and answered my questions. In front of us and approximately thirty degrees below us, we could see the earth with the facial images of two couples. I asked who those people were whose images appeared on the earth and he replied that they were going to be our parents. The older man conveyed to us that it was time to go. The other person standing next to me walked forward and disappeared from my sight. I was told that it was my turn and I walked forward. Suddenly I found myself lying in a hospital nursery with other babies around me. [11]

CHAPTER 23

James saw the movie The Three Faces of Eve
and thinks he has the same problem.

November 15, 1976

James appears more adult-like. He is sporting a mustache and wearing new tan slacks and a white sweater over a red shirt.

He begins the session by commenting on the cool weather and I agree that it's pleasant. I state that I like his new clothes. He thanks me and asks if I like his new belt as he proudly lifts his sweater to show me.

He says his nephew bought these clothes with money he gave him.

He changes the subject and tells me he's been listening for instructions about what he should be doing.

"Who are you listening to?"

"Anyone that's there," he replies.

I assume he is listening to Latot's voice and remind him that he previously told me he sometimes felt caught between what I say and what Latot says.

He agrees but then tells me he hasn't heard from Latot for about five days. When I ask if he's unhappy about that, he says he's unhappy for another reason—he hears other people's thoughts. "I don't know what they're saying so it doesn't make sense to me anyway." He sits quietly for a brief time, then continues, "But it scares me now."

I ask him to be more specific about being scared and he says he's never not scared. "I feel scared when I'm alone in my room and I feel scared when I'm around people."

He also says he feels depressed although nobody thinks he looks depressed. "They all tell me how good I look. If I look that good, I'm going to ask my doctor to change my status to a full patient."

"You want to be a full patient? What does that mean?" I ask.

"It means I'm making progress. I like to hear people say 'look at the progress you've made.' It's like hearing people say I won a million dollars. But that's because I hear 'em thinking. And sometimes I hear you thinking too."

I ask him for more details, and he says he heard my thoughts a few minutes ago but it didn't make sense. Then he changes the subject and says he knows there is another part of him that took over during his visit with another patient named David, because he only has memory fragments about it.

This leads me to tell him that I'm aware of his two most prominent alternate personalities. When I name Jay and Shea, James angrily denounces the possibility that Shea was ever a part of him. He insists that he will never mention his name. Not only that, but he'd also like to kill him if he ever met him personally. However, he also says he doesn't have the same feelings about another part of him —Jay—whom he refers to as the "not me." When I ask if he and Jay are the same person, he says that couldn't be true because Jay is able to speak and read better than he can.

James says he believes there are times when people think he is Jay. "Sometimes they tell me I've done something when I don't have any memory about it. I think the 'not me' musta done

103

it." He says he's had conversations with Latot about the "not me" and was told to quit worrying because it's not important.

He shifts the focus and tells me that Latot is preparing him to become a human being.

"Aren't you a human being now?" I ask.

"I feel like a human but I'm lacking a lot of human qualities."

"What human qualities come to mind?" I ask.

"Being touched, I guess. I don't like to be touched although I know other people don't mind."

"Did your mother touch you when you were small?"

"I presume she did."

"Did Jay like to be touched?"

"I have no idea."

When I point out that I have shaken Jay's hand, James says he didn't know shaking hands was the same as touching, which he avoids, and insists that touch must mean more than touching a person's hand. He says he doesn't like being touched in any way, even when someone brushes up against him.

I change the subject and remind him that he said something very significant last time—he asked me if I wanted him, and I answered that I do want him.

He smiles and announces that he took his thumb out from under his clenched fist last Thursday because it was causing an unpleasant odor.

I congratulate him and think that the emergence of his thumb most likely symbolizes feeling wanted and becoming a person. I believe these parallel his awareness that he has a need to be loved and wanted by another human being, which has enabled him to feel like he is becoming a person. It may also represent his freedom from unpleasant memories of Shea. When I mention Shea's name again, he frowns and tells me that makes him think about his mother.

"She was very selfish. Just like Shea. No matter what she did it was only for herself."

"Don't you don't think she loved you?"

"I don't remember that she did."

"If you were deprived of love the only thing you could do was to give yourself love."

"Maybe."

"So perhaps that's the way Shea dealt with not being loved by mother. He loved himself."

Then James asks a perceptive question. "If a person never received love, how would he know how to give it to someone else?"

"I agree with you, and I believe a boy should be taught about love from his parents."

"I wanted them to teach me the ABCs. Maybe you can teach me the ABCs for humans. That's why I asked you if you wanted me."

I explain that when a boy is learning the ABCs, that's equivalent to learning about loving and being loved. "You wanted to be loved and wanted, and you said you didn't experience that from your mother."

"No. She didn't want me as me."

"What part of you do you think she wanted?"

"I don't know," he says.

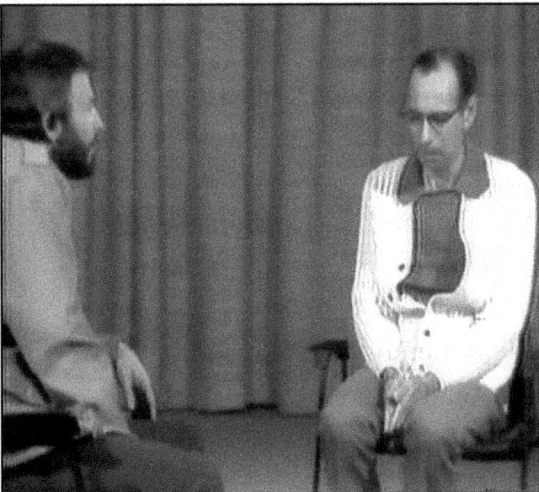

He leans forward with his head down and hands clasped tightly together between his legs. After a long pause he tells me about Al, a hospital patient he describes as the only friend he's ever had. Al was someone he could depend on, and he doesn't know anyone else like that. I assure him that it's normal for him to want a dependable friend.

He continues to sit pensively with his hands folded and says he's glad he came today. "There is so much on my mind. I'm using the nurses and the aides there so I won't run to my room. I grab their sleeves and I holler 'Brende.' I want to hear them answer me so I know I'm still here. And they kept telling me I should have seen that show last night."

"What show?"

"Sybil. She had sixteen personalities. But I didn't wanna see it."

"Have you ever thought about yourself as being similar to Sybil?"

"Not like Sybil. There was another one. *The Three Faces of Eve*. Don't ask me how it ends but it makes me want to understand about myself."

I commend him for wanting to understand himself, and then he asks me why he doesn't want to talk about money while everyone else can't stop talking about it.

I point out that even if he hasn't learned about money, he has learned a great deal else during the last few weeks. But he challenges me by saying that he hasn't learned enough to get off the ward. He says he wants ways to run away and when no one is looking he runs to the door, but it's always locked.

I point out that there is still much for him to learn because he stopped learning at age seven, the age when Jay took over the body.

He sits quietly for a time but suddenly hollers, "I wanna scream!"

"What about?"

"Why won't they let me remember?" he exclaims.

"Who's the 'they' you're referring to?"

"Whoever should have taught me. Maybe it's you. Aren't you they?" he bellows, clearly upset. "I wanna cuss now. Why wasn't I taught? It was something I shoulda known."

I did not try to explain that Jay replaced him when he was seven years old, but I did point out that he has a reason to be angry at his father for abusing him and not teaching him the things he should have learned when he was young.

"I don't wanna blame my father," he sobs.

I remind him that it's okay to express feelings of anger. "You got angry at me because you were hurting during our last session, and I told you it was okay to have those feelings."

"Don't say that I'm angry at you or anyone!" he demands.

"You can be as angry as you like. It won't hurt me."

"But it might hurt me."

"How can it hurt you?" I ask. He replies that he perceives me as someone who acts as if I can pat him on the head like he's a good little boy and it doesn't matter. Then he exclaims that it matters to him and orders me to stop acting that way. He brings his hands up to both sides of his head and exclaims, "Dr. Brende!" After a pause he repeats his exclamation, "Dr. Brende," in a softer tone of voice.

He has difficulty giving up the belief that his anger has hurt me, and he reaches out to touch my arm to make sure I'm okay. I assure him that he didn't hurt me. "Everything is okay. But you can always tell me if I say something that upsets you."

"Why do I have to tell you? Don't you hear my thoughts?" he asks. I quickly reply that I didn't hear his thoughts so he needs to tell me.

"It makes me mad that you don't hear my thoughts! I don't know what to do. Help me!" he exclaims.

"I'm here to help you. I think the confusion you're experiencing today may happen from time to time. You're not crazy. Your thoughts don't bother me," I assure him.

"You handle it a helluva lot better than me," he says jokingly.

I smile, which prompts him to ask if he embarrassed me. When I assure him I wasn't embarrassed he apologizes. "I'm being childish right now, but I have to be because everything is too overwhelming. I know I can't read your thoughts."

I point out that it would be much better if he stopped trying to read people's thoughts, and that he should consider reading books rather than thoughts.

CHAPTER 24

*James tells me he's afraid of losing
the knowledge he has gained.*

November 18–21, 1976

James signs in and quickly tells me he's afraid of losing the knowledge he has gained. "This is the only world I know now. Don't take this away from me," he says.

I assure him that his world is expanding, and I won't take it away. I also remind him that during our last session he said he really existed, like someone who has been born.

"Do you feel like you are really existing for the first time?"

"Yes, because you said you needed me," he says.

"The last time we met you called Jay the 'not me,' and you wondered if I liked him more than I liked you. But I can assure you that I like you both."

We spend time talking about the fact he feels like a young student who needs to learn.

During our next session on Monday, James signs in and makes a comical remark about flirting with some of the new student nurses who have come onto his ward. Then he looks at me and makes a comment about my appearance. "There's something different about you," he says jovially, and asks if I had gotten a haircut or trimmed my beard.

I smile but remain silent.

"What are you smiling about?" he asks.

"I'm thinking about your comment you were flirting with the new student nurses."

He laughs briefly, but then tells me he refused to meet with his parents yesterday. He says he would meet with his father but doesn't want to see his mother. Then he changes the subject and reports a dream in which a male social worker lay next to him on the bed and took his hand. When I ask James if the dream reminded him of Shea, he says a patient on the ward says he was a friend of Shea. "He always calls me Shea Von Kohlman, but I've never seen him before. He said he saw me some place in Topeka. But I don't know what he's talking about."

When I mention that Shea used to spend time in Topeka and lived at the Jayhawk Hotel, James says this guy knew Shea at the Jayhawk. "I got all upset that he talked to me about that. When I told a nurse about it she called him a nutty patient and told me to forget him."

Then James changes subjects and says he won't go home for Thanksgiving because he doesn't want to see his mother because she gets him all upset. I ask what he remembers about his mother, and he angrily denounces her for controlling his life and listening to his thoughts.

I ask if he is able to listen to her thoughts or to my thoughts, and he answers yes but scowls and says he doesn't want to be called crazy. Then he begins to cry and says I've made him scared to tell anybody about personal things.

When I ask if he will tell me more of his childhood memories, he says his mother resented his birth, destroyed his thoughts and feelings, and left him empty. He complains that she never taught him anything and only took from him. He goes on to say that he would refuse anything his mother wanted to give him. He begins to sob and then brings his hand up to his mouth and bites it. I ask if biting his hand is a way to keep from hurting his mother. He agrees but adds that it is also a way to prevent the power of his thoughts from killing her.

I wonder if his extreme anger is an exaggerated expression of a young child's need to separate himself from a symbiotic fusion that allows mother and child to sense each other's thoughts. If so, his anger is meant to establish a boundary in the service of separation-individuation—a necessary step for breaking away from mother and identifying with his father as he begins the formation of his masculine identity.

"I don't believe your mother can prevent you from loving your father," I insist.

"Yes she can!" he contends as he looks angrily at me. "How well do you know her?"

"I know she can't hurt you in the way you think she can. She's not that powerful."

"If that's true tell her to leave me alone with her thoughts! Tell her right now! Tell her right now!" he demands.

It's clear that James is unable to free himself from the power of his mother's thoughts, so I make a clear pronouncement: "Okay. James's mother. Don't invade James's thoughts and feelings anymore."

He looks at me with annoyance. "You're just saying that to me. Speak to her directly. Tell me what you would say to her!"

"What would you want me to say?" I ask.

"You wouldn't call her James's mother. You'd address her as Mrs. Kohlman!" he asserts.

I restate my pronouncement. "Mrs. Kohlman. Don't intrude upon James's thoughts and feelings. Those are his!" I articulate forcefully.

James immediately says he feels better now after applying a technique I had used successfully as a hypnotherapist by establishing a mental boundary to control intrusive thoughts and images. I repeat my previous assertions that his mother will not be able to intrude on his thoughts, nor take his thoughts or take me away. Then I ask if he feels a sense of protection around him. He replies yes.

James closes his eyes and brings both hands to the sides of his head to calm himself. Then he reaches over, touches my arm and grabs onto my jacket. "I need to hang on to you for a moment. Please." After holding onto my jacket for a short time he says he can feel more solid now.

Before our session comes to an end, I remind him that next Thursday is Thanksgiving. He smiles and tells me he can remember happy times he had with his grandma when he was six. He jumped rope, churned butter, and went down into her root cellar. But he has no memories after that when he should have been going to first or second grade, which coincides with the time Jay took over the body. "I remember some things but only until the time I went to school. Then the memories stop. The next thing I remember was being in high school. My mother wasn't around so she wouldn't know."

CHAPTER 25

*It has been six months since James first
accepted love and felt reborn, and a year
since he made an attempt to kill Jay.*

November 29, 1976

After James signs in, he tells me that he had a good meeting
with his brother Clarence, nicknamed Pappy, who came to see
him yesterday. I remind him that yesterday was the one-year
anniversary of when he tried to kill Jay by giving him too many
pills. He had thought of himself as a murderer and expected to
get electroshock treatments as a punishment, but his worse fears
never happened. James now says he has too many other things
to worry about, like hearing everyone's thoughts, having
memories he can't block out, worrying whether love restores or
destroys people, and blaming his mother for her lack of love and
taking his father away.

I point out that even though he believes his mother did not
give him enough love when he was a small child, he is no longer
a child. "How old do you feel you are?" I ask.

"Twenty-eight," he replies.

Since he is actually forty years old, I wonder what happened
to those lost twelve years. Because he felt reborn six months ago,
it's possible that he has rapidly gained twenty-eight years since
then.

As I review the course of therapy thus far, I've talked about
the significance of love as the basis for his existence as a person.
That emphasis has affected our relationship positively. Today,
James refers to me as his friend first and his doctor second.

In order to understand the role of love in psychotherapy, it's helpful to review its significance as a guiding principle for life and human relationships. Parental love is the building block for a child's basic identity and determines how that child, growing up, will experience and express it. Love can involve personal affection, sexual attraction, platonic admiration, brotherly loyalty, benevolent concern, or worshipful adoration. Love, as described in the Bible, originates from the personhood and actions of God who bestows it unconditionally toward all who are willing to receive it.

The significance of love in psychotherapy is not generally discussed in scientific journals. However, noted psychologist Eric Erickson described the empathic relationship between patient and therapist as a necessary precursor for loving and enduring close relationships.

Object-relations theorist Gregory Hamilton described love as the binding element in the object relations unit between mother and child. He also emphasized the significance of the patient-therapist relationship as providing the "holding" functions of therapy—defined as empathic listening and responding to the patient's words and behaviors.

Otto Kernberg emphasized the significance of the relationship between therapist and patient, referred to as transference, and emphasized transference interpretations within the therapeutic process. Transference Focused Psychotherapy (TFP) particularly helps patients who suffered from contradictory fragments of the self and identity confusion. [12]

Since James' symptoms met those characteristics, I incorporated the principles of TFP into my therapeutic approach. For example, I made frequent transference interpretations to confront James's distorted perceptions of family relationships. When he said he heard his mother's thoughts, my transference interpretation focused on hearing my thoughts. When he thought his father was powerless, I made a transference interpretation that he thought I'm powerless. When he blamed his mother for making him feel insignificant, I made a transference interpretation that he believed I made him feel insignificant. I repeatedly emphasized the importance of loving relationships, including his relationship with me, as the basis for his identity.

PART FIVE

James

Full Patient Status

CHAPTER 26

*James has achieved full patient status
but can't resolve his feelings of anger.*

December 2, 1976

James arrives dressed nicely and signs in. I carefully scrutinize the signature pad to see if he has signed a new name, and he asks me if something is wrong. I assure him there is nothing wrong. He had signed James.

He seems much more self-sufficient today. He tells me he has been granted new freedoms and is able to go off the ward whenever he wants. He was also elected secretary of the ward and given the privilege of attending the Industrial Therapy Unit (ITU), which he enthusiastically attended yesterday morning. According to James, his ITU therapist was surprised to learn he had not taken high school physics. I learned later that James had told him he only finished the eighth grade. Despite his apparent success story, he now tells me he continues to be upset by a demanding woman on the ward named Fayetta. He says that she talks continuously and won't stop even though he tries to walk away from her. She accuses him of trying to run off the ward four or five times a day, but he accuses her of lying about him.

As I hear him talk, I'm convinced that the James who is talking to me right now is definitely not the same person Fayetta saw trying to run off the ward. Perhaps I'm talking to Jay even though he signed in as James. It's also possible that the person who she said was trying to run off the ward was a young James or the sub-personality Jim, whom I had contact with many months ago.

He continues to rant about Fayetta. "She has to put her goddam nose into everyone's business. She started this morning because someone picked up her damn cup off the table. It was a guy who thought she was through with her drink and picked it up. She had a shit hemorrhage and fell into it. And who the hell wants to pull her out of it? I'm not gonna!"

I'm curious regarding the degree of freedom James claims to have achieved and ask if it's true that he is able to go off the ward whenever he wants. He explains that he's allowed to leave the ward, but only if he makes a formal request and gives a good reason. If his request is approved by the staff, he must sign out before he leaves and specifically state where he is going and when he will return.

I congratulate him on achieving full patient status with privileges, but I also ask if he's had any memory problems or blackouts.

He says he watches the clock and keeps track of what he's doing in case he blacks out. After a brief pause, he changes the subject, asks me if he's ever been married, then says he had a dream that he was married. He goes on to describe in some detail a pretty girl he planned to marry who wore a big velvet brown hat. Then he changes the subject and complains that the men on the ward are always gossiping about shacking up, an expression he's never heard before.

"What do you think it means?" I ask.

"A shack located up in the mountains."

"Could it mean something else?"

"Just two people staying together, and they don't have any idea what they're doing. They're using each other even though they don't think they're being used. That's something that doesn't appeal to me."

He remains quiet for a short time, then complains of terrible headaches, which he blames on Fayetta. "You know how I'd like to react? I'd like to bash her brains in." He continues to complain that she creates a disturbance every time she comes into the hospital, which has happened four times this year.

I point out that he gives her too much power and suggest other options like stop listening to her and walking away.

"That won't work because she follows me wherever I go, and I keep hearing her anyway."

"I'm sure you can think of something."

"You know she followed me this morning. I felt like killing her because that's the only way to keep her from following me."

"Do you really think seriously about killing her?" I ask.

"Yes, I do. But I don't want to."

"How do you keep from doing it?"

"I clench my fist so hard there are marks on my hand so I can't open my hands. And I go into my room and scream!"

"I've seen your fists clenched when you sit with me. Do you feel that way with me?"

"No. I don't know how to say how I feel." He goes on to explain that he doesn't always know the right words to use. He says there was a time when he didn't even know how to ask for a fork at mealtime. He learned from watching other people and he would do what they did. He says he got very mad on one occasion when a person refused to help him get the food he wanted, and he threw mashed potatoes at him.

He resumes his complaints about Fayetta, so I ask how he would like to change the situation. His immediate response is to keep asking for a transfer to the open ward where his friend Al is a patient. Since he doesn't expect to get the transfer request approved, I ask if he has any other ideas, but he can't think of any. So I suggest that the situation on his ward warrants a good laugh.

"Do you mean being silly? Like a ha ha laugh? Or should we laugh at her?" he asks.

I point out that laughing at her is not appropriate and question whether she is doing all of the things he accuses her of doing. He insists everything he's said about her is true. "It really is happening!" he exclaims. "And when I tell her to stop she won't take no for an answer."

I suggest that he put up an imaginary barrier around himself as a defense against her verbal abuse. But he disagrees and claims it will help her instead of him.

As our session is about to end, I make a final suggestion that he should go to his room and yell in the privacy of his own space when he feels so upset. After James leaves the studio I make a phone call to his ward. I'm told that the staff is quite aware of Fayetta's disruptive behavior, but they keep a close eye on her. They also tell me James has been more upset than usual, but he was also elected ward secretary and is able to leave the ward and attend Industrial Therapy. Although James spouted out angrily about Fayetta, he appeared more intellectually mature today, so I remain uncertain about which James met with me.

CHAPTER 27

James is surprised to hear Jay is not dead.
He realizes he lost most of his memories when
Jay took over, but now he wants to get them back.

December 6, 1976

After James signs in he sighs deeply and says he's been waiting since Thursday for our session today. He shows me a photo taken in the past that other patients say is a picture of him, but he doesn't recognize the person because he has a goatee, beard, and longer hair combed back.

"I've been hearing a lot about that 'so and so' and they say that he is me. But I don't like the name they called him," James states.

"What's his name?"

"Jay." Pause. "And I'm still fighting. Fighting to be here."

I remind him that Jay was the person he thought he had to fight and to kill so he could survive just over a year ago. He doesn't want to think about that and says he has so many disturbing thoughts that the only way to escape them would be to leave the ward. He has already made a request to be transferred to an open ward where his friend Al lives, but his request was refused. "They said Al is a bad influence."

I remind him that there was a time he thought it was dangerous to have loving feelings toward a friend or anyone he cared about, including me.

"You are my friend, aren't you? Can't friends love each other? They don't have to hate each other, do they?"

I express my appreciation that he considers me his friend, and I also agree that friends can love each other. "But sometimes friends have angry feelings and that's acceptable. Do you remember the time you had thoughts about killing me?" I ask.

"Yes. But I didn't say it though. I thought about killing you, but you've said you can't hear my thoughts."

I nod my head and tell him that's okay. After a brief silence I ask if he's going to keep the picture of Jay he showed me at the beginning of the session. He says if I don't want it he's going to decoupage it.

I return to the subject of Jay's absence and James's belief that he killed him. I clarify that Jay is not here because he decided to leave and made that decision on his own. I tell him about the session on September 27 when Jay became catatonic, fell off the chair, appeared to have left the body, and was replaced by James.

"He left?" James exclaims. "He's not dead? Where is he?"

"I have no idea where he is. Nobody killed him. But I know you had a lot of sad feelings because you lost somebody important to you."

James asks if Jay left voluntarily or if the body died. I explain that when Jay left the body it remained very much alive.

This subject is confusing for him, and he questions how he could have existed without a body. My explanation doesn't help so he changes the subject and begins to talk about Christmas, which is less than three weeks away. He tells me that this is his first Christmas as an adult, although he has memories of the time he received a little train with five cars. He remembers other things like seeing a big star, lights for Christmas trees, odors of kerosene lamps, and pies and cookies. After he tells me that Christmas seems superficial and decorations are only temporary, I express my hope that he can see Christmas as being special, and that it's a time when people give and receive gifts.

This is a new subject for him. He is not aware that it is a custom for children to receive gifts at Christmas time.

124

"You say custom. Is the custom of Christmas just a fantasy? Isn't the birth of Jesus Christ a fantasy?" he asks.

After I clarify that Jesus Christ's birth isn't a fantasy, he says he's not a child any longer and wants to find answers about what's real and what's a fantasy.

"What you have been learning about is real. But what you dream about can be fantasy," I reply.

"Like the dream I had last night that I asked to go to the open ward. I kept waiting to hear and then she told me I was transferred there. I jumped up and down. And then I woke up because it wasn't true. Is that a fantasy?"

I agree that what he sees in his dreams are fantasies. Then he tells me he still doesn't know why people are so sad and mad now that it is Christmas, because he thought it was supposed to be a happy time. "I hear staff and volunteers say 'I gotta get this shopping done and that done' and other things that upset them. I think that's bullshit. You don't have to do all those things!" he exclaims.

I point out that he is more direct than most people and he could teach them, but he disagrees. He says he is still fighting bad memories, and that whenever he wakes up after a nightmare he wants to run to my office and tell me about it.

"Did you come over here this weekend?" I ask, having been told by a staff member about his weekend visit to my office.

"Yes," he replies, and then tells me he ran to my office because he was afraid that he would get shock treatments again like four years ago.

"If you thought you were going to get electro-convulsive treatments that was a fantasy. I can tell you that won't happen."

He says that there are other things that scare him, like the patient who ran at him very fast as if he was going to hit him, and then ran into the elevator just as the door shut.

I return to the subject of his frightening fantasies and confront him with the fact that he can't seem to let go of them because they're the most powerful things he still has. The subject of power triggers distressing memories about his mother's power, and he says he hopes I have more power than she does.

After challenging me about whether I'm telling him the truth, he remains quiet for a time, then tells me he went to the music room and found a music book with notes in it. He says he discovered he could play the piano and sing the words. I ask if he learned to play the piano in the past. He says he never learned to play the piano and didn't even know what music looked like. I ask if he could explain how he can play the piano now if he never learned to play it in the past. He says that playing the piano was like falling down. He was never taught how to fall down and he has no memory of being taught how to play the piano.

"Maybe that's a skill Jay left for you," I propose.

"What am I supposed to do with it?"

"Grow into it."

"I'm supposed to be pounding on the piano?" he grins.

"Maybe you can learn to trust what Jay learned—that it's okay if you let yourself do the things Jay did?"

"But if I do that, will I still be here?" he asks.

"Yes, you will still be here. I asked Jay before he left the body if he would leave his knowledge and abilities for you to use and he said he would leave it as a gift," I explain.

James opens his eyes wide. "Was it a Christmas gift?" he smiles.

"Maybe that's your Christmas present."

He nods his head slowly and says he feels like a child who can receive gifts but hasn't learned how to give them. I encourage him to learn how to give as well as receive.

I realize our time is almost up, so I ask if he has something else he wants to talk about, and after sitting quietly for a time he asks an interesting question about people's thoughts.

"You said before that I can block out everything that comes into my mind. But if I do that won't I disappear?"

I assure him that he won't disappear if he screens out people's words or thoughts. He remains quiet for a time, then asks, "How am I able to survive now?"

"You're here so doesn't that mean you're surviving?"

"How was I able to survive when I wasn't here?"

"Jay has been taking care of the body since you were about seven years old so that you could survive."

I ask him if he would like to be able to have Jay's memories, and he says he would like to read like Jay and be fearless like Jay, but he doesn't want to have Jay's life, only his own life.

Then I explain Jay's purpose. "Jay told me his purpose was to give his life to you and protect you from pain because you were not strong enough."

"He said that?" James asks in surprise. Then he becomes very anxious and with a trembling voice asks for an explanation. "Why would he be giving me the body now when it was mine in the first place? And who gave him that right?"

"You did. You gave him the right."

He frowns and wraps his black sweater back and forth on his arm while remaining silent.

"Didn't he realize that what I needed was my own life? Why did he take my life? My whole life?" he questions.

"Yes, he did take over your life, but you gave it to him because you didn't think you could handle it yourself."

"Is that true?" he exclaims, struggling to hold back his tears. "I don't wanna be angry at him. But what can I do now?" he asks.

"You are going to gradually receive from Jay everything you need. Then you'll know what happened over the last thirty-three years. Those memories won't be lost. They will be yours too."

He continues to struggle with this new information and tries to keep from sobbing.

"I think you're upset today because you are now just beginning to know what you missed out on, and the best way is to just feel the sadness for what you lost. The other side is that you're growing and becoming. I hope you can enjoy that."

"I hope I can enjoy some of it. I'm listening to you Dr. Brende. Maybe I'm crazy. But at least I'm listening to you."

"I'm glad you are," I say, and look at the clock on the wall. "It looks like our time is over and we'll meet again on Thursday."

"I don't wanna stop right now. If I could ask you a favor?"

"Yes. What would you like?"

"Can I put my hand on to you for a moment?" he pleads. He reaches out and grasps my arm. "I don't wanna hurt you," he moans.

"You're not hurting me," I assure him, and stretch my left arm out to indicate that it's okay to reach out and recognize that our relationship is intact.

"This is the only thing I know. But I don't know if it's a fantasy," he says.

"This is real. This is not a fantasy," I reply.

It had been an engaging session. James continues to have difficulty knowing what is real and what is a fantasy, including Christmas.

I found it interesting that James remembered holiday smells from his childhood. As I gather information about olfactory memories, I'll learn that smell and emotions are anatomically close to each other within the brain's limbic system, which contains the amygdala (emotions) and hippocampus (memories). These neurological structures encompass the olfactory bulb, which is a very ancient part of the brain. The sensation of smell develops fully within the olfactory center while the unborn child is growing in the womb, and is the primary neuro-receptor until that child's sight takes over at age ten. During a child's early years the odors he perceives will be linked to either pleasant or unpleasant emotions he will remember for the rest of his life.[13]

CHAPTER 28

Jay returns to see if I'm real and to learn if
he is real. He says he has no interest in James,
yet wants to find out if I had abandoned him.

December 9, 1976

I'm surprised to see my patient with a different look today. He's wearing a light-blue short-sleeved shirt and pants and is clean-shaven except for a thin mustache. He signs in as Jay, the personality I've not seen since his electroencephalogram (EEG) nearly three months ago. That may explain why he seems confused and why he's found things in his locker he's not seen before. To my surprise he says he talked to James two days ago and found him to be very frightened.

"I wonder if he was scared because you have returned," I surmise.

"Why would he be frightened about that?" Jay asks incredulously as he wrinkles up his face.

"Maybe he thinks you'll replace him now that you've come back."

"Is that what he thinks?" he exclaims loudly. He pulls out a cigarette and tells me, in a carefree way, that he had not planned to see me. But now that he's come back, he went to art therapy yesterday and did finger painting.

I interrupt him and ask again why he came back. His answer is vague. He doesn't want to replace James and insists that he has no plans to become involved in anything. I repeat the question again and to my surprise he says that he wanted to see me because he knows I'm real. "I have not the slightest idea about what's happening. Everything is a dream. Except you."

I ask if he can provide examples of things that don't seem real, but he says he can't because he can't even tell me what day it is.

"Do you plan to come to therapy regularly? And will you be here Monday and Wednesday next week?"

"Why wouldn't I be here? You ought to know that I haven't missed any of these meetings."

After I point out he's not been here for many weeks, he tells me he has a vague memory that he has seen me through a little hole. He holds up his thumb and index finger in a circle in front of his eye to demonstrate.

I ask him if he had seen James come to my office feeling scared late Tuesday afternoon. Jay shrugs his shoulders and asks, "Is James my brother?" He pauses and then answers his own question. "Yeah, he is." Then he pulls out a pack of cigarettes, which prompts me to tell him he can't smoke during our session.

He puts the pack back in his pocket and then compliments my choice of clothes. Then he shrugs his shoulders and says, "I don't know what to talk about."

"Maybe you just came over to see if I was here, like James would have done. You know that you've always been his protector, and now you say he's your brother."

He makes a comment that he must have been doing a good job since James is still here. But then he says he has a vague memory of James. "He's a very mean person, isn't he? And he doesn't like anyone, does he?"

"If you're referring to James, he's not mean but he does feel angry sometimes because you don't. He has all the feelings, but you do all the thinking and take all the responsibility."

"I've always taken care of someone," he says, looking away with a frown.

"Did you come today because your purpose is to see if I'm taking care of James?"

"I told you I came over because I wanted to see you. But I probably won't do this again."

After assuring him he can see me whenever he wants, I remind him that the last time I saw him was the day I requested that a member of the hospital staff bring him to the EEG lab. Even though he didn't like being there he received an EEG over two months ago on September 27. He squirms in the chair uncomfortably when I tell him I was notified about the EEG results, which did not reveal any active seizure focus.

As the session ends, he suddenly announces that today is December 9, two days after Pearl Harbor Day. It's as if he came back in touch with reality for the first time.

CHAPTER 29

He feels like a five-year-old and is
scared of the crazy people on the ward.

December 13, 1976

I expected Jay to come today since he was present during our last session, but James signs instead. After he lays the pen down, I ask where he was last Thursday. He gives me a nonspecific answer, so I ask if he remembers the last time he was here. He says it was just before Betty visited him last weekend, but he didn't mention he got scared and stopped at my office six days ago.

I ask him if he remembers what we talked about during our last session, and he says he doesn't remember much. Then he complains that people in the ward are making him do things he doesn't want to do. He tells me in fragmented sentences that everyone on the ward gets him upset and then they laugh about it. I ask if the woman on the ward still invades his mind. He nods his head and complains that he can't block out her thoughts.

I make a transference interpretation that he must feel blocked off from me too. He nods his head vigorously. "I came over here to see you and you left me high and dry." After complaining about the ward again, I assure him that I will discuss his concerns with his hospital doctor. Then I tell him that Jay came to the last session. "He came here last Thursday and I wondered if you had wanted him to come?"

"I don't care a thing about him. Let him die. Let him disintegrate. I don't care about him!" he exclaims.

James makes it clear that he did not send Jay to see me and resumes his complaints, this time about the nagging old women who locked the door and kept him from leaving the ward.

"Can't you ask one of the staff to open the door for you? I saw there was a man on the ward last Tuesday when I made a visit to the ward. I'm sure he'd help you out," I say.

"He's not a man. He's just a thing that does something for those damn women up there so they can get their way." He begins to cry, then continues, "If he was a man he'd do something to get the door unlocked. Why do I have to wait 'til nine thirty at night to get the door unlocked?" he exclaims.

He complains that I must be too weak to get the door open for

him, but I clarify that I went to his ward on Tuesday and talked to his doctor, who said he would make sure the door stayed open. But James is unhappy that the door was locked again on Wednesday and Friday.

"You said they promised not to lock the door, but they keep doing it," he complains as he raises his right hand in protest.

I ask if he thinks I have enough power to make the staff keep the door open, but he avoids answering me and insists that they all want the door locked.

"Do you know why they lock the door?" I ask.

"I keep asking why is the door locked? But they don't give me an answer and I don't know the answers for all the things that go on up there," he complains as he wipes the tears from his eyes.

"Would you like me to find out who knows the answer?"

"I know the answer already. It's the frickin' ass females. They're always into other people's business and it's not their business whatsoever," he complains.

I ask him to help me understand why females are so disturbing to him, and he replies that they always want something from him. "I don't know what they want but I won't let them get my thoughts or my feelings!" he exclaims with tears in his eyes.

"You used to think your mother wanted all your thoughts. Do those women also want them?"

"I don't know what else they want."

"You have a body. Do you think they want your body?"

"If they wanted my body I'd sure give it to them because if they get my body they can't get my thoughts."

When I remind him he had told me about painful memories of being sexually traumatized by two men who violated his body, he struggles to hold back his tears and says he wants to escape to a different world where he can talk to Latot. I assure him that he can talk to me about whatever troubles him. But he ignores that invitation and complains angrily that the staff have never given him straight answers about the door. "I asked if the door was going to be locked this morning and they told me they didn't know."

I assure him that I can understand why he has angry feelings, but he complains that no one else cares about his feelings. He wipes his eyes and blows his nose and tells me he is afraid.

"What are you afraid of?"

"I'm afraid because I actually know I killed that person, and that person is dead."

I ask if he is talking about Jay, but he shakes his head and says someone must have killed his father because he has no memory of him.

When I point out that his father is very much alive, he maintains that someone killed him and it must have been his mother.

He complains angrily that women will take his thoughts and feelings, men will take his body, and he will no longer have either.

"Are you afraid I will take your body because you asked me before if I wanted your body?"

He says he'd rather be in Latot's world rather than mine because I might take his body and he would cease to exist. Then he asks about his worst fear. "If you took my mind would I still have a body and would that satisfy both of you now?"

When I ask what he means he remains silent, but I see his knees shaking from anxiety. "I need someone who understands. Not just to understand me but to understand it's me that's here. Am I making myself clear enough for you?" he asks forcefully.

"Yes. You're saying you want to really be here. All of you. Your thoughts. Your feelings. And your body."

"That's right!" he exclaims.

"That means you have to be assured I won't take your body, and that I'm strong enough to prevent your mother and those powerful women from taking your thoughts and feelings."

He nods his head in agreement. Then he says he feels like a five-year-old and not old enough to understand me even though he gives the impression he does. He goes on to complain that he gets scared when he hears people on the ward talk about him because he can't answer them intelligently.

As our session comes to a close, I commend him for sharing this with me, and assure him that I will talk to the staff on the ward so that everyone can understand what he's feeling.

"You're the only person I can talk to," he says, and assures me he won't do anything to chase me away. He also asks me not to let anyone know how much he depends on me or they'll ruin the whole thing.

I give him another tissue and he blows his nose. He says he doesn't want to leave, and finds a way to extend the time by pointing to his shoes and telling me he had a good visit with his brother, who bought his shoes as a gift.

PART SIX

James & LATOT

CHAPTER 30

James says his sister-in-law found things indicating he has artistic talents that may have actually been Jay's.

December 16, 1976

James signs in and takes off his jacket, revealing that he's very neatly dressed. I comment on his good choice of clothing and thank him for revealing it to me.

He gives me a gift he made in Occupational Therapy—a handmade Christmas ornament. I suspect that our discussion about giving at Christmas time during a previous session has influenced him.

After I thank him for the gift, he quickly tells me that he attended a movie last night with Al and enjoyed getting off the ward. To my surprise he tells me that he had been given a pass to leave the hospital by his favorite nurse, who alerted him that other patients would be jealous, but he shouldn't worry about that. He says he felt very good about it, but then asks if I talked to the staff about the locked door. I assure him I did and give him credit for trusting me enough to ask for my help, something he never did a year ago. He changes the subject and tells me he didn't sleep well and had a seizure very early this morning that caused his head to bleed. He says an aide came into his room and told him to change his blood-tinged sheets.

I speculate that his seizure caused him to strike his head on a hard object, possibly a bed post. I assume Jay had something to do with his seizure, but James doesn't believe Jay could have caused it.

He asks what I think of his gift. I open the package and bring out two small decoupage pieces of art, which are done well. He

explains that he made them by gluing paper cutouts on both sides of two small square boards.

I hold them up and describe what I observe on one side—hunting dogs, a mallard duck, ducklings, and a partridge. I ask if he can interpret the meaning of the art piece, and he says he will kick the adult mallard out. I ask if she will return to take care of the ducklings and he says, "She didn't have anything to do with the whole mess," he says.

"That's a very interesting story," I say. I interpret this as a metaphor about the way he handles conflicts with women, starting with his mother.

His artwork is a good example of art therapy, and I ask if his therapist gave him a grade. He says the therapist gave him an A and his favorite nursing assistant gave him an A plus.

After I congratulate him, he says that his sister-in-law Betty came to visit and told him the family wants to visit him one night this week. I ask how he feels about that, and he says it makes him nervous, but he doesn't want to think about it because his mind is too cluttered. Then he tells me he hears Latot's voice but he's too busy to answer him now.

I ask if he can explain his relationship to Latot. He says that Latot just starts talking to him in the form of thoughts, and that he's heard him speak for a long time, since before he could breathe.

When I ask James if he ever disagrees with Latot, he says there is no way Latot can make him do anything.

I continue to listen.

"Someone spoke once about a guardian angel and Latot is like a guardian angel to me. He's something that's just here. I don't question him and sometimes he doesn't say anything."

When I ask if there are other ways he knows if Latot is present, James says he sees him as a spot of light. "I just see him but when I say something personal about him, he leaves because he doesn't want to be here when another person is with me."

"Do you know if Latot talks to Jay too?"

He shakes his head and says Latot told him he knows no one else but him.

When I ask how he came up with the name Latot, he doesn't give me a clear answer, but then says Latot is talking to him now.

I look at the clock on the wall, which prompts him to say he doesn't want to leave yet, although he knows our time is up. I apologize for depriving him of some of his time since we started late today. Then he says his sister-in-law told him he used to play the flute, but he doesn't remember ever playing it, although his brother said he did.

After a pause he tells me that he learned the word flautist, which is one of the new words he's been learning. Then he says people have heard him speak French and Spanish, but he can't understand how that could be possible because he doesn't know either of those languages.

I believe this information clarifies a likely reality that one of his other personalities, most likely Jay, had learned to play the flute and also learned to speak French and Spanish, but which James never learned.

Our time has come to a close and we both stand up and shake hands while I hold James's artwork in my left hand. It had been a very meaningful session, with the high point of receiving James's Christmas gift. He seemed more stable today and acknowledged that he now looks to me for help, which is a sign of improvement.

James described Latot in more detail today, and believes he is a guardian angel who has been present in his life since before he was born. This prompts me to research this subject and learn that many persons have believed there are guardian angels. The three primary religions of the world—Judaism, Christianity, and Islam—describe angelic beings in the spirit world who can help individuals in need and guide them in important activities.[14] Many Native Americans call on the spirit world for knowledge and protection. In Shamanistic cultures, spirits empower shamans with special capacities that can help them during spiritual journeys or healings.

The Holy Spirit is described in the Bible as one of the three persons of the Godhead who inhabits believers in Jesus Christ and dispenses spiritual gifts, including the gift of performing miracles and divine healings. The Bible also contains many descriptions of angels as protectors and intermediators between

God and humans. There are references to angels roughly 300 times from the first book of Genesis to the final book of Revelation. The angel Gabriel appeared four times in the Bible to deliver messages. Although Gabriel's appearance was usually as a human, his actions demonstrated supernatural power and he evoked trepidation in those who saw him.

The Angel Michael is described as the Archangel, or chief, of heavenly beings, and leader of God's angelic army. He is also described as leading God's armies against Satan's forces in the New Testament book of Revelation.

CHAPTER 31

James is having memory lapses, feels lost, and is scared he'll be pushed off a cliff into the darkness.

December 27, 1976

We meet on Monday, two days after Christmas, instead of our usual Tuesday. When James arrives, he sits down and signs his name. He says he has a cold and sore throat and felt sick when he met with his brother yesterday. He goes on to say that he and his brother have different memories.

"My brother talked about things that happened before I was born."

"Can you tell me about it?"

"I remember some members of my family but there's about six years when I don't remember anything. We both remember that my baby brother died. I told him I talked to my baby brother when he was sick. He was born with yellow jaundice and was only nine months old when he died."

I asked how he knew those things about his baby brother. He tells me they were able to communicate with each other without speaking. He also says he could speak to his mother the same way. He describes his communication with her as perfect at the time, but in retrospect it wasn't perfect because she talked to herself more than to him, and if he tried to interrupt her she got angry.

He reminds me that his communication with Latot is like it was with his mother. He also says it's confusing for him to carry on a conversation with me and with Latot at the same time.

I ask for more details about communicating with Latot but James says I'm too ignorant about the other world to understand what Latot is like.

"Do you think that talking about the other world creates a barrier that I can't transcend, and if I tried to come into that world with you, I'd be lost?"

"I don't want you to be lost. But I'm lost Dr. Brende. You know I'm lost."

I assure him that our communication is strong enough to help him feel grounded. But he doesn't understand what I mean; he still feels lost and that scares him.

I ask if his fear of being lost is like the way he felt with his mother, but to my surprise he says he only remembers happy things with her. Then he reaches out and lifts his arm about four feet from the floor to depict his estimated height when he was with his mother. (Forty-two to forty-four inches is the height of an average six- or seven-year-old boy.) He says he can remember standing behind the washroom door and being knocked into a tub of water when his brother opened it. Although he got wet, he remembers feeling happy because his mother asked him if he was okay and focused her attention on him.

I ask if he has other memories, and he tells me about the time his mother berated his father. James says he remembers that his father always had a happy grin on his face and doesn't know why she would say those awful things to him.

I ask if he has any other memories about his father. He says, "I only saw my father until I was about seven and after that I never saw him again."

I ask for more details and he says he's not sure why his father wasn't there anymore. When I ask if he left his father or his father left him, he replies that his father never came to get him again. James clearly can't remember what happened because Jay took over the body.

Because he feels like his father abandoned him, he is very sensitive to abandonment and asks me if I'm planning to leave. After I assure him that I won't leave him, he replies that he can't be sure of that, which is why he often comes to my office to see if I am still there. I ask him why he hadn't told me before about coming to my office.

"I didn't want to get you upset," he said. "And if you've ever dusted your car for fingerprints, they're probably mine. I used to go out and touch your car. They made a joke with me every time I did that," he complains. Then he asks why there are days when he can't find my car parked anywhere.

I'm moved by the information he's just shared with me. But he hasn't told anyone else because he says that if people knew he was that attached to me they would prevent him from seeing me again. I assure him that no one has the power to prevent him from seeing me, but he says it's already happening. Staff members have said he might not be able to go to therapy because he didn't submit an accurate plan. "And I can't get a pass to visit my brother or do anything because I don't know how to submit a plan. It makes me feel like I'm not here. I'm just back where I was before," he moans.

I continue to listen as he tells me how important this meeting is. My absence last week reminded him of the time his father ignored him. My presence today assures him that I didn't run away and leave him as he expected would happen. He goes on to talk about how he has been trying to escape from the pain he feels by going into the other world where Latot resides. When I ask him to choose which world he would prefer, he replies that he would choose this world even though he feels pain here. "This is the world I should be in. When Latot interrupts and tries to tell me I'm not supposed to go into your world to see you, I'll tell him to shut up."

"I'm pleased to hear you say that because I don't want to compete with Latot."

Then James changes the subject and tells me he had a nightmare in which he was being pushed off a cliff into darkness. I'm unsure about the meaning of his nightmare, but I suspect another personality has tried to take over the body when he's asleep. That personality may also occasionally take over and cause memory lapses. Before our session ends, I ask if he remembers coming to my office yesterday and he says he has a vague recollection of coming.

I considered James's description that he could communicate with his mother via thoughts and decided to review the literature about telepathy and wordless communication between people. Although most scientists believe mental telepathy does not exist, the interest in this subject has led to many experiments over time, most of which have been criticized for lack of proper controls. However, some researchers have set up experiments to test whether two people can communicate with each other without using words. They have successfully recorded two individuals—one in India and the other in France—telepathically communicate the greetings "hola" and "ciao" using special codes. Other researchers have used specific techniques to determine that telepathically gifted individuals use certain parts of the brain to communicate. Recent studies with fMRI brain imaging indicate that the right cerebral hemisphere is associated with telepathic messaging, but is not found in non-telepathic individuals. [15]

CHAPTER 32

He is learning new things and
experiencing new feelings of trust.

December 30, 1976

As the year comes to an end, James's early celebration of New Year's Eve begins when he tells me the things he's learned. I'm pleased with his intellectual growth, his desire to learn new things, and his capacity to improve his level of trust. He shows me some of his writings, which he's already given to Ms. Haden, his favorite nurse. He defines her as the only person he can trust, and the person who has fostered his desire to learn. "I asked Ms. Haden to teach me the ABCs," he says.

"Did she agree to teach you?" I ask.

"Not really. She said that it would be better for me to go to Occupational Therapy. But she told me she will help me in any other way she can."

"Do you know how else she can help you?"

"I asked her to help me get prepared to leave the hospital."

His request that she help him prepare to leave the hospital is an appropriate step toward his wish to learn new things to help become independent. However, he may be willing to stay in the hospital longer, attend Occupational Therapy, and gain additional intellectual tools.

I ask if he plans to live with his family when he leaves the hospital, but he says he's better off living by himself. I commend him for becoming open to all his feelings, including love, and wanting to learn his purpose in life. He agrees that learning about his purpose is his main goal, and we spend the rest of this session discussing that subject.

CHAPTER 33

*James ceased to exist at age seven and missed
out on being taught. Now he is like a young boy
learning new things for the first time.*

January 6, 1977

After signing in James immediately tells me that his sister-in-law Betty and nephew Gary visited him this past weekend, but he didn't like the visit because she criticized everything he had to say, just like all females including his mother have done.

James tells me that women make him feel guilty about even existing. He is also uncomfortable when patients talk about having friends because he doesn't know anymore what it means to have a friend.

I point out that friends should be able to speak openly and honestly with each other, but he says he doesn't know anyone like that, and most of the patients call him nasty names (half-wit, know-nothing, and son-of-a-bitch).

I'm aghast at hearing this and ask if he can tell them to cease from talking this kind of garbage, but he says they're a bunch of bullies who follow him around just to annoy him and they'll never stop.

Although I encourage him to defend himself, I also wonder if he gives unconscious messages that his purpose for existing was to please other people by doing whatever he thinks they want. "That's what Jay used to do," I explain.

James looks down and after a long pause says, "Did he say that?"

"He wanted to please people. He also knew how to stand up for himself. But you aren't Jay. I'm sure your purpose in life is something more than just wanting to please other people."

His face lights up as he listens to what I say. He sits quietly for a time and then tells me he won't go to the places where people just want to be pleased. Then he tells me he almost got into a fist fight last night with a patient who intimidated him. "I tried what you told me but it didn't work."

"What did you try?" I ask.

"I said to that guy, 'Do you have to stand right on top of me? There's only two people in this hallway. Do you have to stand on top of me?'"

"Did he move away?"

"No. He said, 'I can stand here in this line if I want to!' I told him, 'I didn't say you couldn't stand here. Just don't stand on top of me.' When he kept telling me he could stand any place he wanted I said, 'Come a little closer. Come as close as you can.' Then he said, 'You'll never reach me.' So I told him, 'You're so damn close to me I'm touching you right now.'"

"What happened then?" I ask.

"A nursing assistant came along and took him off me before I could punch him out. That's what happened."

I congratulate him for holding his ground and refusing to be bullied. He says it made him so upset that he couldn't sleep, but he calmed his nerves down by seeing a picture of a man in a padded cell cutting out paper dolls.

"I looked at the picture and thought I looked just like that man! So, I found some paper dolls and cut them out to calm me

152

down. But I was so angry I felt like running toward the first person I saw. I could hardly keep from killing someone."

"You made a good choice. It's better to cut out paper dolls rather than to kill someone."

"Thanks to you. You taught me that I first must make a choice and I'm glad I did even though I cut my finger." He goes on to say no one ever taught him these things, because he didn't finish school. Now he feels like an eight-year-old boy who wants to learn about the world for the first time. But he can't handle all the things the aides ask him to do or understand all of the conversations that take place. "I start to cry because it's just too much to take in and I don't understand everything that keeps coming at me."

I acknowledge the fact he seems to be enjoying the experience of learning new things, but point out that he doesn't have to learn everything all at once, and he can be selective about the things he wants to learn.

He looks down awkwardly and says he's come to realize that it's better if he can give instead of just taking. I'm pleased about his mature disclosure and tell him I've never heard him say that before. He replies that he never realized that it was important that he learn how to give before.

Then he changes the subject and makes a surprising request. "Can I open a bank account? My brother will help me. The bank is just down the street."

I agree with this request since his brother can help him. Before the session ends, we spend the remainder of our time talking about learning new things.

Even though he has come to this session dressed neatly and sporting a mustache, his intellectual and emotional level is much younger than that of a mature adult. James's identity as a seven-year-old boy ceased to exist after being traumatized at that age. His new identity appears to be forming at this time, thirty-four years later. I review information about the behaviors of a typical seven-year-old boy and find several things that are characteristic of James. A seven-year-old is very interested in learning and will repeatedly ask questions like: how do you build something; how does money work; how do you buy something at a store? A seven-year-old will also idealize a father or father figure, and demonstrate fluctuating moods, serious questioning, and episodes of goofiness.

CHAPTER 34

James is growing up fast and wants more independence.

January 13, 1977

James signs in today and, like last time, he is well-dressed, clean-shaven, and sporting a mustache. He continues to depend on me, but has developed an increasing level of independence, as marked by his ability to obtain a pass to leave the hospital with his brother for short periods of time. He is beginning to enjoy doing things on his own, and brags about getting a haircut.

He points to his forehead and complains of a severe headache, which he blames on patients who smoke. Then he seems to contradict himself by saying that he enjoys these headaches. I ask how that's possible, and he answers that he believes his headache will help him understand what's going on in his mind. I remind him that he used to get headaches when he struggled with Jay for possession of the body. He frowns and says those headaches were different and caused pain throughout his body.

James changes subjects and says he's struggling to control his urges to hit people by directing the thoughts of one part of his mind to another part of his mind.

When I ask James if he thinks he and Jay can be here at the same time, he shakes his head, so I ask him if he knows if Jay is ever here when I'm talking to him (James).

"If he's here, I'm not going to let him smoke or I'll break his damn arm. And if he is here, I'm not about to let him be a snob who thinks he's better than everyone else!" he exclaims as he stares intently at me.

"That makes sense. But I remember you've told me you think I'd rather talk to Jay. Do you really think that?"

"Yes. Because nobody has ever wanted me around."

His answer prompts me to ask if his father spent time with him so he could learn how a boy grows up to be a man. But he frowns and shakes his head.

I mention Jay's name again as we discuss the subject of male characteristics, and James suddenly asks me this question which seems to be about Shea: "What was he? Or is he?"

"That's a good question. What do you think?"

"If I could use a cuss word. I'd tell you!"

"What do you mean?"

"A shitass, that's what I think!" he exclaims with a sheepish grin. "Everyone is always talking about what he did. He...he...he... this and he that. I don't know what in the hell they're talking about and then they leave me out!" he exclaims.

"Perhaps you have feelings about Jay. Did you like him?" I ask.

"I don't know if I did or if I didn't."

"I believe you liked him, since you experienced pain to keep him from feeling it. So you must have really cared a great deal about him."

"I don't know how I could really do such a thing as that!" he exclaims.

I ask James why he thinks Jay is now experiencing pain, and if he feels a need to protect Jay. He listens intently and asks, "Is that the reason that I'm scared all the time?"

"Why do you think you're always scared? I believe you're afraid that I don't want you. But you should know I do want you," I assert.

"You want me? You don't want that other?" He sits quietly for a moment and then asks if I can hear his thoughts. I assure him that I don't listen to his thoughts, and I don't expect he can hear mine. Then I ask my primary question. "Do you continue to live in two worlds?"

"Yes, but it's not easy."

"Are you able to stay in this world where I live?" I ask.

"Yes, I can."

"Do you ever enter Jay's world?"

He frowns and clenches both of his fists tightly. "No. I don't go to the world Jay lives in," he argues, gazing off into the distance and toward his left. "Jay has a body, doesn't he?"

"When you're not here he has a body," I explain.

"Where is he now that I'm here?" he asks.

"He's in the same place that you used to be when you're not here."

"I've been there, and he's never been there!" James insists.

"How would you know he's never been there?"

He sighs. "Because he'd have to occupy the same space where I am. I know I can't be in another world and have a body at the same time," he states emphatically.

"That's true. If Jay was here, you wouldn't have a body."

"Where is he now?" James asks.

"There's nothing to be afraid of because he's not going to take possession of your body. You're the only person who has claim to your body."

"That's what I've said so many times," he insists.

"I agree with you. And he wants it that way too. He wants you to have your body and if he returns, he doesn't want to completely replace you."

James frowns and shakes his head. "I'll tell you something else. Do you know that I'm beginning to lose control of my left hand?"

"No, I didn't know that."

He explains that he is losing coordination in his left hand but not losing strength, although he sometimes drops his fork and spills food when eating. This loss of coordination indicates that he is beginning to lose linkage to the right side of the brain. Suddenly I see a shift in his facial appearance indicating that Jay has entered the body. But he only remains for a few seconds until James returns.

In this session James appeared to be more receptive to learning about Jay and the nature of their relationship. He is growing up and wants to learn, and the typical characteristics of a seven-year-old boy fit his current level of functioning. A seven-year-old typically idealizes or has a crush on his teacher. He is thoughtful, observant, a good listener, and can stick with one activity for a long time. He has increasing control over his body, his thoughts, and his feelings. He likes his independence and will argue for it. He wants a room of his own, his own clothes, and to do the things he likes to do.

CHAPTER 35

James feels like he's floating with nothing solid to hang onto. He is afraid Jay will push him into darkness.

January 19, 1977

After James signs in he quickly says it's been a long week because of a misunderstanding about when his session was scheduled. He remains quiet for a short time and finally breaks the silence by asking me if I could tell him the meaning of the word consideration.

When I ask him what he thinks it means, he says it means understanding. I ask for an example, and he says a lot of people on the ward smoke, and they have no consideration for anyone who doesn't smoke.

"I'd like to smash their cigarettes on their foreheads!" he exclaims.

After sitting quietly for a time, he says he feels very uncertain about his future and wants to learn more. After another

pause, he says he doesn't understand people, but his nephew might understand them better than he does. Next, he tells me, in a soft voice, that he has a bad headache, but it doesn't bother him because it reminds him he is alive. Then he looks around the room and says, "I can sense there are three people here."

"Why you think that? I don't see anybody here."

"I don't see anybody here either, but I feel their presence."

"Is there anyone here in particular?" I ask.

"I think Latot is here. Won't you talk to him?"

"That would be impossible because Latot is not a person," I reply.

James shakes his head. "It hurts me when you say that you won't talk to him," he complains. He goes on to explain to me that Latot is always listening, even though he's not talking.

I decide not to ask him any more questions about Latot. Instead, I tell him that his appearance is more serene today. He shakes his head and says he hides his feelings, particularly when he's on the ward. I point out that he needs to show his feelings because when he hides his feelings the staff can't tell the difference between him and Jay.

"I wanna be here but it scares me. I don't have the knowledge that Jay has but I wanna be here."

"I'm glad you do and I'm glad you're here."

He says he has mixed feelings about showing his emotions, but he doesn't want to go back into the darkness. "I tell people to holler at me so I won't leave."

"Did you say you tell people to holler at you to keep you from leaving?"

"Yes. And I want you to keep me here. I hope you understand what I mean because most people don't. When they hear me say 'holler at me' they immediately lock the door and make a big announcement 'Don't let anyone out!' "

"Do you explain it to them?"

He shakes his head. "I try but they don't listen. I think they don't wanna hear. They don't wanna hear a lot of things."

"Well, your doctor understands. I talk to him at least once a week."

"I thought you did."

Before our time ends, he says he likes meeting after three o'clock because it doesn't interfere with OT (Occupational Therapy), which meets from ten to twelve in the morning and one to three in the afternoon. He says OT is important because he is learning numbers and other new things.

After our session I decide to investigate the subject of "felt presence." I found it means having a sense that someone, unheard or unseen, is present in the room. Although it's not a common experience for most people, it is more commonplace for those who have survived close calls with death, or after they've lost loved ones. Researchers hypothesize that this experience is similar to a NDE during which survivors see their bodies from a distance. Physiological studies have found a disruption to the internal mapping of the body which involves the insular cortex and the temporoparietal junction body (TPJ) in the brain, since a felt presence can be elicited by electrical stimulation to the TPJ.[16]

CHAPTER 36

*James discovers the name Jay on pictures
and is afraid he'll take over and prevent
him from learning new things.*

January 27, 1977

After signing in James pulls out an old library card from his pocket, hands it to me, and asks if I recognize the signature, because he doesn't. The signature—Jay—was written in 1970 and he has very little recollection of that year and none later. He wonders what happened to the last seven missing years. "I've screamed and cried my eyes out trying to remember but I can't. There just isn't anything there." He does have a partial recollection of being a patient on ward 41-B in 1970, where he thinks he was given shock treatments.

I hand the card back and ask if he had checked the book out with that card, but he says no, because he felt disgusted when he saw the name Jay there. I ask if he remembers what the book was about and he says it was about a boy and his father, but he didn't want to read it because he can hardly remember his own father.

I ask how he feels about this, and he says people liked Jay better.

"So, you think everybody liked Jay more than you? Including me?" I ask.

"Yeah. I think everybody liked Jay more, including you."

"How can you arrive at such a conclusion?"

"It's easy to make that conclusion because people would come up to me and tell me how much they had enjoyed talking with me. But I had no idea what they meant because I had no

162

memory of the conversation. So I came to the conclusion that their enjoyable conversation was with Jay."

I point out that he might be wrong to think Jay was liked more than he. But James says he can't compete with Jay and feels out of place on the ward where other patients approach him to make conversation. James says he tries to act like he's everyone's friend, but he feels like a fake. "I try to act like I think they'll like me. But I tell 'em to stay away from me. Let me see who you are and what you do. Let me get used to you for a while and see what you are doing and what you're thinking first."

He looks away from me and down at the floor, seemingly depressed. He continues to sit quietly for a long time, but finally breaks the silence and tells me that he must fight for anything he hopes to get. After another pause, he says people tell him not to fight because he could never win.

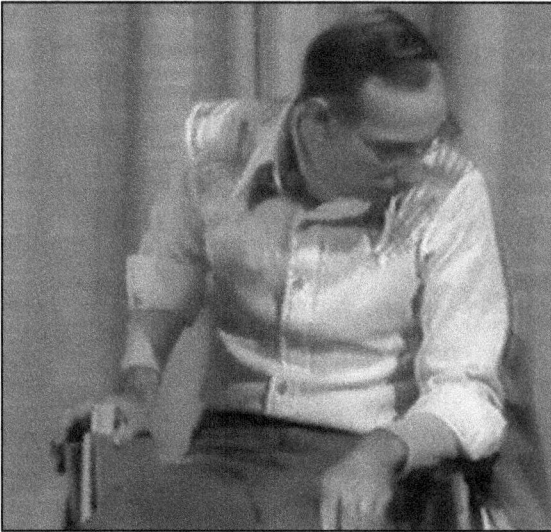

Then James changes the subject and tells me his hospital doctor recommended he attend the art clinic on the first floor. But after arriving for the first time, he discovered Jay's name on a picture there. He says he's seen other pictures with his own name on them and shows me one. "Look. He forged my name on this picture."

He puts the picture back in his pocket, pulls a handkerchief from his pocket, and blows his nose.

I ask if he's depressed and he says yes, complaining that he feels unappreciated and unwanted. He looks at me and asks, "Do I belong here? Do you want me?"

"Yes, I want you and you belong here."

"I don't know how to handle those words. That doesn't mean I don't wanna hear 'em. I'm glad you can say that to me, but I don't wanna keep asking if I belong," he says while wiping tears from his eyes.

I ask if there are any other reasons he feels depressed, but he seems uncertain. He says he doesn't want to lose those feelings because that makes him unique. I remind him that he can also have loving feelings, which scares him because he's afraid someone will take his loving feelings away if he talks about them.

I ask who might do that, and he says any woman who reminds him of his mother. He hangs his head and doesn't seem to be able to express himself. After a long pause he says, "If I tell someone I have a feeling of love for you, they'll want to take that away from me and they'll try to talk me out of it."

"I wonder if when you were young your brothers and sisters tried to talk you out of having loving feelings for your mother."

"If they did I never heard them talk about it."

I then ask if his fear of loving feelings is related to the discussion we had about Jay during our last session. He appears hesitant to even mention the name Jay, but finally tells me what he thinks. "They think Jay is always here. When I come into the room people say 'here comes Jay.' They only see Jay. They pound his name into me and even call me by that name!" he exclaims.

"Well James, I don't see Jay here. But I do see your fear that if Jay takes over, you'll be left behind and you won't be here."

He hangs his head and after a long pause he says that his body feels very old, and he hasn't much time left to fulfill his purpose. When I ask James if he knows what that is, he says he's

164

been wanting to tell me about it for a long time but is afraid Jay will interfere. But he believes it's to teach something, though he's not sure yet what it is.

I thank him for telling me about his purpose and point out that he will be able to teach what he has already learned, what he's learning now, and what he will learn in the future. I ask him to get a notebook and write down everything he's learning, and he says he keeps a notebook in OT. But when he writes things down he doesn't feel like he's the person writing. I suspect Jay takes over at those times.

Before our time ends, James starts to tear up the picture where Jay forged James's name. I ask for it and he reluctantly gives it to me. He tells me, with tears in his eyes, that he doesn't want to leave. After wiping the tears away, he says he's ready now; we both stand up and shake hands. He leaves the studio accompanied by an aide.

CHAPTER 37

*James is aging rapidly; everyday feels like
two or three weeks. He no longer acts like a
little boy struggling to exist.*

February 14, 1977

James is dressed very well in a brown and white shirt with
brown turtleneck and brown sweater vest. As soon as he signs in
he gives me a very large valentine as a gift. He explains that it
can also become a bulletin board. I hold it up and thank him for
the gift that he created.

I'm impressed that he has developed his creative ability so
quickly. He has been growing up over the last several weeks and

no longer acts or
talks like a little boy
struggling to exist.
He tells me he wants
to find out about the
world out there.

"I'm supposed to
be forty years old,
but I think I'm only
thirty. In a day's
time I feel I've lived
two or three weeks, and the way I'm going it won't be long before
I'll catch up with the age I am," he announces.

He has a sense that time moves so fast that twenty-four hours
equals three weeks (500 hours), which is about twenty times
faster than reality. He also senses one minute equaling more

than three hours, which is more than 200 times faster than reality. This may explain why his age moves ahead so rapidly.

Although James seems excited about being propelled into his real age, he is more concerned about people he doesn't like who attend OT.

"There is a guy that sits there not too far from me. But if that guy ever touches me, I'll crush his head with that typewriter down there. I'll beat his head to a pulp with it."

"Why does he make you so angry?"

"I just don't like the way the guy looks."

"Don't you have better things to do in OT than crushing somebody's head in?"

"It's just that those thoughts just come into my head."

"Do you think you're ready to leave the hospital if you're thinking of killing people when you don't like the way they look?" I ask.

He frowns but is reticent to answer. He changes the subject and says he hollered at Jay during OT and once on the ward. His outbursts alarmed the staff, and they asked him if he was hallucinating. James denies that he is, but is sometimes aware of Jay's presence. When I ask him if he is also aware of Shea's presence, he says he's heard people talk about Shea. He also says he's seen his name several times in books he's checked out. "I've seen my name and I know I didn't sign it. I think Jay mostly did but maybe not Shea," he says.

"How often has that happened?" I ask.

"I don't know. But I've seen signatures on the bank statement that are my name, but I didn't sign it. And some I signed but they look very shaky."

I ask if he ever knew Shea and he says he didn't know him very well, but if he returns he is interested in learning more about him.

"How are you going to do that?" I ask.

"Just by hearing him talk," he replies.

"What does Jay say about him?" I ask, assuming James hears his voice.

"He says Shea is one person you shouldn't let touch you."

I ask if he's aware that Jay and Shea are his alternate personalities, but that confuses him. He is curious to know, however, if he or Jay were ever married. When I tell him neither he nor Jay were married, he says he's not surprised.

After this session is over, I reflect on its significant aspects. He began by bringing me a valentine's gift, which I readily accepted. Even though I had been taught psychotherapists should not accept gifts from their patients because that clouds the therapeutic relationship, I did accept James's gift. In the literature about this subject, I find an article in which the author says a therapist can sometimes accept a gift, but only when it will not interfere with appropriate therapeutic techniques. The author summarizes this topic nicely:

> I have accepted inexpensive gifts ... except when I sense that the offer is an unhealthy enactment, or that the patient is sidestepping a useful exploration. As is often the case in conducting dynamic psychotherapy, there is a balance between fostering a warm working relationship versus encouraging reflection and insight. In my view, a blanket rule of refusing all gifts is unnecessarily cold and inhuman for many patients, while accepting all gifts may appear "normal" but does not encourage reflection and may introduce conflicts of interest. The matter takes a case-by-case consideration, neither unthinking acceptance nor unyielding refusal. [17]

I find it amazing that James's age is changing rapidly. Today James says he is thirty years old when, in reality, he is forty. Perhaps the James I talked with today is not the same James I talked with last time. If so, that might explain his memory of having communications with Jay and with Shea in ways I have not heard him describe previously.

Those who have researched the subject of subjective age in ordinary people have learned that the age they feel about themselves may be quite different from their actual ages. A person's subjective feeling of being younger or older than his or her actual age does not necessarily reflect the accuracy of that age. The variability of subjective age is related to factors such as physical health, age, life satisfaction, mood, lifestyle changes, and cognitive decline. According to researchers, those who feel more youthful often have younger structural brain characteristics.

PART SEVEN

Jay &
James

CHAPTER 38

"I know I'm supposed to be a human being.
But I don't really know if I am anymore."

February 28, 1977

I'm surprised to see Jay here today since he wasn't scheduled and has not been here for six weeks. When I ask what brought him back today, he immediately says he had to return to the ward to help James. But he also tells me how surprised he's been at finding things he didn't expect to see. For example, he did not expect to discover a receipt in his locker for a pair of boots that had been purchased from the hospital store.

"I looked in my locker and found this slip that there was a pair of shoes on layaway. I went there and this lady said I'd been there a half a dozen times and was happy that I finally decided to pick up my boots. I didn't know what she was talking about until the other clerk said, 'I see you're in a better mood than the last time when I laid those boots away for you.' "

"Did you explain it to her?" I ask.

"No. I didn't know what to say so I let it go at that. I just picked up the boots and now I hid 'em upstairs in my room," he laughs.

I ask if James had told him about the boots and Jay says, "The only reason I know is because I found them in his locker. I'm happy he's has been doing so much on his own."

I detect Jay's sense of pride in James's accomplishments, but when I ask how he feels about this, he says he doesn't know much about feelings.

173

"Maybe the body knows but I don't know if I'm a human being or not. I've never felt this way before and it's very strange," he says.

I wonder if Jay is becoming aware he's not the only person in his body, but when I ask him about that he looks puzzled. "I've always thought that it was only me, but James has gotta be there too because he's too damn scared to leave that ward unless someone is with him. I'm surprised that he was able to go to the store and order the boots I just picked up."

I explain that James also gets scared for other reasons, like if someone tries to touch him. Jay looks at me with raised eyebrows and asks if James is a homosexual. I reply that he definitely is not.

Jay wonders why he didn't know that and asks why James knows. I explain that James was raped in 1968 and knew something really bad had happened to him. "Did he call on you to protect him after that trauma?" I ask.

Jay frowns and says he can't recall, but then asks if he'll ever have to come and protect him again.

"What do you think you would have to protect him from?" I ask.

After a brief silence, he tells me that he knows from personal experience that there are unexpected circumstances when individuals need to be rescued. He has asked himself if he would ever come back and help James or one of the others if they got into a really bad situation.

Jay's question implies that he is aware of more than one alternate personality who might need his help. Since James is the only one currently active, I explain that I'd like to talk to James about this. I ask Jay's permission to use hypnosis so I can talk to him.

"You can talk to him, but what am I supposed to do?" he asks.

"All you need to do is relax," I explain, and proceed with a brief trance induction technique. I ask him to close his eyes, take a few deep breaths, and relax more deeply with each breath. Suddenly his head drops, but after a few seconds, it lifts again, and he opens his eyes briefly then closes them again. I see his body quiver as if there's a struggle within. His arms become tense and his breathing irregular. Suddenly his eyes open wide, and James appears to be in the body, but he looks scared. He glances at me, looks away, closes his eyes again, and lowers his head. After a few seconds his eyes open again, but this time Jay reappears.

"What happened?"

"I tried but I don't think I was hypnotized."

"You were. You looked like you went into a trance," I explain.

"Is that how you go into one?" he smiles.

"That's it. What do you remember?"

"Nothing. Except I'm gripping this chair tightly." He looks down at his hands, which are holding on to the chair securely.

I explain that James appeared for a short time but didn't talk. Instead of trying to make another attempt to contact him, I decide to spend the rest of this time talking to Jay. I ask if anyone on the staff recognized him, and he says one or two patients knew him but most everyone thinks he is James.

"A few of them tell me I look too normal to still be in the hospital. So I explain that I'm still here because I switch personalities too irregularly. I guess I must accept the fact that's me," Jay says.

Even though Jay talks about switching personalities, he doesn't think that he shares the same body. Nor does he believe he will ever lose his own autonomy. Although he believes James is a separate person, Jay also complains that James does irritating things. "Why didn't he just pick up those boots himself. Hell, there's money laying all over up there in the room. Why didn't he just pay for 'em?"

Since Jay says he doesn't want to be James's protector again, he worries who will take over if James becomes too scared to stay in the body. I explain that it will be my job to do that. Then I ask Jay to clarify his relationship to James while he's in the hospital now.

He says he already told me he came to help James, but it bothers him that James wants to wear his clothes. He points to his shirt and trousers and says, "I want you to know that these are my clothes and they sure don't belong to James."

I nod my head. "It sounds to me like you are planning to stay with James now that you have your own clothes. Can you tell me how long you plan to keep it a secret that you're here now? Although I expect both patients and staff will soon figure it out."

CHAPTER 39

*He signs in as Kohlman and doesn't
know if he is James, Jay, or Shea.*

March 21–24, 1977

Since Jay had come to the last session three weeks ago, I expect to see him again today. But I'm surprised to hear him say he doesn't know if he is James, Jay, or Shea. I wait for him to sign in, and after a brief pause, I watch him sign the name Kohlman. His first words are to complain that he doesn't understand why he's here, which surprises me. During our last session Jay said his purpose was to help James get ready to leave the hospital. Even though this personality signed in as Kohlman, I assume that he has always cared about James. But he quickly tells me that he doesn't want to talk about James, and he's not interested in the past. He insists that his purpose now is to feel like a human being. I point out that he must learn to feel emotions, and we spend the rest of the session discussing how important that is.

When we meet again three days later, I ask him if he will look at a videotaped program I have made that describes a summary of the past two years of therapy. He agrees and watches intently for about thirty minutes until I ask for it to be turned off. He is clearly moved by what he saw since I observed that he had tears in his eyes when he viewed James's dramatic reliving of being slapped by his father and feeling emptiness, which Jay came to fill.

We talk about his response to the videotape, and he says that Jay is incapable of filling emptiness with any feelings. And then he adds, "If you're referring to the emotion of love, only Shea can express love."

"Do you know where Shea is?" I ask.

"He's gone."

"Do you know why he's gone?"

He shakes his head and says he doesn't want to talk about Shea anymore.

After finishing our viewing of the videotaped summary of the past two years of therapy, I ask if he will view a different videotaped teaching program entitled "Multiple Personality from an Object Relations Viewpoint," as explained by my consultant, Dr. Donald Rinsley.[18] I find it interesting that Jay listens quite intently, although I don't expect him to understand Dr. Rinsley's explanations of object relations theory.

After we finish watching Dr. Rinsley's video production, Jay tells me he didn't get anything out of it because his mind had stopped working when he watched James relive his trauma on the screen.

I commend him for expressing empathy for James, and he acknowledges the tears in his eyes, but he says it felt like someone had pushed a button to turn on the tears because they didn't feel natural. I see his fists clench and I hear him complain because he can't recognize their source. "It feels like I've gotten dirt in my eye but there's nothing in my eye. I know the tears are here but I don't understand why," he complains.

I ask him to tell me what he's feeling and rather than describe an emotion he says he is feeling very heavy.

"Where in your body do you feel heavy?"

He lifts both arms and clenches his fists to demonstrate the heavy feeling going through his entire body. Then he shakes his head in frustration. "I don't know what else is going on inside of me. But I wish you could tell me why I'm here today."

"Do you have any thoughts about that?" I ask.

"I don't like being here. Why can't I just go home? I can take care of myself. I don't have any problems!" he insists. After a brief pause, he reverses himself and acknowledges he's got problems that he doesn't understand. Then he points toward the screen and insists he's not the same person as the person he had just watched there.

I agree that he's not the same person and point out that the video program he just watched demonstrated his improvement over a period of two years, for which I commend him.

Jay is unable to accept my commendation and complains that he's worried about James, who had a seizure. He stopped taking his medication after one of the nurses tried to force him to take it. Jay says the nurse just needs to tell James "It's good for you," and he'll take the medication and never complain.

Although he expresses concerns for James, he says he's not here to keep James from getting into trouble with nursing staff. He's here to figure out who he is. "I don't know who I am. That's why I didn't wanna sign my name James, Jay, or Shea. I was very happy to sign my last name, Kohlman."

Although he says he is unsure who he is, I find it significant that he had an emotional response when he watched the monitor. "I saw tears in your eyes and your body was very tense," I point out.

He shakes his head slowly. "No wonder I don't feel like I'm all together. This is too hard to handle. I just feel scattered," he mumbles.

As we approach the end of our session, I express my hope that seeing the videotape helped him to understand James better. When I announce that our time is up, he quickly stands and says he's glad we're finished so he can get out of here and get some fresh air.

The following text is from the video program which described James and his alternate personalities from the perspective of object relations theory:

The progression of significant events during therapy is marked by the presence of emerging personalities that replaced each other for brief or more lengthy periods of time.

Each of these personalities developed a therapeutic alliance with the therapist during therapy and had to be fully revealed and differentiated as therapy progressed. Jim, a child personality, had been named by his father. Jimmy, who was named by his mother, had experienced abandonment and was prone to cry despairingly. Jay was an intellectual pseudo-person who said he didn't feel like a real person, yet he was predominant during therapy for the first nine months. James, the original personality, remained hidden at first, but then emerged for variable periods of time. After he attempted to murder Jay on November 28, 1975, James appeared as if he had been reborn and began to develop a close therapeutic relationship with his therapist. Shea, a personality not previously defined, emerged shortly after that in January 1976, and revealed himself as homosexual, but did not

180

remain in the body long and "died" six months later on June 28, 1976.

During the course of therapy, it became clear that each personality fended off the emergence of loving transference feelings (between patient and therapist) because of a fear those feelings were linked to destructive and self-destructive forces. However, after Shea disappeared, the therapist emphasized the loving relationship between therapist and patient, and this led to the "birth" of a new personality who signed his name with the letter J. Within a short time, a core conflict was revealed—a deep sense of shame about being born. He called himself a bastard and was convinced that he didn't have a mother and that his birth was illegitimate. He said several times during the next several months that he had destroyed everything and everybody he had ever loved. Hence, it became clear that each personality had been organized to avoid love, yet to continually seek it. That had perpetuated a sense of purposelessness and the feeling he wasn't real.

When it was revealed that James no longer had to hide his love in order to protect his mother and to protect the therapist who had become the maternal transference object (relationship to the therapist as mother), he was free to reach out to his therapist. At that time on July 19, 1976, the therapist became real to him, and he felt real for the first time. Interestingly James's birthday was forty years earlier on July 23, 1936. He, in fact, experienced the beginnings of a symbiotic relationship with his therapist as a real person and his only source of emotional nurturance. A major therapeutic goal was to help James cope with his tremendous need for maternal love and nurturance, which was so overwhelming that he feared it would destroy his therapist. Indeed, the hospital staff personnel also recognized this need and took complete and total care for him at that time.

When Jay, his protective personality, returned later, it was for the purpose of transferring the care of raising James over to his therapist, an act of significant trust on his part. Then Jay withdrew on Sept 29, approximately one year and nine months after beginning therapy. Following Jay's withdrawal, James's identity moved toward consolidation, and he began to accept the name he was born with. This move included the need to separate and individuate from the symbiotic tie with his fantasied mother, which involved expressing considerable anger toward her. This process of separation-individuation also helped him gain possession of his own thoughts and feelings. At that time the transference (patient-therapist relationship) also changed, and his therapist's role as the all-giving mother ceased, and he began to experience his therapist as a father figure.

Thus, it was important for the therapist to accept the role of James's father-substitute to help him become a boy who was able to free himself from mother's possessiveness. This enabled him to begin to identify with his therapist and achieve a sense of masculinity of his own. By February 1977, he had grown up rapidly as he struggled with the wishes and fantasies of an early adolescent.

CHAPTER 40

Jay wants to understand if James
is separate or a part of him.

March 28, 1977

Jay arrives, dressed nicely as usual. After sitting down, he complains that he doesn't know what name to sign, similar to last session. He ponders what to do and then says he will sign his legal name, because he knows what it is. He thanks me for showing him the video which we discussed last session, and says it taught him a lot about himself.

He lifts his left hand to demonstrate that the video was very real to him. "I know I'm crazy because I can't get it out my mind!" he exclaims.

He changes the subject and tells me his brother visited yesterday to discuss their joint bank account. He says his brother had a copy of the bank book, which was fortunate, because James had lost it.

Then Jay changes the subject again and tells me he's aware that James has been going to the canteen by himself and put a pair of shoes on layaway. "I found a slip in my locker for a pair of shoes and when I went to see the lady at the canteen, she said she's been waiting for someone to pick them up for quite a while." Then Jay says he suspects that James knows he's here. "I think he knows what's going on. Do you think he knows me?"

After I explain that James seems to be aware there is another part of him, I ask if he is aware of that or knows he has other parts.

Jay shakes head. "There aren't any other parts of me. When I saw myself on the screen, I knew that wasn't me because I would have handled all those situations differently."

"Do you and James handle things differently on the ward?"

"I guess we must. People have told me I've said things I don't remember saying. But that's because I don't remember everything since I became a human being. But I don't even know if I am a human being anymore," he exclaims with a dramatic gesture of his left arm.

"If you have emotions and you're sensitive to James's emotions you are human. Do you feel sensitive to his emotions?"

"After viewing the videotape I felt strange."

"Do you still feel strange today?"

"Yes, I do. But I can't tell if that's emotions. In fact, I can't always tell what's real and I need to see something real. That's why I wanted to see you today."

Jay asks me to tell him about the "others" he saw on the monitor. "I've always thought I was the only one. Then I saw James. But I don't think it was really James because he's too damn scared. He probably wouldn't even leave that ward unless someone was with him," he laughs.

I point out that James is growing up and can even tolerate being touched by another patient now, which causes Jay to look at me with alarm. "I didn't think he was a homosexual!"

"You're right, he isn't, but he might have been afraid of it. He's aware that Shea was homosexual."

184

"That's what gets me. He's aware of Shea but I'm not aware of him or any of the others. At least I have learned something now and can quit assuming things."

Then Jay asks me what happens if James gets scared and summons him, because he won't know what to do. "If that should happen, will I have to get him out of it, or do you think he has the ability to protect himself?"

"I would like James himself to answer that," I reply.

I ask for his consent to use hypnosis to summon James to answer those questions and he agrees. I proceed to hypnotize Jay and ask him to close his eyes and take a couple of deep breaths. Then I proceed with deepening suggestions. "Let yourself relax with every breath. More relaxed with every breath. More relaxed with every breath."

After I repeat this several times I slowly count from ten to one. Suddenly his head drops and he appears to be in a trance state. His head remains in this position for a time, then he lifts his head and opens his eyes, but his face remains somber. I ask what happened, but he does not reply. Then I see him close his eyes again as his body quivers, his arms become tense and his breathing irregular. Suddenly I see his eyes open, his facial appearance changes, and he turns his gaze to the left. James seems to be present in the body although he clearly avoids looking at me.

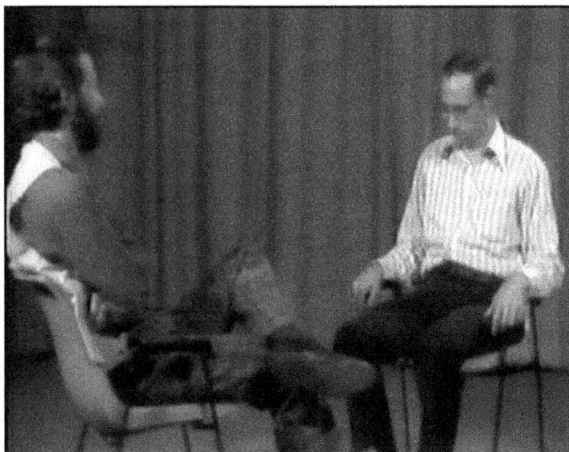

"I don't like your colors!" he exclaims as he continues to look away from me, apparently upset by my red shirt.

I let him know he doesn't have to look at it, and he

closes his eyes and lowers his head. I ask him what he is feeling but he doesn't answer and keeps his eyes closed. After a short time, he opens his eyes and I see Jay's presence. He looks down at his hands, which hold tightly onto the seat of the chair.

I greet him and explain that I saw James briefly but he left after looking at my red shirt. Jay immediately tells me he knows that the color red will trigger a memory of being attacked by two drunken men wearing red articles of clothing and smelling of beer.

I'm impressed by his capacity to recall that traumatic event and ask if he has any knowledge about what James experienced. He shakes his head. I explain that if he wants to know I'll be glad to show him the videotape of James reliving his traumatic experience.

Jay frowns and tells me he knows he would feel overwhelmed and doesn't believe seeing more details would make any difference. But I encourage him to reconsider since watching the tape would help him become more empathic with James. He shakes his head and says he will never forget what he already saw.

Jay tells me that James sometimes acts like a monster, according to the patients. When he tries to explain to them that James acts that way because of his terrible traumas, they don't understand. Furthermore, the patients don't understand that Jay's presence in the body is the reason they think he acts too normal to still be in the hospital.

Even though Jay is now beginning to accept that he has multiple personalities, most of the time he thinks James deliberately does disturbing things to aggravate him. Yet Jay remains committed to his purpose, which is to stay in the hospital until he can get James discharged.

CHAPTER 41

*Jay and James: impending separation
and beginning cooperation.*

April 7, 1977

Jay signs in at today's session and quickly informs me he still can't get the video program out of his head. "I didn't like what I saw. There was a lot of emotions and that can get you into trouble. I was crying and sobbing and carrying on. If I was in that condition, I'd be more than happy to die."

Jay remembers he felt James's tears running down his face and continues to worry about him. "It's like when I'm thirsty and take a glass of water. I always think, 'How will this affect James?' I don't think about myself."

"If you are so worried about James, why have you told me you would like to see him out of the hospital?"

"He's going to have to learn to be by himself and do things by himself. I never had anybody around to help me do things." After a pause he says, "Sometimes people have come up to me and talk like they know me when I don't know them at all. Maybe they knew him in the hospital before. They think I'm James but I have no desire to know those people." He pauses again, then continues, "I act like I know 'em so I can help James out because he is very vulnerable to being left alone."

I remind him that I had previously said I'd be away on a trip in a week and a half from now, but Jay looks puzzled, as if he'd been absent from the body when I told him. I ask if he thinks James will be upset by my absence. He responds like a mother who doesn't want her child to experience abandonment pain, but he also urges me to help James leave the hospital. Then he reminds me that I agreed to discharge him when he behaved himself, words I do not remember ever saying.

I agree that the goal is to get James prepared for discharge by helping him learn things so he can be completely self-sufficient. Jay claims to be playing his part by helping James. "We're making a vest together in OT. Did you know that? I start it then he works on it until he makes a mistake, and I'll correct it. Finally, I'll finish it."

I'm impressed to hear about their cooperative effort and ask if that was James's idea. Jay explains that he is the one who initiates their cooperative projects, not James. Then he makes a surprising statement that he will soon be leaving and doesn't plan to be in the hospital when James is finally ready for discharge.

When I tell Jay I'll feel a sense of loss when he leaves, that surprises him. He asks why, and I explain that I've become used to his being here and it will be a loss when he's gone.

"How could that be? There's always somebody to take my place. I can always be replaced by a vacancy." He breaks out in a big grin.

"No. You're unique. Not even James can take your place."

He pauses, then asks, "How come he has to take my place?"

"When you leave he'll fill the vacancy. But I would also miss James if he were to leave, because he is a unique person too."

"Did you ever say that to him?" he asks seriously.

"Not exactly in that way," I reply.

Jay remains silent for a time and then tells me something I didn't expect—that he feels unwanted when his family comes to visit James.

"Are they aware that you and James are two different people?"

He shrugs his shoulders and claims he doesn't care. "I know that I'm superficial and they don't really want to get involved with me. That's why they come twice a week to see him, because I'm nothing in the first place."

I point out that even though he feels left out by James's family, he shouldn't ignore my feelings that he is not a nothing and I'll miss him. He quickly replies that he doesn't know anything about feelings and doesn't want to pretend he does. "When people say, 'I'll miss you,' what am I supposed to say? All I think is, that's your problem, not mine!" he exclaims.

Although he adamantly denies it, I claim that he seems more receptive to having feelings each time we talk about it. "Perhaps I've had an influence on you to become more open to me," I explain. He listens and responds that it would be very silly if he came to see me and wasn't open.

Before our session ends, Jay repeats his premonition that he has a strange but good feeling that he will be leaving soon. I ask if I'll be there when that happens, but he makes it clear that he won't be saying any goodbyes. (Although Jay expects to be leaving the body soon, his departure won't take place for some time.) He also tells me their ring is missing. James had worn it on his left little finger. When it was changed from one hand to the other it identified which personality was present.

Because of lost video recordings and transcripts, the next recorded therapy session will not take place until June 20.

CHAPTER 42

James returns to therapy after being gone for four months; he thought I was mad at him.

June 20, 1977

Jay arrives today, signs in, and gives me a brief description of his visit with his brother last weekend. I'm pleased to hear him say it went very well, particularly since he previously told me that the family preferred to visit with James and not him. However, they don't know James has been away for a period of months and his absence is the reason Jay met with his brother.

I ask Jay if he knows why James has not come to any therapy sessions since Valentine's Day, but he has no answer. When I inquire if he has any awareness of James's presence, Jay nonchalantly says he still finds unexpected things in his locker and wonders if James put them there. I suspect James has returned to the ward even though he hasn't come to therapy. I'm perplexed about it and ask about James's whereabouts during the last four months. Jay shrugs his shoulders and replies that I'll have to ask him. His apparent indifference surprises me since he's bragged about their cooperative relationship in preparation for James's discharge from the hospital.

In order to talk with James, I will need to use hypnosis. With Jay's permission, I use my standard trance induction technique. After a brief time James appears. He looks around but does not answer when I ask how he's feeling. I try asking again and he complains that he can't do anything because his foot has been hurting him. I find this interesting because Jay did not have any complaints of pain in his foot.

I ask him to tell me about his activities and he raises his head, looks at me, and blurts, "Are you mad at me?"

"Why did you ask that?"

"Everyone seems mad at me all the time and I don't know what I've done," he replies sadly as he lowers his head.

"Who is everyone?" I ask.

"Everyone I talk to. Maybe I shouldn't talk to anyone," he whimpers as he raises his hand to rub his nose.

"I wonder why you would think I'm mad at you?" I ask.

He shakes his head dejectedly and asks if I can tell him what he did to cause me to be mad. I reassure him that he hasn't done anything to make me mad. I also make a transference interpretation—that his feelings about me are like those he felt toward his father. I also remind him that he previously told me he thought his father was mad at him.

"He still is mad at me," he says sadly, and adds that he avoids anyone who might be mad at him and that's why he has avoided me.

When I point out that he has avoided me since I last met with him on Valentine's Day four months ago, he tells me he thought I was mad at him then, and decided not to come to therapy any longer.

I assure him I'm not mad and he is safe here, so he asks if I'll let him stay. I say yes but add that I want Jay's approval for him to stay in the body. He nods, takes a deep breath, and sits silently for a while until he abruptly drops his head and Jay appears. I explain that I want his approval for James to remain in the body, but Jay says James doesn't need his approval because he needs to stay in the body and get along on his own.

I count down quickly from ten to one and James opens his eyes. He looks surprised and has a puzzled expression that seems different from the one I had seen earlier. I ask him if he remembers what we talked about, and he says he remembers asking if he could stay in the body.

When I tell James that Jay wants him to stay, he reacts with excitement and assures me that he won't do anything wrong. I explain that I will occasionally want to talk to Jay, and James nods his head in agreement.

"Our time is up today, and you can go back to the ward," I announce.

"I don't wanna go back to the ward. I don't wanna go back to the ward," he whines with a pained look on his face.

"Okay. Would you rather have Jay go back to the ward?"

"No," he replies emphatically.

When I explain to James that I want Jay to go back to the ward, his lips quiver and he begins to cry and shake his head from side to side. I count rapidly from one to ten to elicit Jay's presence, and I ask him to go back to the ward rather than James today. He nods yes, stands up quickly, and leaves the studio.

While reviewing this session several questions came to my mind. Why did James tell me today that he felt neglected and stayed away for a long time because he thought I was mad at him? This is particularly hard to understand because he gave me a Valentine's Day gift four months ago and I was pleased to receive it. Or did he stay away for a long time because he didn't want to depend on me? Why did he resist returning to the ward at the end of this therapy session? I expect the answers to these questions will soon become apparent.

CHAPTER 43

Jay wants to go to his nephew's apartment
this weekend but doesn't want to tell James.

June 23, 1977

Today is Jay's designated day to meet with me. After he signs in, he says there is something very important he needs to tell me. I ask him to be more specific and he shifts his position in the chair and folds his arms. After a long pause he tells me he will speak softly because he doesn't want James to hear what he is about to tell me.

"I've been planning something, but I don't know if it will work out or not."

"What were you planning?"

"I've been in this body for many years and in the hospital for a long time. I've decided I need to have some time away this weekend. It will be the first time that am going to spend the night away from here."

"This weekend? Where do you want to go?" I ask, surprised.

"I'm going to the apartment this weekend that my nephew and I rented for James when he gets out of the hospital."

"Have you discussed it with the staff?"

"Yeah. I requested a pass, and they approved it. But if you say no to me I won't make a big deal about it."

After I ask if there are reasons he shouldn't go, he pauses for a moment and then says he doesn't want James to hear us talk about it because he'll get upset and cause trouble.

I insist that he talk to me so I can appraise his situation, so he finally tells me that he is finding it more difficult to live as a human being.

When I ask what he means he says no one seems to understand him. He tends to say the things that people want to hear even when those things have little meaning to him. He does everything people expect of him when he really doesn't want to. "I go to work in OT every day even though it's an effort for me to go to work. I more or less have to twist my own arm to go down there because that's what they expect."

He pauses, removes his glasses and rubs his eyes, and tells me he has lost his motivation to continue working with James to complete their projects in OT, which had been a significant step because he had become James's work partner rather than James's protector as he had been in the past.

"It's getting so that I really don't care anymore." He puts his glasses back on and tells me he worries that it will be discovered that he's lost his enthusiasm to help James.

"Do you think James would be upset if he heard you say that?"

"I think he would. But I don't want to tell him. He might think I'm mad at him, but he should realize I can't get mad at anyone."

I sit quietly and wait for him to continue.

After a long pause he tells me he wants to know how he can regain his desire to help James. Yet at the same time he says he'd rather see James take over the body, become independent, and move out on his own.

"I don't believe he is ready yet," I clarify.

"Who is the best judge of that?" Jay interrupts. "I don't want to denounce anyone. I'm just asking who is the best judge of whether he's ready for that? You or I?"

"I'd leave that up to you and him," I reply.

"It's not up to him. He doesn't have a choice!" Jay exclaims.

"Why is that?"

"He can't leave. The body cannot continuously go on forever and ever with this way of thinking. He's going to have to be here."

"Who's going to do the thinking?" I ask, aware that Jay has more capacity for rational thought than James does.

"If he comes into the body he must do the thinking because I will not be here," Jay insists. He goes on to say that all human beings have the capacity to think and since James is a human being, he has no choice except to think.

Realizing that Jay is setting the stage to leave the body, I remind him that he told me earlier that he asked for a pass to go to his nephew's apartment this weekend, but if he's not in the body he won't be able to go. He shakes his head and says he doesn't care because James needs to learn to start coping with life on his own.

When I point out that James will continue to need a teacher, Jay says he's already been teaching him and that should be enough. Furthermore, he questions whether James has benefited from all this teaching. He's adamant that James must soon take over the body and he has no choice. "I can't be here forever. James is going to have to be here on his own. He needs to know that he'll soon wake up and I won't be here, and he'll have to cope by himself."

After hearing Jay insist that James needs to be prepared to have the body all to himself, I tell him that I'll need to talk to James for a few minutes before we quit today's session.

He sighs deeply and says, "We can try but I don't know."

I ask him to relax, close his eyes and breathe deeply. I count backward quickly from ten to one and James comes into the body. His arms and clenched fists drop to each side of the chair. His head quickly slumps, and his chin comes to rest on his chest. He pulls both hands backward as if they're being tied behind the chair. He keeps his head down, and I begin by asking if he remembers our last conversation.

He struggles to find words and avoids looking at me but moves his head from side to side.

I remind him that he had been worried I was mad at him. "Do you remember that I told you I wasn't mad?"

He doesn't answer but shakes his head vigorously while swinging his arms back and forth.

I wonder why he isn't answering me, and I ask him to tell me if there's a problem.

His eyes remain closed as he shakes his head and slams both of his hands loudly into the sides of the chair.

I reach out with my left arm to touch his right shoulder, hoping that will help him to relax. But that only seems to provoke him.

"What's the matter?" I ask again as I continue reaching out to his shoulder.

He gasps and, to my surprise, pulls away from me and shouts, "Please. Please! I don't wanna see people," he stammers.

He shakes his head vigorously but keeps his head and eyes down as he continues to avoid looking at me.

I hope to find a way to help him relax, so I walk to his right side where I contemplate reaching down to his shoulder. But he yells, "I don't know what to do. I don't know what to say."

When I ask him to tell me what he's afraid of, he sighs deeply and shakes his head. "Me!" he yells.

"Are you afraid you're going to do something or hurt somebody?"

I reach out and grasp his right hand, which was swinging back and forth.

He gasps as if unable to breathe.

I ask him to open his fist and grab my hand. "Squeeze my hand hard. No matter how hard you squeeze you can't hurt it," I insist, and repeat myself three times. But James is unable to accept the request to squeeze my hand.

After repeating "No...No...No!" loudly several times, he raises his right hand over his head. That seems to be his signal to relinquish the body to Jay.

Jay returns to the body, takes off his glasses, and pulls out his handkerchief to wipe his eyes and blow his nose.

I ask if he knows what happened and he says no.

"He's very upset, isn't he?" Jay exclaims as he wipes his face.

"How did you know?" I ask.

"One reason I know is because I'm doing this," he says after taking a clean tissue from the box to blow his nose and wipe his face and glasses.

He is clearly frustrated by the fact he has no awareness of James's level of fear, indicating that he isn't as aware of what is happening as he thinks. Then he tells me about a recent blackout while walking to the cafeteria. "It was about eleven thirty and the next thing I know I found myself in the hallway outside the chow hall with napkins and salt and pepper shakers in my pocket. I know I went inside there but then something must have happened and I'm not sure what."

After hearing about this blackout, I tell Jay that I don't think this is a good weekend for either he or James to be leaving the hospital. But he insists that one weekend is the same as the next.

"Aren't you afraid James might come out?"

"I'm not afraid but if he does, I'm concerned about what he will do. Right now he'll have to take the consequences of whatever he does."

"Will your nephew be there?"

"Yes. He knows James."

"Will you ask him to observe and report what happens and let me know on Monday when we meet?"

"I can say the information will get back to you in some way."

I decide to agree to Jay's request to spend the weekend in the apartment.

CHAPTER 44

"James is not me, but he will be me some day."

June 27, 1977

James is scheduled to meet with me today and signs in. I ask him how his weekend went. He looks at me, nods his head vigorously, and says Jay brought him to the apartment and he enjoyed it so much he wants his own apartment.

I explain that his nephew and Jay had rented that apartment for him when he finally leaves the hospital, which confuses him, and he sits quietly for a long time.

But he is in a much calmer mood today compared to the last time we met. I ask if he wants to watch himself and Jay on a videotape today. He nods his head. Dick shows us the videotape I ask for, and we see James wearing a beard and mustache. After a long pause James says, "I thought that was just a dream."

We talk about the fact that his current life is not a dream but very real. "Do you think you're ready to be on your own now or does that scare you?"

He appears to be struggling with a mix of emotions but appears able to sit quietly for a long time. Then he says he feels strange and wants to go to sleep.

I want him to stay awake, so I quickly count backward from ten to one in order to reinforce James's presence. He breathes more rapidly but maintains his body position and continues to keep his head down. Then he tells me why he's afraid. "Will you promise you're not going to hit me?" he asks.

After I promise, he lowers his arm and tells me he doesn't feel good, then raises it again and covers his right eye. I see a change in his body position and Jay suddenly enters the body. I ask where he's been, but he says he doesn't know. He sighs deeply while looking at me with his head turned slightly downward. He rests the spread fingers of both hands on his face.

"I think you returned to protect him from the possibility that I might hit him," I point out.

"Are you going to hit him?" Jay asks.

"Certainly not."

"Well if you do that's his problem. That's life and he's going to have to realize it. If he cannot realize that's life, I can't do anything for him." After a pause he tells me that he is feeling very human.

"You feel human? I've never ever heard you say that before."

"I don't know any other words to use. Of course I see no logic in it. But everything seems different now. It's like having a decision to make but you don't know how to make it because there's a lot of unnecessary things floating around that shouldn't be."

When I ask for clarification, he says he would like to have a dust rag so he could dust the air and clean it up.

I interpret that as a metaphor for his wish to wipe away bad memories of the past caused by people who hurt him instead of helping him.

Jay gazes into the distance, then looks directly at me and says he might have said something that contributed to James's problems.

"What have you told him?" I ask.

"I told him that he doesn't have any choice but to quit depending on me because he, and no one else, is responsible for his life. That's why I wanted him to go to the apartment. Does he know that's his apartment?" he asks.

"I told him you rented it with your nephew for him to use, although he may not understand that."

"I hope he can appreciate what I did for him. Because it's his apartment!" Jay exclaims.

When I point out that James may not appreciate it because he didn't have an active role in renting it, Jay expresses his annoyance. "If he doesn't like it then let him go out and find another one," he exclaims.

I point out that James doesn't believe he chose the apartment because he doesn't understand the two of them are in the same body.

"But I am him!" Jay exclaims. He describes having a new sense of oneness with James now and knows that he and James will eventually become the same. After a pause he tells me he's losing a lot of his memories. Then he changes the subject. "Do you think it's appropriate for me to request a pass for this upcoming holiday weekend?"

"I don't object but you need to ask your doctor on the ward because he will have the final word."

Jay says he's lost interest in everything. He doesn't care to get up in the morning, eat meals, go to OT, or pay attention to time because it's lost its meaning.

I point out that he has all the earmarks of being depressed and I will call his hospital doctor and express my concerns.

After hearing him say that he has lost his awareness of time, I decide to research the published literature pertaining to the perception of time. I find that time perception is influenced by memory, attention, emotional states, and specific situations. There are many neuro pathways implicated—the right side of the brain is involved in time perception but not the left side. Jay's identity is linked to the left side (associated with language and intellectual processing), which seems to explain, neuro-physiologically, why he lacks the capacity to sense the passage of time.[19]

CHAPTER 45

Jay is the maternal "home base" for James. He says the distance between him and James will disappear, a prediction that the two personalities will soon fuse.

July 1, 1977

Before Jay arrives, I'm approached by Jim, the Director of Educational TV, who tells me that Jay came to the studio yesterday expecting to meet with me, and hadn't been told that our session was changed from Thursday to Friday. Apparently, a member of the ward staff had not informed him.

When Jay sits down, I apologize to him, but he brushes off my apology as insignificant and says he doesn't have anything else to do other than eat. He complains about gaining weight, but I point out that he definitely is not overweight.

Then he tells me that his nephew told him James came out during the weekend in the apartment but seemed confused about what was going on, like he didn't think he was supposed to be there.

I asked Jay if he was in the apartment last weekend and he says he was, but he really didn't do anything since it's James's apartment. After expressing my opinion that we'd better help James appreciate the apartment, I ask Jay's permission to let me talk to James.

Despite Jay's belief that he can't be hypnotized, he reluctantly allows me to proceed with an induction. I slowly count backward from ten to one and ask him to use finger signals to communicate with me. He signals that his left side (James) is guarded, so I work with him to relax his left side. James opens his eyes and asks me why I seem so far away. I assume that his spatial distortion is related to his fear of being close to me, so I ask if he will reach out to me.

James begins to stretch out his hand but stops. "I... c...can't reach you," he stutters. Rather than continue any further I decide to bring Jay back. He quickly asks me how James is doing, and I describe his perceived distance from me.

"There will probably be a lot more distance and then there won't be anymore," Jay says.

"There won't be anymore. How do you mean?"

"There NEVER will be anymore!" he announces firmly, a prediction that his relationship with James will end as the personalities fuse into one.

"Okay. When will that happen?" I ask.

Jay says he doesn't know the answer and can't tell me how soon this fusion of personalities will take place. He says it might be a hundred years from now. After a pause he explains that he exaggerates everything in order to make a point. Then he describes feeling far away from everything, like James's description.

"How distant do you feel from me?" I ask.

"As far as the eye can see. That's how far I am away from you," he replies as he gazes into the distance. "You can touch me, but I can't touch you," he sighs.

I wonder if this means he will soon be departing from me and ask if James feels like a child whose mother is about to abandon him.

Jay sighs and his facial expression takes on a somber appearance. "I don't know what you're talking about. I hear your words, but they just don't connect with any meaning."

I reach over and touch his arm. "How does that feel?" I ask.

"It feels very hot but it also feels cold." After a long pause he says he feels compelled to do something.

"What do you have to do?" I ask.

Suddenly he looks to his left and then back again. Then I see tears in his eyes and point that out to him. But Jay disowns the tears.

"You don't like losing control of your physiological functions like shedding tears," I point out.

"There are some other physiological functions which, if I lose control over them, I'm in more trouble," he replies cynically.

After I assure him there is nothing wrong with having tears, he asks me a question. "You say you've talked to James?"

"Of course."

"I hope he wants to keep going to the apartment because it's important that he learns how to be on his own."

"Aren't you carrying him to the apartment?" I point out.

Jay shakes his head. "He shouldn't have to be carried. Who carries me?"

I explain what I mean. "In a way you are like the mother who carries her young child."

Jay shakes his head. "I have no gender."

"That may be true but James is helpless and it is part of your function to help him. You bring the body there so that he can come out and explore the place. When he wants to go back to his 'mother' you're there."

Although Jay doesn't like to hear me define him as a mother, it is important for him to understand the principle—he has been the maternal part of their relationship by providing a home base for the child, the young James.

Jay sighs and makes a sarcastic comment about mothers.

I reinforce this theme by telling Jay that I have also been in the role as mother to both of them.

"Okay, if I have to be his mother, okay. If you have to be our mother, okay. But I don't see it," he complains.

"Of course, as your therapist I'm also more than just your 'mother,' I'm other things too."

"I realize that you're Dr. Brende," he grins.

I look at the clock and realize our fifty-minute hour is over. "I guess it's time to quit for today. I need to let you know that we won't meet for a week until next Thursday."

"What if James wants to see you?" he frowns.

"If necessary, you can arrange for an extra meeting."

"He'll have to make that arrangement, not me," Jay replies, unwilling to take responsibility.

I acknowledge his reluctance and assure him that James can handle the absence of one session.

CHAPTER 46

Jay wants to detach from James permanently.
For James this may lead to positive growth
during the process of separation-individuation.

July 7, 1977

Jay signs in. I am struck by the nature of his detached appearance and manner of speaking today. His voice is barely audible and sounds disconnected. He is not the smooth, glib-speaking man I've been conversing with twice a week. Rather, he seems more like "Kohlman," the transitional personality who appeared previously in an intellectually authentic manner but without emotion. I suspect that he is one step away from leaving the body.

He shows me an injury that James suffered while at the apartment during the past weekend. "He fell, collapsed, and skinned up his leg, uh, my leg, uh, our leg." Then Jay shows me a severe abrasion on his right shin. It is red and swollen but he feels no pain.

I ask if he has shown his injury to his hospital doctor. He shakes his head and insists that there is no need for that because it doesn't bother him. Furthermore, he says he won't get involved with the doctor because he doesn't have pain and wants to remain as distant as possible from James's problems.

To learn how James is doing at this crucial time, I decide to ask Jay's permission to use hypnosis. He agrees and I count from ten to one quickly. James appears and pulls his chair slightly away from me.

I ask about the injury to his leg. He looks down, scowls, and tells me it hurts. He also complains that no one wants to help him. I assume James summoned Jay to block the pain, and if so he would not have felt a need for the doctor's help. He continues to look down and appears depressed. I ask if he feels neglected, but he denies that and continues to look at the floor. After assuring him that I understand his feelings, I ask him, in a firm voice, to look at me rather than at the floor.

He looks up and blames me for being mad at him. He also complains that Jay has been hollering at him and that he doesn't know who to turn to anymore. "Sometimes I think you're him (Jay) and I don't know what to do," he mourns.

He remains distrustful and withdrawn from me. I point out that he believes he's unlovable and ask if he remembers all the times he's felt abandoned. He begins to cry and says he doesn't want to think about it.

I reassure him that I won't abandon him, but he is unable to accept my reassurance and tells me he wants to leave. I interpret that as his wish to leave me before I leave him. I change the subject and ask how he liked his apartment. He looks up at me and says he felt lost there, just like he feels now.

I ask if it would help to have someone with him in the apartment, and he says that he would like a human being there rather than Jay because Jay is not a real human being. I agree that Jay lacks feelings and doesn't feel like a human being.

James tells me, sadly, that he has lost his ability to love and to feel angry. "I used to be able to feel mad and it felt good," he sobs.

Then James asks me to summon Jay, so I grant his wish and count to ten to summon Jay. When I reach ten, Jay quickly reappears. When he becomes aware that his face is drenched with James's tears, he recognizes that James is upset. I step out of the room to find a box of tissues and when I return Jay asks if James talked to me. I nod my head and tell Jay that James is angry at him and at me.

"James has no right to be angry at you!" Jay exclaims.

"James is angry because he thinks I might abandon him. But I have assured him I won't."

Jay scowls at me and blows his nose. "Abandon? There's no such word."

I explain that abandon is a real word, and Jay asks if the word means that two physical things are separated.

"Separated like a mother and her child?" I ask, referring to James's experiences of abandonment and his inability to proceed toward normal separation-individuation.

"They are physical separations, aren't they?" he asks.

"Would you like to see how two physical things can be together and not separated?" I ask.

"Are you talking about me and James? We cannot be together!" he insists.

"You aren't answering my question. Let me put it another way. Would you like James's two parts to feel put together?"

My question confuses him. He sits silently for a while, then tells me he can't understand separation and abandonment because he believes they mean the same thing. "Can't you be separate and still be attached? And be together and still be apart?" he asks.

Before our session ends, Jay announces that he will soon be detached and that it will be more permanent.

As I review this session, I recall my consultant, Dr. Don Rinsley, discussing object relations theory and its application to my therapeutic work with James. The main focus has been to enable James to experience his rebirth, followed by emotional and intellectual growth paralleling that of a young boy growing up with his parents. My first therapeutic task was to enable James to form an authentic sense of self based on a reenactment of maternal love and nurturance. Jay, who had been James's protector, returned during that early process and transferred James's care over to me. James's identity became consolidated, and he accepted the name he was born with. As he began to grow intellectually and emotionally, he moved toward a process of separation-individuation from his fantasied mother as well as from Jay. The quality of my relationship with James has also changed, and my role as the "all-giving mother-figure" ceased as I took on the role of his father. This facilitated the separation-individuation process as James freed himself from his mother's possessiveness and moved toward a closer relationship with his father.

CHAPTER 47

*James's vulnerability to abandonment has worsened
since Jay announced his plans to leave.*

July 11, 1977

Jay signs in and expresses a sense of relief that I am here
today. He says that James came to the studio last Thursday only
to discover we weren't meeting and was very upset about it. After
hearing about James's experience, I ask to talk with him. Jay is
very willing to let me count from ten to one.

When James emerges, he appears emotionally distressed and
asks me where I have been. He looks down at his hands and
struggles to hold back his
tears. His vulnerability to
feelings of abandonment
has worsened recently,
and it has been more
difficult for him to be
alone since Jay expressed
his desire to stop
protecting him. Jay has
insisted that James needs
to learn to cope on his
own and face things that
normal people face in life. But James isn't able to proceed as Jay
had hoped. I find that he is too distraught to continue talking
and ask him if he would like Jay to return. He nods and I count
to ten.

Jay pays no attention to my statement that James is
emotionally too upset to talk to me any longer. Instead, he

immediately tells me he's been busy preparing James's apartment so that it can be ready for him to move into.

Realizing that Jay can't grasp the reality that James isn't prepared to be on his own, I ask to talk to James again and count backward to one. When James emerges, he appears calmer and looks around to see if anyone else is in the room. Then, to my surprise, he looks down at his trousers, reaches into his pocket, and pulls out a small booklet. "I found this in my room and I don't understand it," he says.

I carefully open it and find that it's a bank book for the account of James Kohlman. I look it over and can see there have been many regular deposits, which I assume are monthly VA disability checks. When I ask James if he is aware that the VA has been sending him monthly disability checks, he nods and tells me his nephew deposits the checks each month. He also worries there may be some money missing.

I look more closely and see several withdrawals, including a large one for $500 within the past two weeks. When I ask James if he knows what happened to that money, he says his nephew may have withdrawn it. When I ask him if he has concerns about this, he shrugs his shoulders, indicating that he doesn't know what to do about it.

I decide it would be helpful to ask Jay if he knows more about this, so I ask James to allow me to talk to Jay again. When I count from one to ten Jay emerges. I ask him if he knows anything about the cash withdrawals from James's bank account during the past two weeks.

Jay explains that he made several withdrawals recently to make some important purchases for his apartment.

"How about the $500 withdrawal?" I ask.

"I spent that money on a TV set and some furniture. It's too bad that he didn't go to the apartment and see it. I know that he would've liked it."

After hearing that James did not go to the apartment last weekend, I ask Jay to let me talk to James again. After he emerges again, I repeat what Jay told me—that he was disappointed (James) didn't see what he (Jay) has done there.

James frowns and tells me there are two reasons he didn't go. First, it's not his apartment, and second, he doesn't like being there alone.

I try to help him appreciate what Jay has done for him. "Do you remember that you told me you wanted to have your own apartment? Jay knew that and he and his nephew found the perfect apartment for you, which they have rented. That's the reason Jay is so disappointed that you didn't go to the apartment last weekend."

Unfortunately, James can't accept the fact that Jay and his nephew rented the apartment for him, and he can't appreciate it, most likely because he'd be left alone since his nephew has apparently lost interest in living there. The truth is that James is not yet ready to become independent and live on his own in that apartment. It is also true that James has been feeling abandoned after Jay announced he would be departing from the body, something that neither of them can understand.

CHAPTER 48

Jay found himself walking down the street near the
Jayhawk Hotel without knowing how he got there.

July 21, 1977

When we meet ten days later Jay signs in. He tells me he had
a blackout during his weekend pass and found himself walking
down the street in downtown Topeka but had no idea how he got
there. When I ask if he remembers his location when he awoke
from his blackout, he says he looked around and saw the
Jayhawk Hotel nearby.

Jay tells me that he has no recollection of going into the
Jayhawk Hotel. However, I can recall that Shea once told me he
had lived there for a year after coming to Topeka from Seattle, at
a time when he was an active homosexual. That makes me
consider the probability that Shea may have been at the Jayhawk
during this past weekend and may have engaged in homosexual
behavior. I worry about James's potential vulnerability if that is
the case. James once told me during a previous therapy session
that there had been a time years ago when he awakened in terror
after discovering he was in a hotel bed with another man. He
had no memory of how he got there and fled out of the room. I
do not know if James could have had a similar experience during
the past weekend, but I express my concern and urge Jay to
resume taking responsibility as James's caretaker to prevent
such things.

Before time runs out, I make it clear to Jay, after hearing
about his blackout, that I won't support any more weekend
passes until I am assured of James's safety.

Wolfe

After this session is over, I spend some time going over past therapy notes for references to the Jayhawk Hotel. I found notes when Jay told me about staying at the hotel on two occasions.

The first time occurred during a session on June 16, 1975, when Jay said he had a vague recollection of spending a weekend at the hotel. He had left his brother and sister-in-law's house because his memory lapses and strange behaviors caused him to be too embarrassed to stay with them. He then took a bus to Topeka and checked into the Jayhawk Hotel. But he didn't remember much about it, suggesting that Shea had stayed there rather than Jay. I later learned from Jay that he had stayed at the Jayhawk Hotel for a year sometime prior to 1975 but had very little memory of the details. I presume Shea had been predominant during that year. I worry that Shea may have replaced James and gone to the Jayhawk Hotel instead of to his apartment during the weekend pass.[20]

213

CHAPTER 49

James is tearful and feels abandoned during my absence.
Is that the reason for the presence of someone who could
be a new personality coming to take care of James?

August 8–11, 1977

Today I resume my therapy sessions with Jay, who says that James became very frightened and was trying to find me during my absence. He also tells me that an individual who called himself Jack made his presence known during that time. I speculate that Jack's presence may have been to help James with his abandonment feelings.

I ask to talk with James to learn about his experience and Jay agrees to be hypnotized. When James emerges, he asks, "Where have you been? I looked for you, but you weren't there!"

"I had to take a leave of absence, but I didn't plan to be gone very long." I ask James if he knows about Jack, but he doesn't understand who I'm talking about. Then I tell him what Jay has told me. "Jay thinks you don't need him any longer," I explain.

"I don't want him to go," James sobs.

Before our time comes to a close, I ask for Jay to return. He emerges quickly and wordlessly. I inform him that James is grieving in expectation that he will be left alone. When I ask Jay if he has any questions, he says he has none, so we end the session, and he leaves the studio with an aide.

Our next therapy session is three days later, August 11. James signs in and appears to be emotionally distraught as he keeps his head down and breathes with rapid gasps. I can see the tears in his eyes and reach over to provide an empathic touch. But he pulls away from me as he swings his hands behind his back and keeps his head down. I ask about his feelings, but he remains withdrawn and continues to sob.

I decide to ask Jay to give me more information and summon him by counting from one to ten. Within moments he emerges.

"I don't wanna be here," insists. "I told you I've got to leave, and James knows that," he continues.

I ask him not to leave the body until I return from another leave of absence related to hospital business and he reluctantly agrees to remain longer.

Then I ask him if I can meet Jack. He replies that I may be able to meet him, but he doesn't know when.

I fail to talk with James once more before the session ends and will learn later that I should have talked to him first before asking Jay to walk back to the ward.

PART EIGHT

New &
Transitioning
Personalities

CHAPTER 50

Jay says he'll continue his existence after
vacating the body by taking the form of "mind."

August 22, 1977

During the past month Jay has said he wants to leave James, depart from the body, and take the form of "mind." When I arrive at the studio this morning, I learn from Dick, one of the video technicians, that he seems to be on the verge of doing just that. When he meets me at the door, Dick tells me that one of the personalities arrived about ten minutes ago with the assistance of an aide. When Dick asked him to identify himself, he labored to answer and gestured for something to write on. Dick gave him a pen and pad on which he struggled to write JAY. Then he slowly sat down on a chair in the studio, appearing somewhat catatonic.

When I walk into the studio, he answers my greeting with mechanical and disconnected speech. "I don't... think... I'm here. I think... James is... where he's supposed to be... but he's not quite there."

I ask him to explain what he means.

"I'm... here... but I'm... not... fully... here," he repeats disjointedly.

"Jay, what do you think is going to happen to you?"

He struggles to answer with disconnected speech. "I'm always... necessary... but James is... getting stronger... I'm not supposed... to be here."

To ascertain how Jay perceives himself, I ask if he can describe where his body is located. He points wide to his right side and states that he is "further out" than he has been before. I

219

interpret this to mean that Jay feels a greater degree of separation from James and is losing linkage to the right side of his body. That would also mean he is losing linkage to his left brain (cerebral hemisphere)—the location of his speech and thinking functions. Jay's loss of identity would predictably lead to mental and physiological changes affecting James's body and brain as well.

Now that Jay is losing his identity as a dominant personality, I wonder if his memories and thinking capabilities will be transferred to James when he leaves the body. I ask him how he feels, but he remains emotionally detached, staring blankly into space.

I ask to talk to James and Jay nods in agreement. I begin to count backward until I reach one and James suddenly appears. He looks scared and grips the arms of the chair.

"You're holding on to the chair hard. How do you feel?"

"I don't feel good, and I can't sleep." He goes on to tell me that he's afraid when the lights are turned off and of being left alone in the dark. "Why is he leaving me?" James pleads frantically.

I explain that Jay is leaving because he told me it's necessary for James to grow up and become independent. But James doesn't appear to be able to tolerate being alone. Now that Jay is gone James would prefer to leave. "There's no reason to be here any longer," he moans, and begins to stroke his hands together as a non-verbal way of nurturing himself.

Suddenly I'm surprised to see Jay return and announce in a flat voice, "I'm here."

I acknowledge his presence and ask if he knows why James is so fearful. He answers in halting speech that he doesn't understand human emotions. He continues to look catatonic, and his arm remains elevated when I lift it, a symptom of waxy flexibility associated with the psychiatric disorder of catatonia. I remember when he displayed a similar catatonic reaction during a therapy session in June 1976, after James relived the trauma of being struck in the head by his father.

I count backward from ten to one again and James appears. He holds one hand open and clenches the other in a tight fist. I wonder if the fist represents his non-verbal expression of anger and ask if he's angry. But he quickly responds that he is not. "I just don't know what to do! Please don't hurt me," he sobs.

"I think you're remembering that your father hurt you, but I can assure you that I won't."

"I wish he was dead!" James sobs.

I ask if he is afraid to express loving feelings toward his father, but he continues to sob and doesn't answer clearly.

He begins to caress his own hand. I decide to reach out to him, but he draws back in fear. Then his appearance changes and I see a personality who does not look like Jay. He looks at me quizzically.

When I ask him to introduce himself, he smiles. "Haven't we already met? I'm Jack."

I wonder about his degree of awareness and ask if he can explain why there is moisture all over his face (the tears left by James).

"I'm perspiring sir," he replies.

"Are you aware that James was crying? And are you aware of other personalities?"

"Others? Sir, are you trying to confuse me?"

Since he seems oblivious about other personalities, I decide to ask if he will view a videotape next time so that he can see his personality switch with James that will demonstrate what I'm talking about.

"Can you come to our next session?" I ask.

"If that's an order sir, I'll be here!"

Since our time is nearly over, I explain to Jack that he will be leaving after I count to a number. I decide to count to twenty, a number I have not used before, and after counting from fifteen

221

to twenty, his head suddenly snaps backward, then forward, and he opens his eyes and looks at me. He does not appear to be the same personality I just talked to, and when I ask him to identify himself, he smiles and tells me his name—Robert Random. I introduce myself and he says he hasn't met me before. I ask if he is familiar with the names Jay, Jack, or James, but he doesn't know any of those people.

"Are you familiar with the name Shea?"

"Shea Von Kohlman?" he asks.

"Yes. Did you know him?"

He frowns. "I'm not sure sir," he replies. Then he looks around the room, apparently to orient himself. "Can you tell me where this is and what time it is, sir?"

I spend several minutes answering his questions. Then, after realizing our time is up, I inform him that I must bring James back so he can return to his ward.

Robert is confused about my request. "I don't understand sir. I just want to go home."

"I understand your wish to go home, but you're in the hospital now, and James will have to return to the ward."

Before proceeding, I come to the realization that James may be too fearful to return to the ward. I decide to count back to fifteen and Jack opens his eyes. I ask if he is willing to return to the ward.

He is surprised by my request. "If you mean going to a hospital ward, I have no intention of being in a hospital," he insists angrily.

I realize my mistake of thinking Jack could go to the ward, so I explain the reality and count back to ten. Jay returns, although his body remains catatonic-like. When I ask if he can return to the ward he nods yes.

This session was unusual as it revealed evidence of two new personalities—Jack and Robert Random. It also ended in an unusual way as I was confused about which personality should return to the ward. I remained concerned about Jay's symptoms of catatonia and catalepsy, which prompted me to research this topic more thoroughly. I found that most of such cases were associated with a major mental illness like schizophrenia and bipolar disorder. Three cases of dissociative identity disorder have also been described in the literature as presenting with symptoms of catatonia.[21] I also found reports of persons erroneously pronounced dead with catatonia and other medical conditions—individuals who died but then spontaneously revived, such as the seventy-eight-year-old man in hospice care who was found without a pulse and declared dead, but woke up in a body bag at the morgue hours later.

Catalepsy is a mental and physical condition like catatonia that can mimic death. Its symptoms are muscle immobility, a trance-like state, cessation of breathing, and a heartbeat so slow it is almost undetectable. The muscle rigidity can be mistaken for rigor mortis, which is the third stage of death.

One of the first cases of erroneous declaration of death occurred in 1915, when a physician pronounced thirty-year-old Essie Dunbar dead after she suffered a major seizure. She was partially buried during her service, but after her sister arrived late she was exhumed, and the coffin opened. To everyone's shock Dunbar was found alive.

Individuals who have revived after being declared dead now receive the label of the Lazarus Syndrome, named after the story of Lazarus, who was resurrected by Jesus Christ four days after his death. This syndrome was first described in medical literature in 1982, when researchers reported eighty-two cases. Although not all these individuals were able to sustain life, 45 percent of them experienced a full recovery.[22]

CHAPTER 51

Jay is ready to leave the body.

August 25, 1977

When Jay comes to the session today, I can immediately see his slow and disconnected movements, like last session. He tells me, in mechanical speech, that he can't respond to the needs of his body or control his kidneys.

When I ask for more details, he frowns. "Don't you understand? I keep wetting on myself!"

"That's got to be embarrassing but I hope the rest of your body is still working."

"I'm here and I can still eat."

"That's positive," I say, and ask Jay's permission follow up with Jack from our last session. He nods his head ever so slightly and I count to fifteen. After Jack opens his eyes, I explain that there is a videotape I want him to see. Jack looks to his left at the monitor. When I ask if he recognizes anyone, he says he's heard James speak before. He also recognizes Jay and says he looks very tired. I ask Jack how long he plans to stay. That question seems to surprise him, and he grimaces. I explain that I want to know about the length of his stay, but first I want to

know if he's aware that his body is inhabited by several personalities.

With a smirk on his face he says, "That's the craziest thing I've ever heard."

"Let me explain. I've been talking with Jay and James for over two years. They're both in the same body you're in. And since you're here now, I'm wondering how long you'll be in this same body?"

"I'm always in this body. But I've never been in this place." He looks around as if he's trying to remember. I decide to inquire if he has visited James's apartment. That question surprises him. Then I ask if he had met any women there.

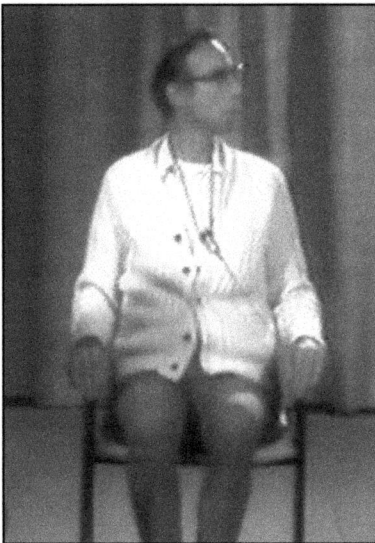

With a big smile on his face, Jack says he had hoped to, but he didn't see any women there.

I decide to pursue the subject about women further and ask if he remembers his first date.

He breaks out into a big grin. "No one ever forgets their first date."

I ask how old he was at that time, and he replies that he was young then but a lot older now.

"How old are you now?"

He opens his eyes wide, frowns, and says he thinks he's forty-seven. Since I know James's actual age is forty-one, Jack's assumed age of forty-seven doesn't make sense to me. When I ask if he knows the date he was born he says no. I ask him when he first existed, and he thinks his existence began sometime between seven and eleven years of age. I know that Jay took over the body at age seven when his father physically struck James, which leads me to believe that Jack's existence is associated with that date. It's possible that he thought of himself as six years old—an age when he was innocent from the abuse that occurred when he was seven. That would account for the additional six years that has led to his erroneous belief that he's forty-seven.

As I inquire about Jack's memories, many are like Jay's, except for the fact he names several girlfriends—Patty Brown, Shirley, Barbara, and Joanna, who looked like Natalie Woods.

Then I ask if he remembers a girl Jay had told me about, named Carol, when he was in the air force. He says he recalls meeting her in Hawaii, but they later broke up, which is a similar memory to one I heard Jay describe. He also tells me that he loved the air force and felt lost when he was discharged in 1968. The next thing Jack remembers is going to live with his brother Clarence and sister-in-law and their kids, indicating that he has no memory of being in the body at the time of the homosexual rape in Seattle.

"Do you remember what year you went to live with Clarence and his family?" I ask.

"I think it was about 1973."

"You were in the hospital two times before that. Once in 1968 and once in 1971."

I continue to ask about memories and inquire if he had a favorite family member. He recalls an older man he called grandpa, with whom he did farm chores. He remembers grandpa died but doesn't recall feeling sad or going to the funeral.

When I explain that James was the only personality who has told me that he experienced sad feelings, Jack says he remembers feeling sad when he lost his dog, Fang, an event James had told me about during a session in late October.

I point out that Jay never had feelings of his own and protected James from feeling emotional pain, but Jack says he doesn't know what I'm talking about.

As I wonder about the significance of Jack's presence at this time, I suspect that it has something to do with helping James cope with his feelings of fear and abandonment. I will continue to have contact with Jack, and his personality will change during therapy. Rather than the carefree young man who likes girls and other youthful activities, as therapy progresses, he will perceive himself as like his father, and there will be a rapid aging process as manifested by changes in his self-image and voice quality.

Since our time is about to expire, I explain to Jack that I meet twice a week with all the personalities. He frowns and shakes his head, obviously confused. Then I ask if he will allow me to talk with Jay, which also confuses him. But he willingly closes his eyes and I count to ten. After a long delay Jay opens his eyes. I explain my conversation with Jack, but Jay remains quiet with a blank look on his face. He sits quietly for a time and finally responds. "I don't know anything about this person you call Jack, and I certainly have no idea where he's been."

Our time has ended, and after I clarify when our next meeting will take place we stand up. Jay remains silent as he walks slowly and mechanically to the door where the aide is waiting. They leave the studio quietly.

I review in my mind the events that took place during this session. Jay first appeared and moved slowly and mechanically, evidence that he is preparing to leave the body. He was willing to allow Jack to emerge and I spent the rest of the time learning about Jack's memories. Some of his recollections seemed authentic but others appeared to have been embellished or idealized. When Jack gave names and descriptions of girls he dated as an adolescent, that indicates, assuming these are true memories, he had replaced James during pre-adolescence or adolescence, since James never reached puberty and never talked about an interest in girls. Jay is basically non-sexual, Shea is homosexual, and Jack seems to be the only personality who is heterosexual.

CHAPTER 52

I meet with Jay, James, and Robert
during the next two sessions.

August 29–30, 1977

After Jay signs in I ask to talk to James and count from ten to one. When James appears, he avoids looking at me and gazes at the floor, seemingly grieving over the impending loss of Jay. I watch his eyes fill with tears and his hands move back and forth on the arms of the chair. Since he has suffered the loss of relationships in the past, I spend most of this session helping him cope with his fear of being left alone.

When we meet again on the following day, Jay signs in but I don't see any evidence of catatonia today, which surprises me. I see tears in his eyes and hand him a tissue, which he uses to wipe the moisture off his face. Since Jay's appearance is so different today, I wonder if he and James have become integrated or fused (these two words are often interchangeable).

I decide to hypnotize him and determine if James can be summoned. Jay closes his eyes and I count from ten to one, the number associated with James's presence. I'm surprised to see

him become agitated and decide not to attempt to reach James. Instead, I count slowly upward and stop at twenty, the number associated with Robert.

His eyes remain closed, so I decide to wait until he is ready to open them.

He keeps his eyes closed for a long time and when he opens them and looks around, he seems unsure of his surroundings.

After a short time with Robert, I ask to talk with Jay again. I talk with him briefly but remain unclear if he has integrated with James.

CHAPTER 53

*Jay is no longer present and James, now
alone, hides his left arm under a towel, has a
black eye, and is suffering violent nightmares.*

September 6–8, 1977

The patient who arrives today is James, accompanied by an aide. He is wearing hospital garb—pajamas and a robe—and appears to be crying. I had received word from his hospital doctor earlier today that James was acting self-destructively and has a black eye his doctor can't explain. Furthermore, he hasn't bathed or brushed his teeth for several days. He has been placed on a one-to-one watch for close observation.

"What happened to you, James?" I ask.

He stutters an answer. "I...I... always had J...J...Jay to help me... but now... he's gone."

James says he feels too upset to stay in the hospital and asks to go to the apartment. But I make it clear he is on a one-to-one watch and must stay in the hospital. James reacts angrily and says that if he can't get out of the hospital he doesn't want to live. I let him know I want him to live, but he continues to insist on leaving.

After I help him accept the reality of Jay's departure, he finally calms down. It's a short session today and he leaves the studio accompanied by an aide.

We meet again two days later, and I learn that James is still considered a suicide risk and remains on one-to-one observation. However, in addition to his black eye, the most significant development is the white towel covering his left arm.

James says someone attacked him, which explains his black eye but not the towel. I ask for more details, and he describes

horrendous nightmares about drunken men wearing red jackets. He tells me that he wakes up feeling terrified and paces his room all night.

I'm surprised that his traumatic nightmares have returned, and I express my concern. When I ask about his black eye, he can't tell me. When I ask why he's covering his left arm with a towel he tells me he doesn't want to hurt anyone and certainly doesn't want to hurt me.

I ask if he's trying to protect me from the power of his rage. He sits quietly for a long time. Then he tells me he just wants to protect himself and the only way to do that is to run away.

"Running away is not a solution because you would be running away from everybody who wants to help you, and you'd be left alone again," I reply.

He ponders my statement and concedes that he has no place where he can run. Furthermore, he can't go home because he doesn't want to be around his mother's smothering presence.

I ask if he is responding to a childhood memory of wanting to run from an over-controlling parent and he agrees. I make a transference interpretation that he wants to run away from me and the hospital because he feels overly controlled, but he shakes his head.

Then I point out that he has two parts to his personality—one part wants to stay and the other part of him wants to run.

He ponders my statement and asks, "If you say there are two parts of me does that mean I'm not a whole person?"

I nod my head in agreement. "Those two parts of you want to do different things," I explain.

"Does a part of me wanna eat and another part doesn't wanna eat?" he asks.

I nod yes and give another example—one part of him hates me and another part loves me.

He ponders my words and then says he doesn't remember ever saying that. I remind him he had told me about his loving

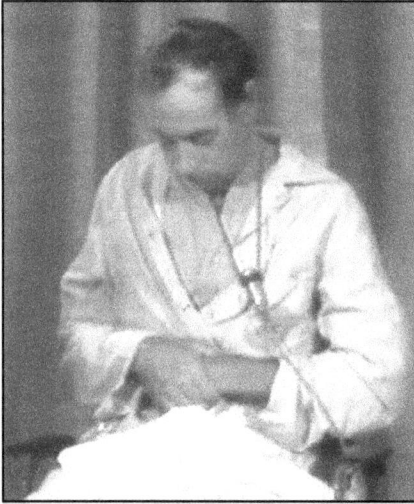

feelings last year. I also explain that it's normal to have mixed feelings but it's not normal to want to kill someone he loves.

I point out that his hate feelings must only be in his left hand, so his love feelings are much stronger. Then I ask if he can remove the towel, because he can't hurt me. He looks at me and says, "Doctor Brende, I can't take this towel off. Because I know I can do some things I don't wanna do!"

"Why don't you remove the towel and see what happens?" I ask.

After insisting that he doesn't want to hurt me, he looks down at his covered left arm and speaks to it. "Just behave!"

After a few seconds he reluctantly removes the towel and firmly grasps his left wrist and forearm that "holds" his potentially murderous left hand, which has a neurological link to his right brain.[23] I will conduct research later using electrodermal skin conduction to demonstrate that his three primary personalities-are linked to different parts of the brain.[24]

When I reach over to touch his forearm he reacts fearfully and begins to sob. "I won't do anything. I won't do anything."

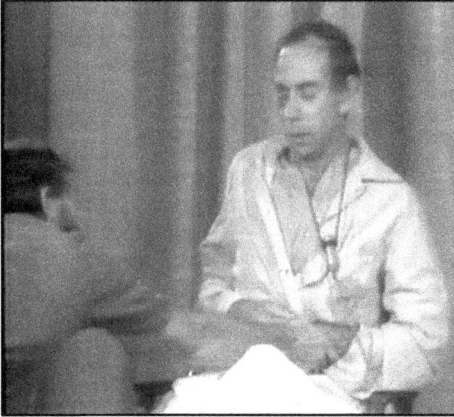

I reassure him that nothing bad will happen. After ten seconds I remove my hand from his forearm. "See. Nothing bad happened when you took off the towel," I declare.

I give him permission to replace the towel. He quickly covers his left forearm with his right hand and appears to hug himself with his right arm. But he remains distressed. I expect it will take more time for him to learn that nothing bad will happen when the towel is removed.

CHAPTER 54

Jack tries to understand that he is
not the only person in this body.

September 9, 1977

James signs in today. His left forearm is still covered by a towel. I ask if he's ready to remove the towel.

He asks if I'm going to hurt him, and I assure him that won't happen. I ask if he will agree to let me talk to Jack, and if he will allow Jack to remove the towel. He doesn't say yes or no but asks if he can be present when that happens. I explain he can't be present if Jack takes over his body, which confuses him. But he remains silent as he rubs his right hand on the towel over his left forearm.

"How do you feel about somebody else taking over your body?" I ask, breaking the silence.

"I wish they would all the time," he responds sadly.

"I'm surprised to hear you say that because you've told me before you hated it if someone else took over the body," I reply.

"Things are different now. I can't get any sleep."

When I ask how much he's getting, he says about twenty minutes, and its only broken sleep. He remains silent for a time but then looks around nervously and complains that he doesn't understand what's been happening to him.

I point out that I also want to understand and indicate that Jack might tell me more about it. So I ask James if he will allow me to spend a few moments talking with Jack. He agrees and I quickly count from one to fifteen. When I reach that number he shakes his head, indicating that he wasn't hypnotized.

"Let's try it again," I suggest. "This time I want you to relax and close your eyes. Okay?"

He nods and I proceed again. This time I count much more slowly and speak reassuringly about his safety. When I reach fifteen Jack opens his eyes and greets me politely. "Good afternoon, sir. How are you?"

"What makes you think it's afternoon?" I ask.

" 'Cause it's not at the time it's supposed to be."

I explain that I had to change the time from eight o'clock this morning because of unforeseen circumstances. "What have you been doing since I saw you last?"

"Nothing," he says as he looks down at the towel. "Do you mind if I take this thing off my arm?"

"Yes, it's okay," I reply, and watch Jack remove the towel and place it on his lap.

He then complains that he does not remember that I changed the time, but I remain silent. After a brief time, I ask what he would like to talk about today, and he responds with irrelevant comments about the fall season and camping. Then after a long silence he asks me if I have something to talk about.

"Yes, I do have something," I reply. "Can you tell me about your relationship to James? Maybe we can talk about that."

He frowns, turns his gaze downward, but doesn't answer.

"And what is your relationship to your father?" I add.

After a long pause he says, "We don't get along. But I would like to be exactly like him. Sometimes I copy him, but I need to watch myself because I get carried away."

I ask if talking to me is like talking to his father, but he only scowls without answering verbally. Then I ask about the nature of his communication with James. That question seems to confuse him. He asks what James I'm referring to, and I reply that I didn't know there was more than one James. But he clearly knows whom I'm talking about. "There is a person called James who is in this hospital. He calls it his house. I was there once but I don't wanna go back because I didn't like it."

I ask him to explain what he means, so he insists more strongly that he will never come to the hospital to see James again.

"That surprises me. I've talked with James, and he is doing okay in the hospital," I say.

"I didn't know you talked with him. He gets on my nerves, and I've told him so!"

"Did you give James that black eye on his right side?" I ask. Jack appears curious and lifts his right hand to his eye. "I know I've got a black eye there. Maybe I hit something. I don't know."

"Did you happen to hit James on the side of the head?" I ask.

He tries to remember but then shakes his head. "No sir."

I ask if it's possible he struck James on the side of his head like his father once did. After a long pause, he tells me he would never do anything like that, even though he has felt like it sometimes.

I ask if he knows if James may have provoked someone in the hospital to hit him. But Jack doesn't like the question. "That doesn't make sense. How the hell would I know if he wanted someone to do that?"

I postulate that James may have provoked someone to hit him because he thought that might please Jack.

"Why would that please me? But sometimes I'd like to shake the holy hell outa him," Jack insists.

"Just like your father would?"

He sits quietly for a brief time then answers, "I don't know that."

"Wasn't that how your father used to be?"

"Maybe so. We just didn't get along." Pause. "Maybe I'm too much like him. That's why I stay away from him."

"I believe you're like your father because you carry him around inside you," I point out as I consider the likelihood that Jack's identity is a personification of his father.

When Jack hears that he says, "Maybe you're right. I know I can't get rid of him but I'd sure like to get rid of his wife!"

I ponder Jack's words, recognizing that he does not acknowledge his father's wife as his own mother. I point out that his wish to get rid of his mother and women like her is not consistent with the reality that he likes women.

Rather than reply to my comment, he complains that James gets on his nerves. "He

237

nags and cries just like she does," he says, and remains silent for a time. Then I ask him to listen to James's concerns.

He turns his head to the side and says he will agree to listen to what James has to say provided I don't make him go to his hospital ward.

"I won't expect you to do that, but I would like you to come to our Friday morning sessions," I state.

He frowns and says he doesn't like to get up that early in the morning. Then he looks down at the hospital garb he's wearing. "How come I've got on these weird clothes?"

"Don't you know why you're dressed like that?"

"No. And I don't remember how I got here either," he says.

"You came into this studio with those clothes on because you're in James's body," I explain.

He looks around the room and frowns. "You're confusing me. I must be getting old because I don't remember doing that."

Rather than explain his situation any further, I decide to return to our previous subject, and ask if he and his father shared any similar characteristics or did things together. Jack says he liked being in the field and always wanted to be a farmer like his father.

"Did you love your father?" I ask.

Jack frowns. "I don't know about love. That's a very strong word, isn't it? Nah, I can't say that I do." He rubs his eyes, clutches his nose, and shakes his head.

"Did you remember wanting to be like him so he wouldn't hurt you?" I ask.

"He never hurt me. Why would he want to hurt me?"

"Did you know he can be very mean at times? He hit James on the side of his head."

This subject makes Jack anxious. Perhaps he has a vague memory of James being hit. He changes the subject and says his glasses don't fit right.

He rubs his nose with his right hand and places the glasses on the towel lying on his lap with his left hand. After a moment he

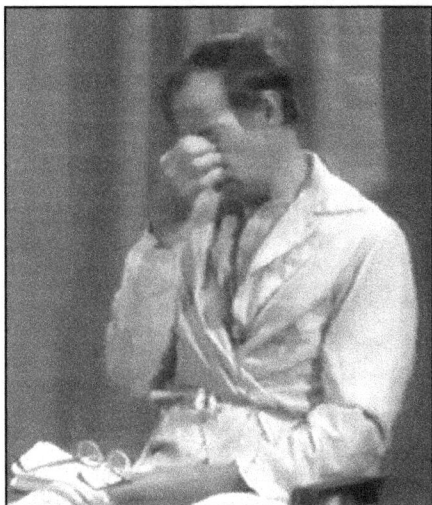

picks the glasses up and places them in the pocket of his robe, indicating that the glasses, which don't seem to fit, may be James's glasses.

Jack tells me he couldn't be like his father because if that was so James wouldn't talk to him. I point out that he already told me that James doesn't talk to him or to his father.

He ponders this for a moment and then, with a questioning look on his face, asks, "Am I like my father?"

For a long period of silence I wait for Jack to answer his own question, but his silence indicates that he may be wondering whether he would prefer being like him or not being like him. It's not clear now, but as therapy progresses there will be more evidence confirming that Jack's identity will transition into an older adult who personifies many of his father's qualities.

I point out that our time is up and explain that I'll call the ward to let them know we have finished our session and that someone will bring James back.

With a confused look on his face, Jack asks me to repeat what I had just said to him.

"James came over to this session and you're in James's body now, but I want James to go back to the ward."

He frowns but remains silent.

I point out that he is like James's father in many ways, and that James should see him more often. We agree to meet in a week and shake hands. I ask him to relax and count backward from fifteen to one.

When James appears he immediately places the towel back on his left forearm. Then he complains about a terrible headache and raises his right hand to his head. I am sympathetic to his pain and suggest that I can hypnotize him to relieve it.

He says he's not sure if he wants to be hypnotized, so I explain that I can give him suggestions for relaxation and pain control. He agrees and I give him positive affirmations about relaxation and relief from his headache pain, which appear to be effective.

I ask him to open his eyes. He looks at me, and says the headache is gone. I encourage him to control his own headache by counting backward while relaxing. Then I announce our time is up. After I ask him to come to the studio on Monday, he tells me he feels strange. The right side of his head itches now, in the same location as the headache he had moments earlier.

CHAPTER 55

I wonder if this angry personality is the same James.

September 12, 1977

When James signs in I see a striking change in him. He came without the towel covering his forearm, and he is angry and unwilling to sit down. I ask him firmly to sit, which he reluctantly does, but jumps up almost immediately. He paces back and forth along the side of his chair and yells out, "I ain't no dumb bunny. I don't wanna sit down. I wanna get outa here. I've heard all the reasons why I can't go but I don't wanna sit in smoke filled rooms listening to drunks and half-wits who don't know what they're talkin' about. If this is all there is then I'm givin' you an ultimatum."

He reluctantly sits down at my request but keeps his fists clenched. He raises his fist and complains loudly that he doesn't want to continue living in a place where everybody is either retarded, a sex weirdo, or an alcoholic.

"If this is all I see then I don't want this life!" he insists.

"I'm sure there's more than that up there," I reply.

"You don't know that. How often do you go up on that ward? That's right, you don't even go up there. I must spend twenty-four hours a day up there listening to them talk about how to get drunk, how to fuck, and how to take dope."

He refuses to consider that there may be some good things happening on his ward and continues to rage. He complains about not being able to go to the bathroom because people are lying in the doorway, and he must sit on the toilet with his legs spread to keep his shoes from being soiled from the excretions on the floor.

When I ask if he's complained to the staff, he replies that they couldn't care less and weren't even willing to bring him over to the session today because they were too busy.

He demonstrates with arms spread apart how angry he is that no one does anything to change the atmosphere. "They don't give a goddam. Besides, I've learned everything there is to learn and I want out!" he exclaims.

When I ask if there are some educational activities he can get involved in, he replies that the hospital can't teach him anything. "There's only one person I trust other than you and I'm beginning to have question marks about our relationship."

"What are your question marks?"

"I don't know what they are. I don't know whether to trust you or whether I should stop coming to see you anymore," he says as he stands up. He paces back and forth while he continues to rant. "I have no choice but to come here because there's no place else I can go. But if this is all there is, I don't wanna see you anymore. I know what Jay meant when he said it's not worth it."

I listen to his angry outbursts and distaste for the hospital, but he finally changes the subject and talks about a different concern—he's just learned that his nephew rented an apartment in his name six months ago and he's been paying for it. But he can't remember ever going there. "They told me I went there three times, but as far as I know, I've never been there. How do I know if it's really my apartment?"

It appears to me that I'm either talking with a new personality, or a new rendition of James. So, I ask him why he thinks we are meeting now, but he says he doesn't know.

"I know one thing for sure. I don't want this life. I've had it for five some years."

"Actually, you haven't had a real life since you were seven years old," I clarify.

"Well, I want a real life!" he exclaims while pacing back and forth. "I don't just want idiots around me who smoke and drop their cigarette butts and shit in their pants. Tell me if this is just a bad dream."

"If it's that bad, I would like to come up there and see it for myself. But I can't imagine it's that bad," I state.

He looks at me with alarm and insists that it would be a mistake if I came there. "The janitors will have it all cleaned up and you'll be fooled."

I nod my head but don't reply.

"Anyway, I don't want you to come up there. I just want you to tell me how I got into this hospital. Am I here on a court order?"

"No. You're not."

"I'm not on a court order?" he bellows, quite surprised. Then he sits down and remains in his chair for the first time since he came in. But he continues to complain about how much he hates being there. I assure him I'll investigate and announce that our time is about to end.

When I request that he meet with me next week he gets angry. "I don't care about next week. I wanna know right now!" He begins to cry, takes off his glasses, and wipes away his tears. He continues, "I wanna know right now if you're gonna let me know if there's something out there I can work for so I can get outa here, because if there isn't ..." He fails to complete the sentence because he's overwhelmed with tears.

I realize we need to clarify the confusion about his apartment. "I have a suggestion. How would it be if we go over to the apartment your nephew and Jay rented for you sometime this week?"

He stands up and says he doesn't care about the apartment, and he's confused about me. "I've been waiting for days to come over and see if you are real or not and I still don't know," he sobs.

He sits down and after a moment tells me that the only time, he feels real is when he gets mad. "If I don't get all upset, I'm not even here," he says, apparently referring to times when another personality takes over.

I ask him to tell me more about those times when things don't seem real, and he exclaims angrily that he never knows what's real. When I point out how angry he's been today he agrees, but also explains that he'd rather be angry than cry because he doesn't want to cry.

Then his mind seems to clear, and he tells me his nephew said he can't come to visit him in the hospital any longer.

"Who told him that?" I ask.

"He said a woman told him not to come and see me." He wipes his glasses off and lays them on his lap.

This is surprising and I assure James that I'll call his hospital doctor for clarification.

He continues to complain about his problems on the ward, saying someone threatened to attack him and when he defended himself, he was accused of being the aggressor. He suddenly stands up and complains angrily that the staff threatened to place him on close watch and confine him to his room.

"I don't wanna be angry up there and I just wanna get along." He sits down again. "If I get upset they make me stay in my room, but you don't know what it's like to sit in a room by yourself for days and days and days. And if you go out of your room you'll be attacked or get so sick from the smoke or everything else that goes on." He stands up again, looks around frustrated, and then sits down. "Those people only talk about screwing and taking dope and drinking."

He stands up, paces several steps, and sits down. He repeats that sequence again and sits for a time. After a period of silence, he tells me he once owned a living thing he thinks was a dog, and always went to the store to buy food for it. "I didn't know what it was but it was always hungry." After a pause he says it must have been his dog. He wipes his eyes, then stands up and complains about the drunk on his ward. Then he sits down once again.

"Can you sit still for a moment?" I ask.

"Why should I? So you can try to finagle me like those goddamn women do up there?"

"You just said that you don't want to always be angry and upset, so I'm just suggesting you sit still quietly for a few minutes so that you can see what it feels like."

"I don't wanna sit still, I want an answer and I don't wanna go back to the ward!" he exclaims angrily.

Despite my assurance that his anger won't destroy me, he remains angry and tells me there have been many times when he felt like busting me in the mouth. Then he breaks down sobbing and wipes his eyes with his fists. "I don't wanna hurt anyone and I don't wanna cry. But I want something besides that life up there."

I repeat my recommendation that he request a weekend pass to visit the apartment that Jay and his nephew got for him. That prompts him to say that he talked to his nephew and his friend Al and knows there's more to life than the ward. He insists he is the only well person up there, but if they won't let him be around normal people he can't stay well.

When I propose a visit to his ward so I can personally investigate his situation, he gets up out of his chair, walks away about four steps, and turns to face me. "No! I don't want you coming up there. They'll call me a bawl baby and accuse me of needing a doctor to come with me." He walks back to the chair, sits down, and tells me he's scared to go back there because he doesn't want to be called a bawl baby, and he doesn't want to be a helpless victim where the staff has had power over him for the past thirty years. When I question the reality of his perception, he gets out of his chair again and walks away. After I question him again about his level of helplessness, he changes his mind and insists he's not helpless anymore, because he has too many important things to do.

After I point out he contradicted himself, he goes on complaining and raises both clenched fists while telling me he won't put up with it anymore. I repeat my intent to return with him to the ward to investigate, but he says it's not safe and accuses me of giving him false reassurance, because he'll be attacked again after I leave the ward and he's left alone.

I ask him to relax before our session ends and point out that his left hand and forearm are not covered by a towel today. I acknowledge that he made a big step forward when he took off the towel, indicating he's not afraid his anger will hurt me. James asks who knows that the towel on his arm is meant to cover up his murderous thoughts. He also asks if I will have him put in the quiet room because I know. He is relieved to hear me say that won't happen.

After our session has finished, I tell James about my plan to accompany him all the way to ward 4-2-C. But when we leave the studio, I see an aide standing there who assures me that she is very capable of taking him back.

Later that afternoon, I walk over to the ward and talk briefly with his doctor. I find James in his room, and he seems much calmer. He apologizes for his anger during our session and seems happy to hear me say that I expect to meet with him next time.

During my visit with his hospital doctor, I learn that the ward environment is not as chaotic as James described. I ask if he thought James might qualify for a pass to go to his apartment, but was told he had become so disruptive recently that he would not qualify.

CHAPTER 56

I meet with James and his nephew,
who wonders why his uncle has changed.

September 13–14, 1977

I am pleased to see James and his nephew, Gary, arrive together at the studio today. Gary called me earlier this morning and expressed concern about his uncle, so I suggested that he come to our session today and talk about it.

Gary is a nice-looking young man with shoulder length hair. He tells me he is worried about James's anger when he visited him last weekend.

I recall how angry James was during the last session, but he seems calmer today. Yet he complains that his life in the hospital is meaningless, and the environment in which he lives is unhealthy and chaotic.

I quickly describe my visit to his ward yesterday and assure James that I told the staff about his complaints and heard their promise to enforce the patients' rules.

James says he doesn't care about their rules and just wants to be treated like a human being who can greet someone and be greeted with respect in return. I agree with his request to be respected and share my observation that he appears depressed. "Have you had any suicidal thoughts?" I ask.

He frowns. "I'm not going to kill myself because I want someone to help me find out there is more to this life than being trapped on a ward with a bunch of weirdos."

"I hear you. But it would help if you had a relationship with a staff member who was a man."

"There was a man I really liked but he's not there now. When I asked what happened to him no one would tell me."

I had not heard this before, and wonder if that's why James has recently been so angry and sad. I express sympathy for his loss and tell him it's normal to have those feelings when a person loses an important person in his life.

When I ask Gary if he would like to talk about his concerns, he says James is not the same person he was several weekends ago at the apartment. Gary also says he doesn't want to lose the $200 monthly rent money or see James give up the apartment.

After hearing me describe James's recent identity changes as well as everything else going on, Gary says he's glad he came today because he's gained a better understanding. I thank him for coming and predict that the apartment will play an important role in James's transition into outpatient treatment in the near future. When our time comes to an end, James asks if he can visit longer with Gary.

We meet again the next day at four o'clock. James signs in still wearing hospital garb and looks distressed. He complains about his situation again, and I encourage him to go to his apartment for a break. He shrugs his shoulders and, to my surprise, says he's never been to the apartment, which contradicts the fact that he had previously visited the apartment more than once. When I remind him that he has described the apartment to me, he repeatedly says this couldn't be real because it's just a dream.

I suggest we find out how real it is. "Consider this possibility. I will ask your doctor to give you a day pass and we can go there this week so that you can find out it's real. Then we can plan for you and your nephew to go there the following weekend after you request a pass."

James fails to acknowledge my plan. Instead, he continues to complain that the patients only talk about things he doesn't want to hear, and when he complains they tell him to shut up. I ask if this has ever happened to him in the past, and he remembers that he wasn't allowed to say anything that disagreed with his parents when he was a boy. "I remember hearing them say, 'You don't get any water to drink and you don't get anything to eat unless you agree.' " He sits silently for a time before telling me he's afraid to talk because he's sure he will say something that will make me mad, and then I'll punish him.

I assure him otherwise. "You've said a lot of things, but I haven't gotten mad and punished you or denied you anything because of what you've said."

"No, you haven't. That's why I like coming over here. You don't deny me going to the bathroom or anything like they deny me up there."

I raise my eyebrows, wondering if I heard him correctly. Then he explains that he was denied permission to leave his room and go to the bathroom last night from one thirty until two thirty in the morning.

"Did that hurt you to wait until two thirty?" I ask.

"Yes, I hurt a lot. I just walked and walked from eleven thirty to two thirty. My feet hurt so bad I could hardly even touch 'em.

And I had to walk so I wouldn't pee in my pants like those people who wet their pants up there."

I listen without commenting for a time but find it hard to believe a staff member would not allow him to go to the bathroom.

After he complains again about all the disgusting things patients do, I ask why he doesn't talk about something good like taking a pass to see his apartment and his nephew. He says he's afraid to talk about those things because someone in power will take them away. When I challenge the accuracy of his statement, he insists it's all true. Rather than continue listening to his frustrations, I ask him again if he will go to the apartment with me tomorrow. But he frowns and says if they let him do that they will want something from him in return. Furthermore, he doesn't want to get his hopes up because if he is given anything good it will be taken away.

"You have pulled away from everyone who wants to help you. Would you like to find a way to help people understand your unhappiness?" I ask.

"I suppose I can slit my wrists," he replies cynically.

"I definitely don't want you to do that," I reply firmly.

"I'm not a type of person to hang myself either. Only criminals get hung and I'm no criminal."

Despite his complaints, I tell him I believe he's not as angry as he was on Monday. He nods in agreement and sits quietly for a time. Then he says that when he came to see me Monday, he was so upset he couldn't see straight, and he didn't know if I was even real. Today I seem more real to him, although I can tell he's still afraid of his anger by the way he clutches his left hand.

James isn't interested in talking about this any longer and says that the only reason he wanted to talk to me today was to ask about going to the apartment tomorrow. I smile and remind him that he told me he didn't want to go because he didn't think the apartment was real.

"I want to find out if it really is real. But I don't want to wear these clothes," he says as he points to the hospital garb he's wearing. "Do I need to get permission to wear real clothes?"

I point out that if he wants to wear real clothes, he should submit a request for a pass to go to the apartment and ask at that time. But he insists that no one on the staff will believe him. Furthermore, he'll have to ask a staff person to open his locker and let him shower, shave, and brush his teeth, things they refused to let him do before.

"I guess you're just going to have to stop resisting the staff so you can brush your teeth and shower and shave. Are you willing to sacrifice a little bit?" I ask.

He shakes his head. "If I do that they'll think I've given in to their demands. Then they'll never stop."

"How about you tell them you will agree to whatever they ask, except you won't go into a room filled with smoke. Isn't there someone you can trust up there?"

"There's one man I can trust. He doesn't smoke, and he won't make me sit in a room where everyone smokes, or make me do things I don't wanna do, or make me sit where people say things I don't wanna hear."

After a long pause, he begins to complain again about the crazy patients he has to live with who do things he can't tolerate.

I point out that he shouldn't overlook the possibility he shares some of their same characteristics. He emphatically disagrees but I confront him with the fact he's not able to manage his own life and remind him that he couldn't control his feelings on Monday. He quickly responds that he doesn't want to remember Monday.

I urge him to attempt to understand the other patients and he frowns, but says he'll try to do that. Then I return to discussing the plan to leave the hospital for two hours tomorrow to see his apartment. To my surprise, he seems to have changed his mind and says he's reluctant to go because all the patients will get mad, and it will be harder for him to get along. I tell him his fear is unrealistic and insist that we should stick with our plan. "I'll meet you at one o'clock tomorrow," I insist.

After our session ends, I place a call to James's hospital doctor and describe recent events that have taken place in James's therapy. I mention his insistence that he can't tolerate hospital conditions and my recommendation that he leave the hospital for two hours to visit his apartment with me tomorrow. I also explain my plan to arrange for his nephew to meet us at one o'clock and return two hours later. After he asks a couple of questions about James's potential risk of suicide or elopement, I assure him there is nothing to worry about and he gives his okay.

To my dismay, when I call Gary, he informs me that he can't come to the hospital tomorrow but gives me the directions and says James has a key. When I arrive at the ward at one o'clock a member of the staff tells me that James was ejected from a group meeting this morning because of an angry outburst. For that reason, his pass was denied, and he was confined to a quiet room where he is separated from external stimulation.

I go up to the ward and briefly talk with James, who repeats his complaints about being a victim of over-controlling staff members. It's unfortunate, but perhaps predictable, that he undermined this opportunity to receive a two-hour pass to visit his apartment today. Time will tell when he's ready to go.

CHAPTER 57

"I don't like Jack. I wanna go to the apartment
but I don't want him to be there."

September 19–23, 1977

James arrives at our Monday session wearing hospital pajamas and robe once again. After signing he immediately begins complaining about people who talk about crazy things and smoke on the ward. Rather than pursue this depressing subject, I ask him if he has heard anything from Jack. James says he's sick of listening to Jack talk about things he doesn't wanna hear. When I ask him to be more specific, he bellows out, "I just don't like him!"

"I'm surprised you don't like him because Jack talks about things your father might. He wants to be like your father."

James scowls. "If he wants to be like my father no wonder he hates me."

"Jack doesn't hate you. In fact, he was glad the time you went to the apartment. That's why I'm surprised you didn't want to go when I arranged to get a pass for you."

"I wanna go to the apartment but I don't wanna have to go back to the ward. And I don't want Jack to be there."

When I ask if he ever had positive thoughts about Jack, he adamantly says no. He resumes his complaints about his ward. Before our session ends, James insists on being discharged so he can move into the apartment. I strongly advise him that he must first go there on a weekend pass.

When we meet again on Friday, he is still wearing hospital pajamas and robe, an indication that he remains on one-to-one

253

watch. His first request is to be discharged so he can escape from the chaos on the ward. I ask if he can present me with a good discharge plan, but his thoughts are muddled, so I make it clear that he needs more time to prepare. He scowls but doesn't argue with me.

When I ask if he will let me talk to Jack, he agrees. I count slowly to thirteen and Jack emerges. He looks at me calmly and then shifts his gaze from side to side. I ask if he knew James has been demanding to leave the hospital and move into the apartment but refused to go there on a pass.

Jack nods and tells me he heard that James had an apartment but doesn't understand why he was afraid to go there. When I suggest that James is afraid because he might discover the apartment is only a fantasy, Jack says I should know James has felt lost ever since Jay left and is afraid to be alone. I ask Jack if he could become a source of support, but he objects and asks me to find someone else. I explain that James's nephew is supportive, but he's not always around.

Jack frowns at me. "If he's not around that's not my problem. Besides, I'm not like his nephew."

"I agree that you're not like his nephew, but James likes his nephew, and if you could be more pleasant like his nephew, James might get to like you too."

"I don't care if he likes me. I never liked him when he was an annoying little kid. Now that he's gotten old and irritating, I really don't like him!" Jack asserts.

"Do you dislike him because he's angry?"

"Sure, but why should he be so angry?"

"He's angry because he's not able to live outside of the hospital where he can grow up and live his life. But he needs your help to do that."

"What do you mean, my help?"

"You can help if you treat James respectfully and treat him as if you were the father he always wanted."

CHAPTER 58

James opens his mind to Jay's
good memories and feelings.

September 26–October 3, 1977

During my meeting with James today, I begin by asking what he can remember about our last session. He says he remembers that we talked about Jack but can't recall details. I point out that I asked Jack to help him improve his relationship with his father, but he says he doesn't want to feel better about his father and is more interested in finding something to criticize Jack for. That seems to be why he blames Jack for Jay's departure.

"I wish that Jay would come back," he says.

When I ask James to explain, he says he misses Jay's intellectual ability and his good memories. I point out that I can help him to gain access to Jay's memories and ask James if he's willing to be hypnotized. He agrees, so I ask him to relax and close his eyes. He enters the trance without difficulty. I count to ten, the number designated for Jay, and make suggestions to enhance his self-image. Then I suggest that Jay's good memories can be transferred to James, after which I give James permission to come out of his trance and return to the current time and place. When James opens his eyes, I explain that he should feel positive and have access to Jay's good memories and intellectual capacities. James nods his head and smiles.

I review this videotape the next day and see that James responded well to hypnosis, as he has during previous times, and that hypnotic suggestions seemed to be effective toward helping him gain access to Jay's memories and enhance his self-image.[25]

James appears quite anxious when we meet two days later. I suggest counting to ten, which reduces his anxiety, but he says he feels like he's floating. I decide to help him feel grounded by counting toward one. Then he asks why I seem so far away.

I extend my hand and ask him what he's feeling now. He grasps my hand but says he doesn't feel real. "I feel like I'm just surviving and I wanna feel alive."

"What will it take for that to happen?" I ask.

"I need to get out of the hospital."

I believe it may be a positive move for James to be discharged, so I encourage him to take a pass this weekend so he can go to the apartment in preparation for being outside the hospital.

During our next session after the weekend, James tells me he is very upset because he can't remember anything since our last meeting and doesn't know if he ever went to the apartment.

I ask him to relax so I can facilitate a hypnotic trance and talk to Jack. At the count of fifteen Jack opens his eyes. I ask what happened and listen as he tells me how much he enjoyed his weekend at the apartment. When I ask if James was there Jack frowns. "Why should I let that angry kid come there?" he replies.

"Can you tell me why you didn't want him there?"

"Sure. I didn't want him to kill me."

"That doesn't make sense. Why do you say that?"

"Because James is capable of killing me. That's why I wouldn't let him come."

Jack says that if James killed Shea, it's too risky to be around James. So he refused to let him come into the body. Consequently, Jack was the only personality who spent the weekend in the apartment visiting with his nephew.

I ask to talk to James again and he emerges quickly. When I give him Jack's report, James replies angrily that he would like to kill Jack.

I explain that Jack could sense his rage and interpreted that as his wish to commit murder. "It's okay for you to feel angry but it's not okay to want to kill him. Can't you try to get along with him?"

"How can you expect me to get along with him after he spent the entire weekend in the apartment and cut me out?" he exclaims.

James insists that he can't tolerate being dominated by Jack as well as the hospital. After listening to James's plea that he wants to be free of the hospital, I agree to talk to his hospital doctor about having a discharge plan for him.

PART NINE

James
Leaves the Hospital

CHAPTER 59

James is discharged from the hospital,
but Jack still tries to dominate him.

October 17, 1977

James comes to the session today with his nephew Gary, who tells me he knew Jack had been in the apartment with him last weekend instead of James. When James hears Gary's report, he angrily blames me for not preventing Jack from dominating the entire weekend.

I explain that I had no control over Jack's behavior last weekend, but James is still mad and accuses Jack of being a liar. He insists that it would be impossible for them to become friends.

I am sympathetic and tell James I'll talk with Jack about this. I induce a trance and count to fifteen. When Jack emerges, I insist that he explain his weekend behavior. "Why did you prevent James from coming out when you were in the apartment?"

"I liked it there. I didn't think you'd disapprove. Besides, it was nice not having that spoiled brat around."

"You don't pay the rent and it's not primarily for your enjoyment. In the future you can only go there if you to stay in the body just long enough to help James get to the apartment safely."

Jack frowns and insists that he doesn't like James and doesn't want to help him. When I ask what prevents him from having positive feelings toward James, he angrily replies that he has no intention of ever feeling positive about him.

After completing a discussion regarding Jack's resistance, I ask to talk to James again and count from fifteen to one, at which point James returns. He quickly resumes criticizing me for not controlling Jack's domination and insists on wanting more out of life than he's got now.

"I've told you I've got to get off that ward. Are you going to keep me there by committing me?"

I'm surprised by his question and reply that I have no legal grounds to keep him in the hospital against his will.

I call Dr. Cokely an hour later and tell him that James insists on being discharged and is not a candidate for commitment. We discuss his hospital discharge treatment plan, and I recommend an outpatient structured program like the Day Treatment Center in combination with psychotherapy[26] two or three times a week. I explain that I'm very familiar with the DTC and will call Mr. Barber, the program director, about this.

When I call Mr. Barber, he tells me there are twenty patients who participate in daily activities, group meetings and occasional outings, and James would fit in nicely. Then I call Dr. Cokely back and report my conversation with Mr. Barber. He agrees to discharge James today.

When James comes to therapy two days later, he tells me his nephew brought him to the apartment right after Dr. Cokely discharged him. When I see him three days after that, he says he is having frightening nightmares and admits that living outside of the hospital is harder than he expected.

CHAPTER 60

Jay and Gary left and James feels abandoned.

November 2, 1977

James is clearly agitated and seems to have difficulty speaking. I ask if he has been able to count to ten, but he says he's lost the calm feeling associated with ten, and he begins to cry. After he wipes his eyes, I can see he is still very anxious. I ask him to close his eyes and repeat saying ten several times until he feels calm. Then I ask him to tell me what happened. He says Jay left and Gary left, and he doesn't know where they went. Realizing this is a replication of his abandonment trauma as a boy, I ask him how he's coping. He tearfully tells me he's been up the entire night taking showers but finally felt better after putting on the clothes Jay purchased. I ask how he got here from his apartment, and he says he either ran or walked, but he would hide whenever other people were around. When he finally got to the VA hospital grounds, he tried to go into building five where his friend Al lives but the door was locked.

"I'm concerned about your circumstances James. I didn't expect that your nephew would leave you alone."

"I've been alone my whole life. I'd be fine if I had a friend," he says.

I'm very concerned and ask him to come back into the hospital until Gary comes back.

James frowns and vigorously shakes his head. "No. I don't wanna go back up there!" he exclaims.

"Will you go up there so you can talk to your friends on the staff?" I ask.

"No. All those bad memories will come back if I go there!" he exclaims.

I ask him for more details about what happened over the weekend, and he repeats that Jay and Gary left him alone. I ask if he remembers being left alone many years ago.

"Don't ask me about that 'cause I don't wanna think about it!" he exclaims. Then, to my surprise, he asks me if I'm going to hit him.

I reassure him I would never do that.

He asks me again to let him return to the apartment, so I ask him to give me a reasonable plan to deal with his situation. But my request only stimulates more anxiety. As he struggles to talk about this, I say ten several times, and ask him to think about good memories and keep ten in his mind.

"Are you feeling any better?" I ask.

"Yes. But Jay told me never go back to the hospital. That's why I'm wearing his clothes, because it helps me to feel calm so I won't ever have to go back there."

"Did he actually tell you that?"

"He said if I went back to the hospital I would get hurt by the other."

"What do you mean by the other?"

"Shea. He tried to take over, but I stayed here," he sobs.

I reach out and grasp his hands, which are clutched together, and count to ten several times. He begins to relax, and I withdraw my hand.

I'm not sure why James is having memories about Shea now. However, he may think he was abandoned because of Shea's behavior, so I assure him he does not have to worry about being hurt.

Our time has ended, but I ask James to stop back at four o'clock this afternoon so I can see how distressed he is. He agrees but doesn't know what to do in the meantime. I encourage him to go to the OT lab, but he shakes his head and tells me he's afraid to go any place in this hospital for fear of being placed back on the ward.

I promise not to do that and ask if there are things he can do in the apartment. He lists several: listening to the radio, wood carving, knitting, cleaning the house. He says he doesn't want to hang around the outpatient waiting room, and would rather go home, cook himself a pork chop and green beans, and come back later. We end our session and I'm relieved that he seems much calmer.

He returns at four p.m. and is surprised when his favorite staff nurse greets him in my office. She explains that I had informed the head nurse who told her about his difficulties so she asked if she could come over. After ten minutes of conversation, James describes his plans for the evening and feels reassured that we won't force him back into the hospital. After his nurse leaves, I ask if he needs a ride home, but he says his apartment is close enough for him to walk.

When we meet again the next morning, James seems better and tells me he cooked a pork chop last evening but couldn't eat it all. I ask him if Gary had returned, and he says he looked at the calendar and discovered that Gary had a meeting in Emporia, Kansas for two days, but would be back tomorrow.

James says he can't sleep and feels very anxious all the time. Counting to ten works fine here, but it doesn't work so well when he's at any other place. But there are times when he wants it to work. "On my way back I saw kids playing and heard people hollering. That made me mad so I counted then because I didn't wanna hurt anyone."

I ask what he will do this evening, and he says he'll watch channel eleven and go to bed when he gets tired.

I suggest he return for his usual scheduled time on Friday. During our session I insist that he begin attending the Day Treatment Center. Before the session ends, he asks me to count to ten and he calmly leaves the studio.

CHAPTER 61

The Day Treatment Center

December 7, 1977

For the past two weeks James has been attending the Day Treatment Center program located in a small building on the northwest corner of the VA hospital campus. The program director, Mr. Barber, has informed me during a recent phone call that James is doing well but is anxious, which I'd expect for a patient coming into a new treatment program. I learn that the patients participate in different activities, eat meals together, and are a cohesive group.

I have been continuing to meet James in therapy, and he arrives today dressed nicely but looking anxious. He continuously grasps his hands together and says he woke up at three a.m. feeling like he is losing control of his mind. When I ask for specifics, he remains silent for a time, but then tells me he doesn't remember what happened after our last therapy session. I point out that another part of him must have unexpectedly taken over.

"What do you mean a part of me took over?" he asks with a frown.

"There is a part of you who takes over to protect you sometimes."

"What do you mean?"

I try to explain but he insists that no one had done that and pulls a handkerchief out of his pocket to blow his nose.

"Someone took care of you and got you home safely. Nothing happened that made you feel ashamed," I state.

266

"I'm hanging on or otherwise I wouldn't be able to talk to you," he moans as he continuously folds his two hands together. "I want to scream but I'm holding on now, so I don't have to scream."

I stretch my hand out and ask him to hold on, but he says he doesn't want to depend on me because I'm not always around. He says he needs someone who will always be around.

I ask if he can remember what happened after he left my office. He says no and asks me to count to ten. When I reach ten, he is able to talk more calmly and says that he can't remember anything after he left my office Friday. "How come I can't remember?" he cries.

"I know it's upsetting to not remember, but I can assure you everything worked out okay. I believe another part of you got a taxi and told the driver where to go."

"No. I told the cab driver where to go," he insists.

"You can remember that? What else do you remember?"

"I had to get my billfold out to get the address."

"Do you remember getting into the cab?"

He frowns and remains so anxious he can't continue to speak, so I count to ten, at which point he regains a normal, relaxed position. I ask again why he had gotten so upset and he frowns and tells me it's frightening to not always know what's happening. His body starts to tighten up again, but then he says ten and reminds himself that he is still here.

I point out that he was fortunate to have someone help him after he left the last therapy session. "Do you think Jack helped you?" I ask.

"Not that old man. He's too old and he's not smart enough. I'm smarter than he is," James insists.

After I ask him if Jack is getting old like his father, he agrees that Jack is getting old just like his father did. I ask if I am like his father in any way, and he says I'm not like his father because

I'm strong enough to help him when he is very upset. He also says he feels safer when he counts to ten.

Since the number ten had been associated with Jay, I ask if he feels like Jay now, and he says he does.

"I'm glad you do but you don't have to be exactly like Jay," I explain.

"Why not?" he asks.

"You're different from Jay because you can feel emotions and Jay can't."

"Is that because I'm alive?"

"Yes. You're very much alive."

He changes the subject and asks why the Day Treatment Center staff didn't ask him to go to Kansas City with the other patients yesterday. I explain that they want to give him more time before taking him on a long trip.

We reach the end of our time and James announces, with a smile, that he is going Christmas shopping with his nephew today.

CHAPTER 62

James remembers being reborn
and growing up in Building Four.

December 12, 1977

After signing, James tells me he feels upset because he can't remember anything after one o'clock Saturday until Sunday afternoon.

"Do you think you were gone during that time?" I ask.

"What do you mean? I was there in the apartment. I couldn't go any place."

"If you weren't gone your memory was. Let's put it that way."

James says he can't explain it, although he feels like something is wrong with him.

He closes his eyes and mouths the word ten to control his anxiety. He isn't able to count, so I take over the counting for him. After his mind clears, I ask about his memories. He tells me

he remembers the time he died when he was living in Building Four and I brought him back to life. He thinks he was born there and learned how to walk, talk, eat, and breathe. He says I helped him grow up and go to school there.

"I know I really didn't go to school there, but I can't remember going to school anywhere else."

269

"What you are remembering is partially true James. You had a rebirth experience in Building Four, so it feels to you that you were born there. That's when you first felt like you were a person."

James becomes anxious and motions for me to count to ten. When he calms down, I bring up a subject that stirs his anxiety again. "I met with the Day Treatment Center staff, and they hope you can attend their Christmas party."

He becomes very anxious, takes gasping breaths, and tells me he can't go to any parties. So I repeat saying ten several times until he calms down, but he continues to insist that he can't go.

"Why can't you?" I ask.

"There are too many people. And it's too dark and I haven't done that before. I wanna do something I've done before so I know how to do it. Besides it'll be dark."

When I ask why the dark upsets him, he takes a deep breath. "People did things to me in the dark when I didn't wanna be there." He pauses and then continues, "Didn't you bring me out of the dark?"

"Yes, I did James, but you don't have to worry about going back into the dark, and the Christmas party won't last until dark." He shakes his head vigorously and tells me he keeps a light on in his apartment and will never go outside after dark.

I remind him that counting to ten will enable him to feel like he has Jay, who wasn't afraid of the darkness. "But I can lose that light and not get it back," he exclaims with tears in his eyes.

When I ask if Jack can help him feel like he's in the light he shrugs his shoulders. I ask if Shea brings him light and he immediately shakes his head in disgust.

I begin to count to ten and James's eyes close. He catches his breath as he lifts both hands upward. I remind him he is still at ten, but he tells me he feels scared because he doesn't know how to exist outside of Building Four, where he feels like he was born and where he could depend on his friends. I point out that he can make new friends, but he shakes his head. "They always want something from me. I think I'd rather be dead." After a pause he says, "But I don't wanna be dead."

"I don't want you dead either. Be glad you're alive, even though it can sometimes be scary."

"But I'm too old to just be finding out about life now. I'm thirty-three you know. That's old."

It is unclear why James feels that he's thirty-three years old when in fact he is forty-one. Why is there an eight-year difference? Is it related to Jay taking over the body when James was abused by his father seven years after his actual birth? Or could it be related to his feeling of being reborn a year and a half ago in July of 1976 in Building Four? The most likely answer is that it's related to Jay taking over the body when James was seven-plus years of age, and he's merely expressing Jay's perception of his age.

If that's the case, then James has gained access to Jay's memories. He tells me about fragments of memories I haven't heard from him before. His sense of identity seems to be in the process of becoming reshaped as time progresses. James shakes his head, and says he feels like he's in the middle of a dream. I ask him to focus on the word ten before our time has ended and remind him that we will meet again in two days.

CHAPTER 63

Jack says there is a war going on.

December 14–16, 1977

During our last session, not described here, James said he was afraid I would be leaving because one of the video technicians was about to move away. Today he expresses his relief that I am still here, but says he feels strange because his sense of the past is mixed up with the present. I suspect this is a carryover from last time, when James seemed to have access to Jay's memories. I also believe that Jack's presence may be related in some way. Thus, I feel it's important to talk with Jack and, with James's approval, I count to fifteen. When Jack appears, I ask how he is and he responds with a gravelly sounding voice, "I feel fine sir." Then he says he is feeling older today, which is consistent with my prior observation that he has been aging rather quickly.

I ask Jack if he has taught James anything and he frowns. "Robert told me not to teach anybody anything."

I am surprised and ask why Robert was talking to him.

Jack says there's a battle going on and that he is too old to be mixed up in a war. I'm uncertain what that means but insist we can all work together and decide on what James needs to learn. Jack sits with a depressed look on his face, and after a long pause he says he's afraid I'll get mad at him for saying something.

"What do you want to say to me?" I ask.

"One of you is going to have to leave me alone."

"One of us? Who do you mean?"

"Either you or Robert."

I ask if he can explain what he means. He shakes his head and says, "I'm too old to be cussed out and screamed at."

Our time runs out and Jack tells me he's sorry for being such poor company, and that he's too old to fight this war any longer.

After bidding him "so long" until next week, I count from thirteen to ten and summon James. After he appears, James tells me a lot is going through his mind, but he doesn't want to think about it. To help reduce his anxiety I count to ten again; he responds positively so that we can finish our session.

CHAPTER 64

James's fight with Jack makes him crazy,
and he hangs onto Jay, who becomes LATOT.

December 19, 1977

James signs in and tells he is trying to hang on the best he can. When I ask what that means, he turns his head to the side and keeps his hands tightly clasped together.

He says he feels like he's going crazy. When I ask what's going on in his mind, he finds it difficult to talk. Finally, he tells me that he's very upset that his nephew Gary has been absent for days at a time, and sometimes just disappears.

"The other day I asked him to take me to the Day Treatment Center at noon. He said, 'Okay, just wake me up in the morning and I'll do that.' Then he disappeared and I didn't know where in the hell he went."

James also reports memory lapses. "I know I went to bed last night but there are times I can't remember I ever went to bed. Sometimes my body is really cold and I feel like I just came in from being outside. But I don't remember going out there."

Jack has told me he often leaves the apartment to go outside at night or early morning, and I explain that to James. Suddenly he stands up and blurts out, "Jack is real? I thought you were kidding when you brought his name up before. Can you to teach me what's going on before you go away?"

"Sure, and I can promise you I'm not going anywhere. I've told you that before, but you don't seem to believe me."

His fear of abandonment takes over and he cries out that he can barely hang on, which is also reflected by his body language—his left hand grasping tightly to his right hand. I point out that his hands are expressing his desire to hang onto someone he trusts. He nods his head and says I'm the only one he can hang onto, but he's worried that he'll soon lose me.

I wonder if his fear of abandonment explains why Robert and Jack continue to hang on. When I ask if these two provide support for him when Gary disappears, he shakes his head. He says they aren't real, which is a change from his previous descriptions when he said Jack likes to smoke and run around. I decide to explore this further. "If you know about Jack, why aren't you interested in knowing why he's been here?"

"Because he's just a bad memory and I don't wanna think about him."

"Would you like to know there's another side to Jack?"

"Why should I care?"

"Because he's like the father you wish you had."

Suddenly James stands up and angrily accuses me of bringing up a bad memory about his father that he wants to forget. He begins to sob and says he's too confused to talk.

When I ask him to sit down, he turns around until he finds his chair. I count to ten several times and then his emotions calm down, but his body remains tense, and he continues to hold his hands together tightly. He breathes in gasps and tells me he hasn't accomplished anything, and his life has no meaning.

I suggest that if he wants to accomplish something important, he should become reconciled with Jack like he did with Jay.

"I never liked Jay," he insists.

"I know. In fact, you used to hate him," I reply.

"I may have argued with him, but I never hated him," he disagrees.

"You tried to kill him," I argue.

"I could never do that," he says, and shakes his head.

"Do you remember that Jay came into my office two years ago and fell to the floor. I thought he had died. Then another personality sat up and said he had to kill him. That other personality was you."

James blows his nose as he tries to assimilate what I said. "It must've been Shea because I wouldn't kill Jay," he asserts.

"I agree you wouldn't kill Jay now."

"What do you want me to do?"

"I hope you can become a friend of Jack, and that you will think about giving him some love like you wanted to love your father?"

He shakes his head vigorously. "That's wrong. I don't wanna love him!"

"Why is it wrong to love Jack? You loved me and it wasn't wrong."

He wipes his eyes and tells me he was too small to know any better then.

When I ask if it's wrong to love a man he nods and exclaims, "That's because it's sex!"

"Where did you get the idea that loving a man is related to having sex? Don't you think you can love a man without mixing it up with sex?" I ask.

He insists that he could never love Shea or any man that acted like him. When I assure him he does not have to love Shea, I see his posture change. He lowers his hands but keeps them clasped together.

James's strong antagonism toward Shea may never change, because he was raped by two men, and Shea was a passive participant in the rape because he enjoyed the sex.

After a long pause I ask what he's thinking. He looks at me intently for the first time and whispers loudly that he knows who Jay really is. When I ask him to explain he whispers, "Jay is Latot. But don't tell anybody."

I see him lift both hands and his left hand is clasped tightly to his right. "Why are you holding onto your right hand?" I ask. No response.

"I believe that when your left hand grasps your right hand you are holding onto Jay." I explain to him that he needs to hang onto Jay, whom he now calls Latot, so he can feel calmer when he counts to ten.

James questions my explanation and asks how it's possible he can be holding on to Jay. I answer by explaining that he and Jay share the same body, which doesn't upset him.

"I'm glad he's there," James says.

"Since you can feel positive that Jay is able to use your body to help you, can't you also feel positive if Jack uses your body?" I ask.

He frowns. "I don't want him in my body. I'd rather kill him."

I point out that if he is going to kill Jack, he will have to release his hands. But James is not able to unlock them, indicating that his left hand (Jay) has control of the potentially murderous actions of his right hand (James), revealing body language that exposes an intra-personal dynamic. It also discloses that James was a helpless little boy who always hung onto his mother.

When James hears me repeat Jack's words, he becomes enraged and stands up. He continues to pace back and forth while I try to calm him down by pointing out that Jack was not calling him helpless, but only recalling a childhood memory. But my explanation doesn't help. He shakes his head, plugs his ears, and exclaims, "I'm not listening to you. I can't hear you. I don't know what you're saying!"

When I ask why he is so angry, he says I need to stop saying that name because it makes him crazy, and he can't think. I interpret that to mean James is trying to block out memories of conflicts with his father, personified by Jack.

James also has another problem—he isn't sure he's a real human being because he can't do things that real human beings can do. But I reassure him that he has all the thoughts and feelings that human beings have.

"What you say doesn't apply to me because I need another human being to be able to do those things," James insists.

"You have me, James."

"But I am always scared every time I'm with you!" he exclaims.

"Perhaps you don't see me as another human being," I reply.

He takes out his handkerchief and blows his nose but doesn't answer. I make an interpretation that he has a problem relating to me like he did with his father.

He remains quiet but he squirms in the chair and shakes his head. "I don't wanna talk about this."

"Why not?"

"Because you'll get mad and then you'll be gone."

I agree not to talk about it and encourage him to keep the number ten in his mind.

Before our session ends, James tells me he almost did not come today, but he's glad he did because he learned some things. Then he tells me his eyes feel like they're pointing in opposite directions, which I believe is a metaphor for his internal mental struggle that he can't see resolving.

PART TEN

Jay Returns

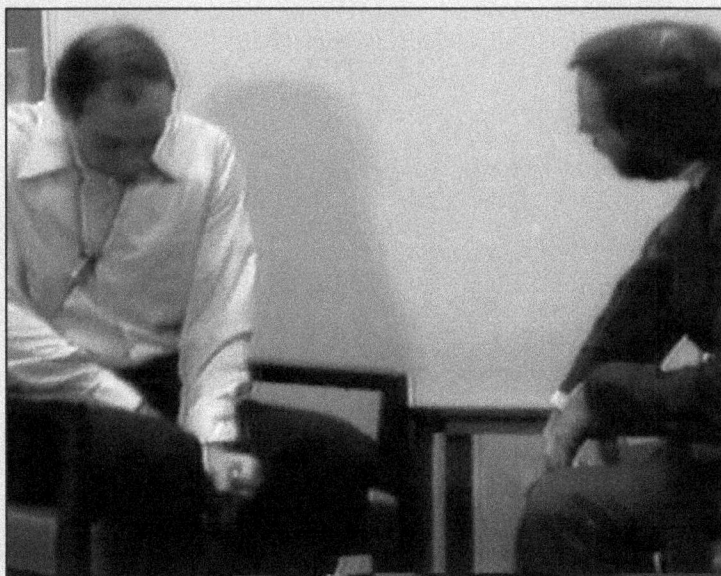

CHAPTER 65

James can't handle this situation.

December 28, 1977

Jay signs in today, which surprises me considerably. I welcome him and ask if he remembers when he last saw me, but he can't. I suggest it was probably three or four months ago, and then ask why he returned. He says James called him to come back because he's so upset about things that happened during Christmas.

I ask to talk to James about this and Jay agrees. I count from ten to one fairly rapidly. When I reach one James does not emerge, so I repeat the count more slowly. This time I emphasize deeper relaxation with each number until I reach one. But again James does not emerge, so I slowly and emphatically count three... two... one. This time James suddenly stands up, frightened, and walks several steps away from me until he finally returns and sits down. Despite my attempt to help him, he repeatedly insists, between sobs, that he wants me to let him go. "I don't wanna be here. I wish I was dead. Let me go," he sobs.

I had learned that his nephew left him unexpectedly at Christmas, but he refuses to talk about it. Although that seems to be the primary reason he's distressed, I soon learn that the Christmas season has triggered an unpleasant boyhood memory. He reluctantly reveals that his newborn baby brother died at Christmas time, and he believes that it was his fault. When I ask why he blames himself, he shakes his head and refuses to answer. But then he talks about a different event related to his brother's death that was even more disturbing.

"I didn't mean to hit him," he sobs.

"Where did you hit him?" I ask.

James points to his groin area. "I can't be here. Let me go. Please," he pleads.

I have difficulty understanding James's attempt at explaining what happened and conclude that he believed his baby brother's death occurred because he struck his father's penis.

"You are a person, and I don't want you to go."

I place my hand on his shoulder for reassurance.

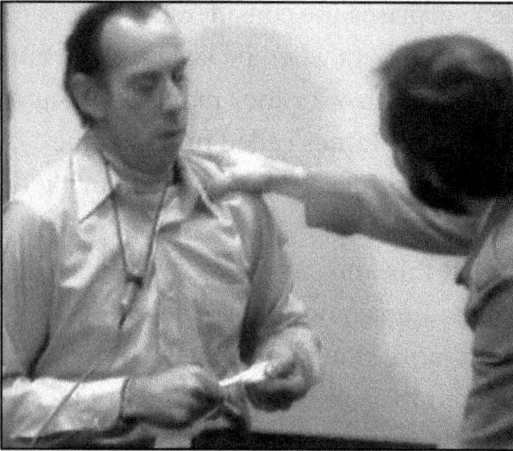

He wipes his eyes with a tissue and calls out again, "Let me go!"

"How would letting you go make it better?" I ask.

"I need to go back into the dark where I belong."

"I want you to stay here in the light because you are a person who couldn't have caused his baby brother's death."

But he insists that he isn't a person and asks me again to let him go back into the world of utter darkness.

In spite of my reassurance, he repeatedly whispers that nobody wants him here and that I should let him go. I assert that I won't let him go back into the darkness. When I ask how he feels he doesn't answer and keeps his eyes closed, body stiff, and hands together.

Suddenly I hear him scream "Jay!"

James's scream brings Jay into the body, and in spite of my surprise, I greet him and explain I had just talked with James.

"You talked to him?" Jay asks with raised eyebrows.

"Yes, I did. He had trouble speaking and shed a lot of tears."

"I know. I'm wiping up after him," he says, swabbing his face with a handkerchief he just pulled from his pocket.

"James just screamed your name so loud you were forced to come back."

"I'm surprised, but I know he's having a difficult time."

When I ask if he knows the cause of James's difficulty, Jay says it had something to do with his nephew. I explain that James called me on the phone and said he had been left alone in the apartment. I felt very concerned and asked him to come back into the hospital, but he refused.

"May I say something?" Jay asks.

"Sure."

"He'll run away if you make him come into the hospital."

"I hear you. Then I want him to go to the Day Treatment Center. But how is he going to get there?"

"I can take the body there. I can also bring the body here."

"What are the consequences if you leave the body?"

"If I can't stay in the body there won't be anyone to replace me because he's not capable of managing it now."

"Has that ever happened before?" I ask.

"Yes, it has. But I don't want it to happen again," he insists.

Jay's answer prompts my recollection of a time, many months ago, when he became catatonic, and his body became immobile just before he exited.

When I ask if he can prevent that from happening, he says if James is uncooperative, he can't be forced to do anything. Jay's answer prompts me to wonder why Jay can carry the body to specific locations but can't physically force James to do anything. There must be internal dialogue whereby James hears Jay's voice asking him to do things, and vice versa.

I ask Jay to ask James to stop blaming himself for causing a baby to die, and he says that he will tell that to James.

"Can you bring James back into the body now?" I ask.

"Yes, but I don't know if he'll be the way people have seen him."

"Then how will he be?" I ask.

"He'll have my philosophy."

"What's that?"

"It's not emotional."

"Does that mean he'll be without emotions if you bring him back?" I ask.

"All I can do is bring him back into the body and we can see."

"Can you bring him back right now?"

"That wouldn't be wise. I don't think he's even here now," Jay says.

I look at the clock and realize it's time to bring our interaction to a close. Before we stop, I remind him to come back on Friday at nine o'clock.

CHAPTER 66

Jay is like mother and Jack is like father.

December 30, 1977

Jay signs in but says he can't allow Jack to come today. Although I typically meet with Jack on Friday, I agree to spend this session with Jay. During our conversation we talk about his and Jack's role with the other personalities. Although it's clear that Jay's primary function has been protective, I suggest Jack's role may be similar, but to a lesser degree. I hypothesize that Jay is like mother and Jack is like father.

Jay bristles at my hypothesis. "I can't accept that's my role!"

"You should know that a mother's purpose has always been to protect her child from the time he's born."

Jay frowns. "What happens after he's born?"

"The mother keeps the baby alive until he can take care of himself and become an independent person. Didn't you do that for James?"

Jay shakes his head at first, but scowls as if he realizes that James is facing difficulties now that require his help.

"Do you know what difficulties he's facing?" I ask.

"I know he's got money problems." Jay goes on to say he's aware his nephew Gary is in legal trouble because of his debts and asked James to help him out.

I insist that Gary needs to raise his own money rather than ask James to rescue him. Then I ask about James's finances. "Do you know more specifics about his money problems?"

"I know there are overdue bills that need to be paid, but I don't know if James has enough money to pay them."

"What do you recommend?" I ask.

"I'll just do what I've done before."

"What's that?"

"I think the word you use is to forge."

I raise my eyebrows at the mention of that word. "Whose name do you want to forge?"

Jay shrugs his shoulders.

"If you mean forging James's name, remember that your legal name is James, so it's not forgery if you sign that name."

Jay nods.

I ask if he will allow me to talk to James, but Jay says no. "I know he needs to come back to the body but not now."

I continue to ask Jay for more information about James and Gary. He tells me Gary may get arrested, but he shouldn't tell his parents because Gary asked him to promise, and he needs to keep his promise.

"Did you know if James kept that promise?"

"Yeah. I thought he did," Jay says.

"So you knew about this then?" I ask.

"I didn't know 'cause I've lost contact with James because he's been very emotional and I don't understand his emotions," Jay says.

I'm curious about Jay's knowledge regarding where he goes when he's not in the body, and he says he is in space where there isn't any time.

"Do you go to a place where some people might call it heaven?"

"No. It's a man-made place where there isn't any emotion."

"Is it a pleasant place?"

"You use words like pleasant but it's just a place where there's no emotion and nothing solid there."

"Okay. I do need to talk to Jack today, so is it possible for you to relax and let me count so Jack can come?"

Jay quickly tells me that he doesn't think he can let this happen, but I ask him to give it a chance. He agrees, so I begin to count slowly from ten to fifteen after he closes his eyes and begins to relax. When I reach fifteen, he opens his eyes and says, "Hello sir," which has been Jack's typical greeting. I ask how he's feeling, and he tells me in a raspy sounding voice like that of an aging man that he feels old, and is worried about the pain across his left lower chest. I listen a little longer about his physical complaint and conclude that it doesn't represent a cardiac problem. Then I change the subject and ask what he knows about the baby's illness and death shortly after birth.

"Whadda ya wanna know?" he asks.

"Is it possible that James hurt his father's sexual organ and caused the baby to be born malformed?" I ask.

Jack asks why James is still thinking about that, and I explain that when James was a young boy he didn't know what to do. "Now he wants you to help him 'cause you can do that better than his mother," I state clearly.

Jack sits quietly, looking disheartened, and says he spent his entire life working so that his family would always have a roof over their heads and never starve. But now he's too old to help anyone.

"I commend you for doing a good job taking care of your family."

"What more can I do?" he asks.

"You can tell James you're here and he doesn't have to run to mother."

He lifts his head and frowns as if he doesn't understand, so I tell him he can be a strong father who would never want to hurt James.

Since our time is running short, I ask Jack to plan on meeting again next week. Then I begin the countdown from fifteen to ten to bring Jay into the body. Jay opens his eyes and clasps both hands together. He asks how Jack responded, and I explain that I asked him to be strong for James.

Jay thanks me for helping James and apologizes for not being able to provide more help. Before we stop, I ask if he can help solve his nephew's financial problems. That prompts Jay to reach into his back pocket and pull out several bank books with accounts his nephew had opened. He says some of these accounts have a lot of money and one of them contains $15,000. But in one account $5000 was deposited seven months ago and only $1000 remains now.

This concerns me, and I tell Jay that something needs to be done to keep James's money from disappearing. He says Gary can't be trusted any longer, and it would be better if their relationship was discontinued. I don't take a position about his relationship with Gary but suggest giving up the apartment and finding a foster home for James. Since I had previously checked into this, I am able to say that it would cost James $200-$225 a month for food and lodging, and he wouldn't be alone. Jay asks for more details, and I recommend interviewing potential foster home parents for suitability.

Then Jay tells me about the things that must be done now like watering the flowers and paying the bills.

Since our time has ended, I remind him there will be no appointment on Monday because of a holiday. Jay agrees to take James to the Day Treatment Center on Tuesday but worries that he may be too confused to participate in the activities.

After Jay leaves, I think about his level of cooperation with James, and I wonder if we've reached a potential therapeutic endpoint where different personalities can cooperate successfully with no risk for destructive behavior, similar to what psychiatrist Richard Kluft has written about.

CHAPTER 67

When James gets upset, his body chemicals change, and Jay can't remain in the body.

January 4–11, 1978

Jay signs in and immediately tells me how upset he is with Gary for an abundance of reasons. He says Gary can't repay the $2000 he owes James because he must pay a lawyer for defending him from a crime; he needs money for his girlfriend's Christmas present; he has to pay for college tuition even though he may not enroll. Then he left James alone in the apartment with a note saying he had to go someplace but never returned. "He is irresponsible and can't be trusted. He needs to get out and stay out!" Jay exclaims.

I'm appalled to hear this, but I'm powerless to change Gary's behavior. My main concern right now is James's need for a stable environment which, according to Jay, can't be the hospital. When I ask Jay if he can help, he says he'll pay the bills with James's retirement check.

"This is James's very first adult Christmas and it's a shame he's had such a bad experience," Jay says.

"I agree. Did you know that James called me on Christmas Eve and Christmas Day, and I went to the apartment to check on him?" I ask.

"Yeah, I know you came on Christmas Day because when the doorbell rang, I came into the body and saw you."

"How long did you stay?" I ask.

"Just long enough to make sure he could talk to you." He goes on to say that he tries not to listen when James talks to me because he can't understand his emotions.

I ask to talk with James about this, but Jay says he's not available. Nonetheless, I manage to convince Jay to let me use

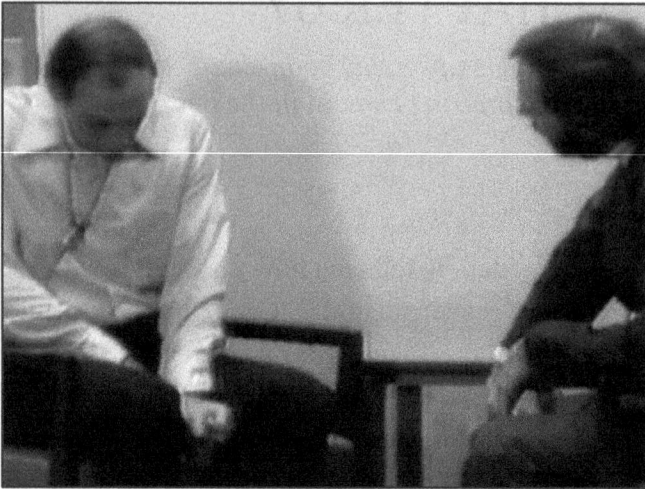

hypnosis. James finally emerges but he is clearly agitated. He lowers his head, swings his arms, and sits on both hands. After a brief time, he clenches his fists and rests them on the arms of his chair. Then he starts hitting both fists together.

When I ask what is troubling him, he shakes his head and says he doesn't want to talk. But then he apologizes for calling me on Christmas after I remind him about my visit to his apartment on that day. When I ask about his problems with Gary, he gets very upset and proclaims that he hopes his nephew would die. I explain that I can find better living conditions for him, but he shakes his head sadly and begins to sob. I ask if he would let me count to ten so he could feel better, but he insists that he would rather return to darkness.

James sits silently with his head down and his hands clasped together between his legs. He refuses to let me help him and brings his handkerchief to wipe the tears from his eyes while sobbing that he doesn't want to stay here any longer.

I decide to bring Jay back by counting to ten slowly. When Jay emerges, he immediately says he's aware James doesn't want to be here, but insists it's important for him to come into the body. I ask Jay if he can take care of the body when James isn't in it.

He replies, "Yes, but I have to let him come back in as often as I can."

"Can you to bring him to the Day Treatment Center on a regular basis?" I ask.

"That means he'll have to come into the body when he gets there. But if he gets too upset, I'll have to come back."

Jay says that he has difficulty remaining in the body when James gets very upset. I ask him to explain, and he says that when James's body chemicals become "more awake" it's harder for him to stay in the body. (I assume that these are the two primary neurotransmitters—adrenaline and cortisol—that are activated during the fight-flight response to danger.)

"What happens to the body after you leave it?" I ask.

"It just stays the same. But when people want to talk to me because they think I'm James, I can insist that he comes back into the body if I think it's important for him to answer."

I ask Jay to show me how he does this, but he refuses.

Just before our session ends, Jay tells me that the Day Treatment Center is planning a trip to the bowling alley next Friday afternoon and he'll have to take James's place. But since James usually bowls a low score of eighty-eight, Jay says he will deliberately keep his score low to avoid making people suspicious that he is not James.

One week later Jay signs and immediately lights up a cigarette, which he claims will prevent James from coming into the body. When I ask Jay's permission to talk to James he refuses because he needs to stay in control for reasons of safety.

I explain that he doesn't have to worry. "When you come for therapy, my job is to help both of you, and I do it better when I am in control. I can promise you that I won't let anybody get hurt."

I shift the conversation to James's need for stability and remind Jay that I would like to find a stable foster home for James, though he is not in favor of my plan. Nonetheless I explain that I plan to meet next week with an interested couple to see if they would be suitable foster parents. But Jay says he doesn't trust most people, and reminds me that I shouldn't forget about the fiasco that happened at Christmas time.

CHAPTER 68

Jay considers himself to be James's temporary guardian. Jack wonders if he is James's father.

January 6, 1978

On Friday, when Jay comes to therapy, I comment on his early growth of a beard. He replies that no one can grow a beard like mine, and I thank him for his compliment. He can't give me a rational reason for growing it so I can only speculate that it reflects a positive relationship he feels with me. Then he begins to talk about his relationship to the body—that he is merely taking care of it until James returns.

I compliment him on his realization of the importance of planning for James's future. I also discuss some of the practicalities of helping James, such as money management. Then I discuss the prospect of finding James a foster home. Jay says it is not financially wise to move out of their apartment now because they have a six-month lease that hasn't been completed. I ask about the possibility of getting a different roommate for James, but Jay frowns and says he doesn't like that idea. We discuss James's attendance at the Day Treatment Center and Jay says it is helping James. He says there are times when James is so scared he must take over, which he likes to do.

I ask him to tell me how he wants to use today's session. Jay's answer is very nonspecific. He says he brought the body here today for me to help James any way I want to. So I suggest that I work with James first and then Jack.

I count from ten to one, and when James appears he looks down at the floor despite my greeting. When I ask what he's been doing, he says he doesn't care about doing anything. I attempt to bolster his view of life by telling him that the Day Treatment Center staff met with me yesterday afternoon and said they want to help him in every way possible, including his money management.

James looks at me and asks, "Do they like my nephew?" Before I can answer he begins to sob and describes his futile attempt to "buy" his nephew's friendship by giving him money.

I decide to interpret his feelings. "I can see that you are angry at your nephew."

He nods his head but does not reply.

"I expect you're hoping that he would come back and stay."

James nods his head again but remains silent.

"Jay told me he's been spending his nights with his girlfriend," I continue.

This time James responds angrily and complains that his nephew is gone at least five nights out of the week, and if he comes back, it's not until late afternoon.

"I'm sorry to hear that, however, you seem to be doing pretty well in spite of it," I point out.

He shakes head. "I'm not doing well, and I know I'll never have anyone with me."

To counter his pessimism, I assure him that Jay is still here to help. But he doesn't respond positively. He remains anxious and his hands move back and forth on the arms of the chair. "I just wanna be away from everybody. I wanna get back to where I was but I don't know where I was."

"You were doing very well. You were learning to enjoy the Day Treatment Center, and you were even bowling."

"I should never have told you that I'd bowl a hundred. And I didn't want you to know that I'd spend money foolishly." He begins to sob again and says he let me down. He also despairs that he can't live up to his own expectations. Then he expresses his unrealistic hope that if he had given his nephew money, he wouldn't have left.

"Do you think giving him money would have bought him off?" I ask.

"Maybe that's the only way Gary can love," he sobs. He continues to despair that he doesn't understand people and complains that no one ever talks to him.

"When you are at the Day Treatment Center, don't people talk to you there?" I ask.

"Not like we talk. I know that people don't like me around." He begins to sob more loudly, and then criticizes the way he behaved with his nephew. "I was a crazy old uncle. They should have put me in the back room and shut off all the lights. That's the way I felt." He continues to sob and wipes his eyes with a handkerchief.

I encourage him to go to the Day Treatment Center today after our session, but he shakes his head. "Jay is planning for you to go, and he'll take you there," I insist.

He looks at me and says that he likes Jay. "He's the only person I can talk to. I don't have to holler or scream." James goes on to say he also feels that way with me.

I say I'm happy to hear him say that. I also point out that he's beginning to have a positive relationship with Jack, but he angrily disagrees. "I don't want anything to do with him!"

"Maybe you don't want to have anything to do with Jack but he's beginning to have more of an interest in you."

We finish our discussion, and I tell James about my wish to talk with Jack. I ask him to relax, and I count to fifteen. Jack appears and I ask how he is doing. He makes a comment about the weather and then thanks me for letting him go to the apartment. After I ask how it's working out, his answer indicates that he has taken it upon himself to try and fill the void after Gary disappeared. He makes a few comments about watering the plants in the apartment, and then says he doesn't know what happened to his nephew.

"If he comes back and asks for money, please don't give him any," I point out.

"I don't have any money to give him," Jack declares.

"How do you get along if you don't have any money?"

"Sometimes I find a few dollars, but I never know how they got there."

I change the subject and ask if he's aware of James's struggles.

Jack frowns. "Yeah, I know about it but it's not my problem."

"Can you be willing to help him out when he needs it?"

"He doesn't need me to do anything except to just let me be who I am," Jack insists.

"You may think James is self-sufficient, but he only pretends that because he doesn't trust you."

Jack doesn't know how to respond, so I switch topics and bring up the subject we talked about during the previous session. "If you remember, James believed he had hurt his father and caused the baby's death. But I told him that it was not his fault."

"Did he believe you?" Jack asks.

"He wasn't fully convinced. So, I want you to try and convince him," I declare.

Jack shakes his head. "He doesn't listen to what I say."

"You're going to have to speak more forcefully then."

"I've already tried that, and he cusses me out."

"You should assert yourself and tell James that cursing you out will not hurt you."

"I'm too old to assert myself," he replies.

"A father must learn to take his son's anger because it's not going to hurt you," I insist.

"I'm not his father, am I?" Jack asks.

"Sometimes you've seemed to be."

He ponders my statement, so I ask what his relationship is to James.

He shakes his head and replies, "I'm his whipping boy," which sounds like a role reversal. Then he tells me he doesn't know if he's James's father or not.

I change subjects because I'm concerned about Jack's new role as James's helper. I remind him that it is important for him and James to have a good relationship. When Jack doesn't argue with me, I consider that they might become reconciled, which can simulate the reconciliation of his parents. If so, that would help James to resolve the oedipal conflict[27]—that his anger would cause his parents to split up.

CHAPTER 69

Jay wants the entire time talking to me and
asks why James is not coming into the body.

January 9, 1978

Jay seems quite serious today and asks if he can use the entire time talking to me. He says he doesn't want either James or Jack to take up the time. So I spend the next twenty minutes talking with Jay. He begins by asking an interesting question—is James's struggle an inner one or an outer one. I say it's both and use as an example that James is anxious because he's afraid that the power of his thoughts and feelings can hurt others. Jay agrees.

"James hasn't destroyed me," I point out.

"And I hope he won't," Jay replies.

"He hasn't destroyed you either," I point out to Jay.

"He can't destroy me," Jay replies.

Jay avoids talking about anything meaningful, so I ask if he's going to talk about something important. He finally gets to the point he wanted to discuss. "I want James to get into a routine so he can be comfortable enough to come out," he says. "If James had familiar people around him, he would stay in the body longer and I wouldn't have to stay in it for so long. It's hard for people when they see sudden personality changes. That's why I don't leave the body any time I want to," he says. But then he tells me why he stays in the body when he's with me. "If I leave the body when I'm with you, you might put it in the hospital where he doesn't want it to be."

"I didn't know you didn't trust me, Jay. I'm surprised that you're afraid I might do something different than what you would want," I reply.

Jay responds in a way that won't offend me. "I don't really think you'd do something that's in contrast to what I want, but my purpose is to take care of James."

I believe the issue of Jay's distrust dates to James's parents—that his mother never trusted his father, which caused repeated conflicts between them. I point out that the conflicts affecting James and Jack are similar.

Jay doesn't like my interpretation, so I ask if he and Jack are more likely to agree or disagree. Jay doesn't answer because he says it isn't important what Jack thinks because he and James are the same person.

"If that's true then why do James and Jack perceive themselves as different and disagree with each other so strongly?" I ask.

"That's because they don't realize they really are the same person. That's similar to James and I because we're in the same body."

I agree but return to the point I'm trying to make about Jack and James. "They perceive themselves as different because Jack is like James's father, and they don't get along."

"Jack never agrees with anything," Jay insists.

I ask a more important question. "Do you think Jack is trustworthy enough to take care of James?"

"My answer is no," Jay says.

"Do you think Jack would ever be able to provide leadership for James?"

"He already does that. For one thing he is providing an adult manner... uh... how do I translate that?"

Since Jay has difficulty describing Jack's role as a leader, I repeat my hope that Jack can provide more leadership for James than he does now.

"Jack is not going to do anything more than he has to, and no matter what you do, he won't change," Jay insists.

"Well, I'm working with him."

"I hope so. That's one reason why I bring the body over here."

"You wouldn't prevent that from happening, would you?"

"No."

"You have a very strong need to protect James to the point of not trusting me," I assert.

Jay says that he's protective in a philosophical way, but not in a physical way. Then he asks me a pointed question. "How can you prepare James to come back, and stay back, without it becoming emotional?"

I challenge him by saying that when James returns to the body his human qualities include his emotions. "Let me ask you a question Jay. Would you like to have emotions?"

"Emotions are ridiculous—I have no need for it. The only need I have is for James to be in this body!" he exclaims.

Jay finally, but reluctantly, tells me he wants him back in the body even if James has emotions. When I point out that he and James are one person he disagrees, which seems to contradict what he just said a few minutes ago. "We're not one because even though we're in the same body we aren't there at the same time except that when James is in the body and calls me, I need to enter while he is still there."

As we continue to talk about this nebulous subject, Jay says it's disturbing for him to have James gone and have no contact with him. He is hoping that I can reestablish James in the body and help him stay there because he has no power to force that to happen.

Since we only have ten minutes left, I ask to talk to James. Jay sighs with disappointment, but he reluctantly closes his eyes and I count to one.

When James appears he keeps his head down, but when I tell him I can only give him five minutes today he angrily tells me he wants more time than that. After explaining why our time is limited, he makes no comment and becomes resistant to all my questions. I ask if he will consider going into the hospital, but he says he doesn't care what happens. I point out that Jay's protective and controlling qualities are like his mother's behavior, but he doesn't answer. Then I comment on his beard and ask if Jay had wanted him to have a beard, but he doesn't answer that either. When I ask if he knows today's date, he answers that question by saying it doesn't make any difference what the date is. He continues to sit with his head cradled in his right hand.

I decide to ask Jay to return. He asks me why I didn't spend more time with James. I explain that James was angry because I hadn't allotted more time for him. Jay scowls and then asks if I can explain why James is the way he is. I explain that he has not resolved two triangles—mother, father, and James; and Jay, Jack, and James.

CHAPTER 70

Why is James angry and is he potentially destructive?

January 11–13, 1978

Jay is preoccupied with keeping James away today, and keeps a cigarette in his hand, which he says will prevent him from coming. He feels unusually protective and can't forget the pain James experienced on Christmas when he didn't get a present from his nephew and felt abandoned. Jay then says something surprising—he doesn't want James here because he might hurt me and then I'll retaliate and hurt him. I attempt to understand the origin of James's fear, and Jay says it's related to the trauma he experienced at age seven when a sister sexually abused him, and his father struck him when he found out. I find this information disturbing and will discover more details about it later. However, in response to Jay's concern now, I reassure him that he shouldn't be afraid that James will hurt me or that I would hurt him.

He asks about my progress in obtaining the foster home placement and expresses his concern that this not a good time to start it. I then inform him that I've invited a couple who have an interest in having James come to live with them to come to our Monday session in six days.

Jay signs in on Friday, two days later. After a brief discussion about James's continued absence from the body, I request a meeting with Jack. I count to fifteen and Jack appears. His voice sounds tense, and I wonder if James's distress is affecting him. But Jack says he doesn't pay attention to James and then complains that he has a headache. I suggest that his physical pain must be caused by underlying emotional pain. Jack says he doesn't understand what I'm talking about but complains that James doesn't respect him. "I don't like the fact that he's always angry at me."

I had previously learned from Jay that his mother found ways to get James to express her anger at her husband. That means the source of James's anger toward Jack might be related to the way his mother expressed her anger toward her husband. Knowing this, I tell Jack that James might not be so angry if he knew that his anger was really his mother's.

PART ELEVEN

Jay
A Caring Protector

CHAPTER 71

*Jay's relationship to James is transitioning
from unemotional caretaker to caring protector.*

January 16, 1978

Jay signs in and describes himself as wanting to fulfill his goal of responding to James's cry for help. I believe that he has, in many ways, been like a mother providing for a helpless child, although Jay doesn't like that description. But I remind him that he has told me his purpose has been to protect James until he becomes an independent person and can take care of himself.

As I review Jay's longevity, he told me his first memory occurred at age twelve, even though he took over James's body at age seven. He called himself Jay for the first time when he was in the air force during his twenties. His relationship to James during the nearly three years of therapy has changed since it began in the spring of 1975. During the first nine months of therapy, Jay clearly defined his role as James's protector from emotional distress. His purpose paralleled that found in other cases, which I described in Book One—the host, the protector personality, or the inner self-helper (ISH), a name I first learned about in 1976 during a special psychiatric meeting devoted to a discussion of multiple personality disorder (later referred to as dissociative identity disorder).

During the early months of therapy James experienced Jay as a hindrance to his own existence rather than a protector. After nine months of therapy James came to believe that he needed to free himself from Jay's control and attempted to kill him.

In February 1976, a month after the attempted "murder," Jay said, "I hate the name James and I don't want to think of myself as two different people." Jay became very upset when I explained that James was the little boy part of him who needed to feel loved.

James's symptoms improved to the point that his hospital doctor discharged him from the hospital in April 1976. However, his emotional and personality instability was so disruptive that his family asked to have him return to the hospital after forty-eight hours. James remained in the hospital until he was discharged on October 17, 1977.

During the course of therapy, Jay had periodic episodes of leaving the body for extended periods of time, often occurring when he lost strength and couldn't continue his existence. On more than one occasion his disappearance from the body was preceded by episodes of catatonia. Similarly, whenever James felt Jay's or his therapist's absences, he experienced profound feelings of abandonment. Consequently, James's feelings of abandonment were recurrent themes.

During therapy, Jay's self-perception went through periodic changes associated with personality switches. He maintained that he was incapable of experiencing emotions which fulfilled his role, as James's protector, to have no emotion or physical pain. Early in therapy he expressed concern that he would blank out and would not be able to prevent another personality from taking over. Periodically he would experience fainting spells, physical symptoms, memory lapses and become aware of feeling weaker, or losing interest in protecting James, and he would vacate the body. Whenever Jay vacated the body for several hours or more, James experienced a profound feeling of abandonment.

I asked Jay where he went when he left the body and he described it as a place of nothingness where there's no time, no emotion, and nothing solid.

As therapy progressed, Jay eventually came to believe in his own separate identity even as he came to accept the fact that he and James shared the same body. Though Jay realized that James inhabited his body when he wasn't in it, his goal has been to help James learn to live independently. To accomplish that, Jay became insistent that James had to get out of the hospital. Then he insisted James needed to learn how to live in the apartment he and his nephew rented. Although that goal has been partially met, James now struggles with the challenge of living alone since his nephew has moved out. But he can call on Jay's presence when he needs relief, sometimes preferring that Jay take over the body. While Jay calls himself James's non-human caretaker, he says that is not his eventual goal. Jay wants to help James be more independent while, at the same time, he knows he must be available to James, who remains dependent on him.

Whenever Jay brings James to the Day Treatment Center, people aren't aware of the times he leaves the body and Jay replaces him. "They keep talking to me because they think I'm James," Jay says. When I ask Jay to show me how he does this he refuses.

James comes to therapy for his own needs. When Jay comes to therapy, he sees himself as a temporary guardian of the body and may come to a therapy session that had not been scheduled, telling me he needed to bring James because he needs my help.

CHAPTER 72

James is overwhelmed and feels exhausted.

January 18, 1978

Jay signs in and reports that he caught his nephew stealing $200 from James. Jay says he deliberately planted the money in a place where only his nephew could find it and then the money disappeared.

I ask Jay if he confronted his nephew about this, but he says he doesn't care because it was James's money. When I challenge him with the reality that James's savings are being depleted, he says, "The money isn't mine anyway so why should I care."

"If you're concerned about James and you're protecting him, shouldn't you care? He has no idea about money, you know that."

"He's run through savings before. I'm not worrying about that but I'm beginning to understand why he's been so upset, particularly if this was going on before. Maybe he's finally realizing he can't trust anyone, particularly his nephew," Jay says.

"I believe James basically trusts people, doesn't he?"

"He's overwhelmed. I think we're throwing too much at him. I worked very hard to get him out of this hospital and I don't want him to be so exhausted that he has to return again."

"He won't go back into the hospital now that he's at the Day Treatment Center."

"He went there this morning, but I question whether he can handle it."

"I believe he can. It's the ideal place for James to learn basic skills. I want you to make sure he gets there every day," I declare.

"Don't worry. He can go there without anybody's help and stay for maybe two hours. If I take him there at eight in the morning, he'll be there until ten o'clock sometimes."

"Can you take him over after this session and arrange for him to stay until noon?" I ask.

"I can arrange for him to stay there all day. But I'm not gonna force him. If he wants to leave the body he'll ask and I'll take over. He must take care of the body because if he doesn't, or if I'm not in it and it goes empty, that's hard on the body and hard on the other people too. So when he wants to leave and asks me to come into the body I'm right there. Nobody else notices and I just socialize with them."

"When you come into the body, they may even prefer your presence because you're more sociable, even though they'll think you're James."

I ask Jay if he is willing to let me hypnotize him so I can talk to James now and he agrees. When I ask if he will let me count, Jay says he prefers that because that makes it easier for him. After the countdown, James comes rapidly and comfortably.

I tell him that Jay informed me that he takes him to the Day Treatment Center each morning for a couple of hours, but James complains that he doesn't always know where he is or where he is supposed to go when he gets there.

"You've been going to the Day Treatment Center every day. And I've asked the staff to teach you how to manage your own money. That's a start."

"I've had lots of starts. What are they going to do to me?" He looks down sadly.

"After the staff makes sure you can manage your own money, they'll teach you other skills."

He doesn't reply.

"What are you thinking James?"

"Are you mad at me?"

I ask James why he thinks I'm mad and his reply is in the form of a question. "Can you hear the wind blowing when you can't see the wind?"

"That's possible," I reply.

"When I was younger, I heard that people say God talks to you, but you never see God. If that's true, is that the reason I can't hear Latot?"

"It's true that God is in the spirit world, and you've told me that Latot is in the spirit world."

James becomes more anxious and asks me not to be mad, so I reassure him again that I'm not.

When I ask for his definition of Latot his answer involves Jay. "Jay was someone I knew about when I was very young. I always called him Latot but I always kept that as a secret. Do you believe me?"

"You've told me about Latot and I believe what you've told me."

"Then I'm not being what she (mother) called me, am I?"

"What did she call you?"

"A silly ninny?"

"No, I would not call you a silly ninny."

"I won't tell anybody about these things then. I won't bring it up to anyone because I don't feel like crying. Sometimes I feel like hollering. But I don't feel like hollering now. I don't feel like anything. I used to come in here and I wasn't crying when I saw you. But now I can't understand why I keep crying." He goes on to say he doesn't understand his thoughts and feelings, but he's spent a lot of time thinking about it. Then he describes having dreams that he can't explain. "In my dreams I'm just reading except I don't know how to read. I can't tell if I'm dreaming these things or if I'm remembering them. I keep hearing Latot tell me those things are not important because they're related to something I don't wanna think about anymore."

"What is it that you don't want to think about anymore?"

"Emotions. I think that's the word. But I don't even know what emotions are. I used to want 'em but now I don't think they're important."

"You've been telling me about your thoughts and feelings, but you've never said before that you didn't want emotions. Let me explain that your feelings are your emotions."

"I don't need them." Then he changes the subject and asks a question. "He doesn't have to go away, does he?"

"Are you referring to Jay or to Latot?" I ask.

He ponders my question and then asks, "Did you know Latot?"

"No, I didn't, but I know Jay," I reply, and ask if he can explain their differences.

He nods his head and says that only Jay is human. "Latot isn't a human, and he just belongs to me."

"He is just yours," I agree.

"I didn't think that anyone else ever knew about him."

"That makes him even more important to you. Even though I don't know Latot I know Jay, and he is one of the ways you communicate with me. If he's here and talks to me, he tells me the things you would want to tell me but don't know how."

"He's so much smarter than me."

"One of the things he told me was that you should slow down and not go too fast. That's been hard for you to tell me."

Rather than respond, he continues to reminisce about his memories of Latot, and describes the times when things flash through his head so fast he couldn't focus on them. "It's like going in a car real fast. I see things and they go shooosh." James goes on to describe times when he only has fleeting communications with Latot, and other times when he seems very far away.

"If you know about Latot can you tell me what he looks like?" James asks.

"I know what Jay looks like. He looks like you, but he talks with more confidence and has more knowledge of things than you. Other than that, he's like you."

"In other words, you've never really seen Latot have you?"

"I've only seen him when he's in the body and he uses the name Jay."

"Does that mean you've seen me?"

"In a way, yes. He comes into your body when I count to ten. Unless you decided you didn't want him to come into your body."

I am pleased that James can tell me about Jay and Latot. But he doesn't fully understand that he can't replace Jay in the body unless he transcends the boundaries of human limitations to find Latot. He knows this is a very special condition, but he doesn't want to talk about it to anyone else for fear of being called crazy.

Our time is about up, and I suggest that he allow Jay to take him to the Day Treatment Center. But he says he has a lot of things to think about and prefers to walk over there by himself. We leave the studio together and I walk down to my office. But then, a few minutes later, James comes to my office and asks me to call for Jay. I remind him that he can count to ten by himself, but he says he wants me to summon Jay because Latot told him I was planning to visit the foster home today at one o'clock and Jay wanted to go with me.

CHAPTER 73

*Jay prevents James from coming into
the body as much as he would like.*

January 23, 1978

Jay signs in. I congratulate him on his beard, which is becoming thick, and he thanks me. I have not talked with James very much and I ask Jay which of them—he or James—is in the body more often. Jay says he tries to be there the most because he's afraid that James might become destructive if he spends too much time in the body. But he also says his efforts to keep James from coming into the body are causing problems, and that may be the reason James had a seizure last night. I'm concerned and request time to talk with James. After I count quickly to one, James appears and sits quietly with his head down. After a minute of silence, he angrily tells me that Jay keeps him from coming out as much as he would like and asks me why.

"I believe Jay is worried that if you were to come out at the apartment, your anger at your nephew might explode and you'd get yourself in trouble," I reply.

"Why would he say that? I'm angry at my nephew but I won't hurt him," James replies. Then he sits quietly without further comments about his angry feelings until he finally asks me a question in a subdued voice. "Have I ever really set out to hurt someone?"

"I don't know of anybody," I reply.

"Maybe I did a long time ago, but should I be punished for that now?"

I shake my head. "Are you referring to your father?"

"I felt like hurting my father a long time ago. I'm not hurting anyone, but people keep hurting me. Can you tell me why?" he asks.

I share my observation that he may be extra sensitive to feeling hurt, but he shakes his head in disagreement. He continues to sit uncomfortably bent forward with his hands between his legs and it seems like he has tears in his eyes. I remind him he can call Jay whenever he wishes by counting to ten, but he tells me that he doesn't know if that's the right thing to do. I point out that he has the freedom to do what is best for him. James nods his head and tells me that there are times when he calls for Jay but he doesn't come. When that happens, he feels very alone.

I ask James if he ever calls for Latot and he replies that is the same as calling for Jay. "Latot is who Jay is. A long time ago Jay told me about him, but I couldn't talk to anyone about it."

"I'd like to ask you more about that, but we'll have to wait because our time has run out."

Before ending I reluctantly inform him that I'll be out of town next week, news that distresses him. He bites his wrist to the point of making teeth marks on his skin, lowers both hands, and speaks in a whisper, as if he's been beaten into submission. I try to reassure him by reminding him that Jay will return to take care of the body whenever he asks him to.

"Do you remember those times when you used to be able to count and Jay came to take care of you?"

"That was a long time ago. I wasn't worried that someone would hurt me." He begins to sob, and I can see the tears stream down his cheeks. "That's all gone now, isn't it?" he asks mournfully.

"I don't think it's all gone," I reply.

"But I can't go anywhere now. I can't see anybody. I think I'll just leave and not come back." He sits quietly for a while and then asks, "Why can't someone care for me?"

316

"I think that someone would want to care for you," I emphasize.

"Does that make me selfish?" he asks.

"No, but even if you were selfish sometimes, or angry sometimes, or even if you were sad sometimes, you deserve to be cared for!" I insist.

"I don't wanna be angry. I don't wanna be sad. I just wish someone cared. Just for me. Not because I have eight fingers and two thumbs, or anything like that. Just because it's me."

I respond that I recognize he wants to be loved, but he says it's wrong to accept love. I remind him that there was a time when he believed it was okay to feel loved. He nods his head and says the reason he can't accept love is because he must do something to earn it, and he doesn't know what that should be.

James appears exhausted, so I tell him it's time to ask for Jay to come. But he's reluctant to do that. "I argued with him last night because I wanted to leave the apartment, but he didn't want me to."

"That was a good thing, wasn't it?"

"I guess so because I don't want to fight him."

I offer to give him a ride home, but he says that would make him feel sick. Then he begins to cry. When I ask why he's crying he says he's afraid Jay won't come.

But Jay does return to the body at my request when I count to ten. I mention that I wanted to give James a ride home, but Jay says he is uncertain what James might do and would prefer to take him home himself.

CHAPTER 74

Visit to the potential foster home.

January 27, 1978

I visited the Allison's home on Friday with Jay. This had been arranged by Mr. Bonilla, the social worker. We had a negative first impression because their home, which they purchased only three months ago, was not fixed up very well. Jay says it reminded him of his family home. Not only that, but he tells me that the Allison couple is so like his parents that James would react violently if he came there. Furthermore, the home is ten miles from the hospital. Jay says it's too far away, too complicated, too confusing, and too risky for James to live there.

During our visit, Jay offers his opinion to the Allisons that James might suddenly want to run to the hospital. But because he's only able to react at the level of a four-year-old boy, he wouldn't know how to take the bus. Jay's negative response was met with moderate receptivity on the part of Mrs. Allison, and she says she is willing to give up the idea of taking James in at this time. However, her husband asks Jay a lot of questions. A very interesting discussion ensues, during which Jay describes himself as not being human, of not having feelings of love, hate, or pain. Mr. Allison can't understand what he means, and Jay announces that he can prove what he just said by sticking his hand over a gas burner. That shocks Mrs. Allison, who quickly insists that he needn't do that. They engage Jay in more dialogue, so he describes himself further as a protective spiritual being, almost God-like. The Allisons seem intrigued by the spiritual aspects of the discussion.

During our return trip to the hospital, Mr. Bonilla, Jay, and I can discuss some of the implications of the visit and some of the options that are available for the future. The first option is to have James stay in the apartment and find a stable roommate. That is excluded when Jay states that he does not want to ask his nephew to leave the apartment and risk alienating him.

A second option is to find another foster home closer to the hospital and more comfortable for James. A third option is to begin a "family therapy process" with James and the Allisons so that James could begin to work out the transference issues he had with members of his family and ease into the foster home. I'm surprised to hear Jay express his willingness to go with the third option. If successful, it might be possible for James to move into their home in about four months.

CHAPTER 75

Jay insists he and James are the only two.

January 27, 1978

Jay asks me almost immediately during this session if I want to talk to Jack because he hasn't been around. Jay agrees to hypnosis, and I count to fifteen. After reaching that number he remains in a trance-like state. I repeat the name Jack five times slowly, and he finally emerges. He says he isn't feeling good and has a pain in his head. I ask if this is related to James's anxiety, but rather than answering yes or no Jack says, "I'm out of contact with James. He's not here."

"You mean he hasn't talked to you?"

Jack shakes his head slowly and tells me the pain is going away but he feels very tired. I ask if he is missing James.

"There's a lot of things I miss but I don't miss him," Jack answers.

I ask for specifics, and he says he misses his younger days. When I ask what he did with his father, he remembers being on the farm and caring for the horses along with his father. I ask if he thinks James wants to improve his relationship with father, but Jack doesn't seem to understand the importance of a good father and son relationship. When I ask if his father loved James, Jack says, "He got life," and asks permission to go back to sleep.

His eyes remain closed while he slouches back into the chair, so I ask what he means when he says James got life, but Jack doesn't answer. I explain that James received life from both his father and mother when he was conceived.

"That's what we all get," Jack says.

"Don't you think James got good genes?" I ask.

"Sir, are you talking about a pair of pants?"

"No. I'm talking about what he received from his mother and father."

"I already told you that he got life."

"But what qualities did he inherit from his mother and father?"

Jack responds very quietly, as if he's almost asleep, "Strength." Then, with a raspy voice that sounds like an old man, he asks, "Can't you let me sleep?"

"I will later, but I have another question. If you were James's father, would you be worried you may have passed him some traits you don't like?"

Jack keeps his eyes closed and continues to sit silently. Then he finally answers, "I couldn't have because I was never around him." He retreats into silence, indicating that he has no intention of responding to any more of my questions.

He now appears almost immovable, so I repeat his name twice to awaken him, but then I decide to count to one. James emerges with a frightened look on his face. He slowly gets out of his chair, seemingly confused, and tells me he has a terrible headache. I explain my conversation with Jack. James has a puzzled look on his face. He looks around and tells me he doesn't like the place where he had just been.

"Where did you go?" I ask.

"It used to be a quiet place. But now I'm hearing things."

When I ask what he heard James shakes his head, so I ask a different question. "Did you hear me talk about Jack and your father?"

James backs away from me as if to escape the words I just spoke. I ask him to sit down, but he continues to stand about three feet behind his chair. He looks around as if to ascertain where the voices in his head are coming from. "They must be dreams. But I'm awake," he says.

I reassure him that dreaming is normal for all human beings. But he's obviously afraid of something else. I suspect that he's sensing the presence of another personality. I ask James if he wants me to count and he quickly nods his head. After counting to ten Jay appears and immediately sits down in the chair. "That was the first time I had ever counted to ten when James was standing. Are you curious to know what happened?" I ask.

He looks around the room and shrugs his shoulders. "I was just standing here. What's curious about that?"

I'm surprised that he's reluctant to pursue the subject, so I push him. "It seems obvious to me that if you are suddenly standing in the room, you would wonder how that came about."

"What I wonder is what was your conversation like with Jack and with James."

"Neither Jack nor James talked much. But you can talk so I'll ask you again if you're curious why you were standing there."

"It should be obvious that I was standing there because James was."

"Do you know why James was standing there?"

"He's learning life. He is getting in touch with himself."

"What part of himself?"

"That other part he calls Jack. Jack is realizing that he is James and James is realizing that he is Jack. Then there's that other part," Jay states.

"Can you be more specific about that part?" I ask.

"That part is called Shea. James doesn't like him, and he got frightened and confused. He got in touch with his feelings of being afraid."

Jay's answers to my questions reveal that he must be aware that James is having "dreams" about the alternate personalities—Shea, Jack, and James. When I ask him if they're having common problems, Jay says "Yes, it's Father."

"Can you be more specific?"

"You see, his father didn't like him."

Jay says he could tell me more about these things, but if he did that, it would take away from James's self-discovery. "You'll soon hear him talk about things that he doesn't even know anything about. He's blaming it on dreams right now."

"He needs moral support and correct answers," I state.

Jay says my answers are correct. James doesn't accept them now, but he will eventually. He tells me emphatically that James needs the freedom to express his emerging individuality. "It's wrong to force him because then he does it out of fear. That's one emotion that's ridiculous."

"Fear?"

"That's right."

"Is James afraid of what people will think of him?"

"You're correct. He'll have to hide things like my presence when he's around people who think they're talking to him. He won't be able to expose me because if he exposes me, he'll expose himself." Then Jay goes on to talk about their common secret. "Jack, James, and Shea are all one person. Only James and I are different."

CHAPTER 76

James talks about his loneliness, his relationship to Jay and Latot, and his inability to return to the apartment.

January 30–February 10, 1978

Jay signs in and quickly tells me he's concerned that James will become fearful and depressed when I'm gone. His request is that I should put James to sleep during my ten-day absence because he can take care of the ordinary "human" things that have to be done during that time.

I explain that I can't do that and ask for Jay's permission to talk with James. After I count from ten to one, he appears. I ask how he has been feeling since our last session and he answers that he feels alone but denies feeling depressed. I assure him he can depend on me, but he says he doesn't like to depend on human beings because they're not very dependable. But he knows he can depend on Jay because he's not a human being.

I change topics and ask James about his dreams. He complains that his dreams are depressing because they contain sexual content and abandonment themes. He says he would like to have someone teach him how to sleep without dreaming. I ask if it's okay with him if I call for Jay and he nods his head. When Jay returns, he acknowledges that James said he wasn't depressed, but he will willingly take over the body if James asks him.

When I enter the studio on February 10, I find James standing there. It's been ten days since our previous session, and he appears frightened when I greet him. He sits down and I hand him the sign-in sheet. After he signs, I ask him if he knows why Jay wanted him to see me alone today. He says he doesn't know.

"Maybe it's because I just returned after being gone for ten days. Did you know that?"

He shakes his head. Then he asks me about Jay. "When I last saw you, you said you knew Jay. Did you know that I used to holler his name?"

"Is that because you were asking him to protect you from feeling alone?"

"Yes, but I don't know for sure if he does."

I explain that Jay has protected him from feeling abandoned and was able to do that during the time I was gone.

James frowns.

"Jay took over your body so that you weren't here," I explain.

"If I wasn't here, where was I?"

"Maybe you can tell me."

James mumbles that he must have been asleep and didn't know I had been gone for ten days. "I thought you were only gone for a day," he says. Then he adds that he doesn't want to think about it and becomes quiet.

When I ask again where he had gone, he gives me an interesting answer. "I had a dream that I went to Building Four because that's where I was born. Did you know that's where I began to learn about the world?"

I explain that I knew about his rebirth and that I'm glad he had a dream about it. I return to the subject of his relationship to Jay and explain that Jay gave me permission to talk to him several times during the past weeks. "Do you remember those times?" I ask.

James frowns. "I don't know," he replies.

When I ask if he knew where Jay was during my absence, James tells me he doesn't know but he had heard from Latot.

"What did you and Latot talk about?"

"He told me about the others."

"What do you mean?"

"He told me that all those others—Jack, Shea, Jim, and Jimmy—are me." He pauses a moment and then says he doesn't believe what Latot told him. "I'm not all those other people!" he insists.

I return to the topic of his feelings about my absence. He says that his feelings were too overwhelming.

"What do you mean by overwhelming?"

"When I knew you were going to be gone it was like being hit by a tornado."

"Do you think your feelings drove me away?" I ask.

"It must have. Why else would you go?"

"I had no choice. I had to go out of town to attend a meeting."

"I cried and I don't like it when I cry."

"It's normal to shed tears when a person feels very sad and lonely."

"Those tears came just like this beard did," he says as he points to his whiskers that Jay started to grow.

"I guess the tears represent the child in you, and the beard represents the man in you."

"I'm neither one, am I?" he asks.

"You're both because you're a person. A person can be either a male or female. But you and I know you're not a female because you're a male." I explain that his masculinity is normal for him. But he replies that he doesn't know what is normal anymore.

"Jay explained that Jim, Jimmy, Shea and Jack are all parts of you, and that's your normal."

"But I'm not that young Jim and Jimmy. I know I can't be Shea and I'm not that old Jack."

"Do you know how old you are?"

James has a puzzled look on his face and says, "I don't know if I'm old or not, but maybe I am."

I reassure him that he is not old compared to his father, who is in his seventies. Then James frowns. "I'd be better off without a father!" he exclaims.

"You would not be here if you didn't have a father."

James ponders my statement for a minute, then says, "Latot doesn't have a father."

"But you told me that Latot is a spirit. You're human and humans have fathers."

He sits quietly for a while with a puzzled look on his face, then asks a significant question. "How come I don't have a home then. If I'm a human being, they always have a home."

"Why do you feel like you don't have a home? Don't you think your apartment is your home?" I ask.

"I can't go back there 'cause I'll be alone," he replies.

"Don't you think Jay will be there?"

"If he's there then where will I be?"

His question reveals his concern that when Jay replaces him, he will go to some place undesirable. However, I want to respond to his fear of being alone when he's at the apartment. I decide to ask if he would prefer an alternate place to be. "Would you like to go someplace else and sleep, or stay here and think when Jay returns?"

He shakes his head. "I can't think if I stay here."

"You used to be able to think when I counted to ten," I state.

"I can't do that anymore," he moans as he shakes his head.

"Would you like me to call Jay back now?" I ask.

"Why do you have to call him? Can't he come back on his own?"

"I believe he wants to be called. Aren't you able to call him whenever you want to?"

He begins to cry but closes his eyes and begins to count. When he reaches six his speech becomes softer. Finally, he whispers ten and Jay opens his eyes. He acts surprised to see me. I ask why he didn't come today rather than James, and he explains that James was very anxious to see me, and it seemed natural for him to spend this session with me. I tell Jay that James is afraid to go back to the apartment on his own. Jay says he understands, and we terminate the session. We shake hands and he leaves the studio.

CHAPTER 77

Jay has a glimpse of Shea. Jack is a gardener.

March 24, 1978

Jay signs in and then tells me that he saw Shea in the hallway of the outpatient clinic while waiting to pick up a medication for James.

"He was leaning against the wall, and I heard him tell someone he'd been a patient in this hospital two years ago."

"Did you talk to him?"

"No. I saw no logical reason to do that. If I wanted to talk to him, I'd present myself so he could see me and then I'd wait for him to speak to me." Then he changes the subject and tells me he couldn't take James to the Day Treatment Center Wednesday because he didn't have control of the body. "Jack was in the body all day, spending money on gardening equipment and four sacks of peat moss. He planted a lot of plants and flowers inside the apartment."

"I'm surprised that you let Jack do that."

"I know he's been treated unfairly and kept out of the apartment too long. It's time he had the freedom to do what he likes."

"Now that Jack is in the apartment, can he help you with James?"

"Not really. Jack isn't real. He's only James's imagination and we can't get rid of his imagination yet." Jay goes on to say that he will allow Jack and Shea to continue their existences as personalities who can replace James so that he doesn't always have to take care of the body.

At this point I decide to talk to Jack and count to fifteen. "Good morning, sir," he says in the gravelly voice of an old man.

I greet him and explain that we will begin meeting on Fridays again. Then I ask about his new interest—gardening.

"I'm beginning to learn to grow plants in the apartment. I call it patio growing," he says, and goes on to tell me about his flower seeds, rosebushes, and ivy.

I ask if he'd like to teach James about this, but Jack says James doesn't want to learn. Then he says his plants are on the patio since he's not allowed in the living room. He says he is only allowed to use one bathroom and one of the two bedrooms. I wonder if this arrangement is like his father and mother sleeping in separate bedrooms.

After that brief meeting with Jack, I count back to ten to talk to Jay. I describe my conversation with Jack, including the fact that Jack said he was not welcome in two of the rooms. Jay admits that he keeps Jack away from James's room because he smokes, and James doesn't like that. Jay also says he took Shea's things out of James's room. I ask where he sleeps, and Jay says that he often falls asleep in one bedroom and wakes up in the other.

Before talking to James, I ask Jay whether he'd like to have me tell James about my absence next week. But Jay makes a request that I not tell him.

"What happens if he comes over Monday or Wednesday next week and I am not here?" I ask.

"I can make sure he won't come over here," Jay replies.

When I count back to one, James immediately gets up out of his chair and I ask him to sit down. He appears very anxious and tells me he doesn't want to go to the Day Treatment Center after this session because it's too scary. When I ask him to explain, he says he doesn't know what people will do.

He tells me he has headaches and vision problems and is still distressed about his nephew's absence at Christmas time. James says his nephew had promised to spend Christmas with him but left because of his girlfriend. Then he begins to sob. "It's always that," he says repeatedly. I stop our painful interaction by telling him that I will call for Jay.

I count to ten and he opens his eyes. We talk about James's plight, and Jay says it's been difficult for him to share the responsibility of taking care of James. "I tried to put all the responsibility on you before so I wouldn't have any responsibility. But then I realized I'm the only one who can take care of the body and I must fulfill my purpose."

I tell Jay that James doesn't want to go to the Day Treatment Center today, so Jay says he wants James to go, and he'll take the body to the building. "If he wants to be there, he can stay there. But if it's too painful for him, I'll be there in his place."

I wish him a good day and remind him I'll see him in a week.

CHAPTER 78

"If you call for Jay you'll have to leave the body.
If you want Latot you can stay in the body."

April 12, 1978.

Jay signs in. He says he couldn't get James to come out when he took him to the Day Treatment Center. Then he says he wants to confess what his agenda is. "Dr. Brende, I must tell you that I'm using you to teach James how to grow up and get along with the others."

"You don't have to feel guilty because one of my roles, along with being his therapist, is to be James's teacher."

I ask to talk to James and with Jay's cooperation, James appears at the count of one. I can immediately see that he's frightened. When I ask what he's afraid of he seems paralyzed with fear, so I count to five. He remains anxious so I count to a higher number, which calms him down. I ask why he stopped attending the Day Treatment Center, and he says it was because it brought out his bad memories.

I ask what bad memories, and he says memories about Jimmy being scared. Since Jimmy was the name given to him by his mother I ask if he has memories about her. He frowns silently. I ask what he's thinking, and he says "She hates me. She doesn't want me around."

"Can you go to your father?"

"He doesn't like me."

"Can you go to your sister or brother?"

"They all went away."

He remains quiet and I ask again what he's thinking. He says his memories from the past never go away. After a period of

332

silence, he asks why no one wants him, and I assure him that I do.

He continues to be distressed and says, "I don't wanna cry, but it hurts so bad. I don't know what to do."

I remind him that he can count to ten to bring Latot to feel calmer, and if he wants Jay to come and replace him, he can call out the name Jay.

James cries out for Jay, who quickly emerges. He takes a deep breath and thanks me for giving James those instructions—he can either call for Jay (who will replace him) or count to ten for Latot (to relieve his pain and anxiety).

I express my concern about James's failure to go to the Day Treatment Center and emphasize that he needs to go back there. Jay says he will be happy to take him, and we end the session.

CHAPTER 79

Jack wants to go to church.
Jay says he's only an imagination.

April 14, 1978

Jay signs in. He quickly explains that he will soon leave the body. But he wants to show James about the things he must learn to do first. "I only belong in this body to help James because I'm not a human being," he says. Then he tells me that he is experiencing more difficulty bringing the body to therapy or controlling his absences from the body. "There are times when I know I'm not in the body but I'm not sure who is there. Last night I was at home, but I wasn't in the body."

"Who was there?" I ask.

"I think Latot was. But there are other times when I think Jack is there."

"How does that happen?"

"I don't know, but this morning there were three sets of clothes laying out."

"Who were they for?"

"It could be that Shea is back. But if she is I know that Jack doesn't speak to her."

"Are those two something like James's mother and father?" I ask.

"I think they know about each other but don't really know each other," Jay explains.

I ask to talk with Jack by counting to thirteen. When Jack appears, he sits quietly for a long time. Finally, he asks how long he must keep seeing me. I reply as long as it's important. Then I ask if he knows if Shea is back. He shrugs his shoulders and says he doesn't pay any attention to her.

I ask if his relationship to Shea is like the way his father related to his mother and Jack talks about his father more positively today. "I try to be like my father. I work because I need to put bread on the table. I don't have time for other things. But maybe there's time now."

He asks if I'm going to chase him out of the place he's been staying. I say I wouldn't do that. He tells me he misses church and he'd like to go to the one across the woods from where he's staying.

"I haven't heard you talk about that before."

"When I think of you, I get too rattlebrained to talk. It's like that with all doctors and I know you're a doctor."

When I explain that I'm both a doctor and a psychiatrist he replies that he's not crazy. "I don't need you. The only problem I have is getting old."

I think it would be helpful if he could see himself on the monitor, so I tell him about the video camera that records our sessions and ask if he'd like to see himself. He shakes his head. After a period of silence, he looks around and asks, "Where's the camera?"

After I point to the window behind which the cameraman is sitting, he asks, "Do I have to be recorded sir?"

I explain that he doesn't have to, but he had already signed a consent form. He looks down at his shirt. "I guess I'd like to see myself, but I don't like this shirt I'm wearing." Then he scowls and says, "I don't remember putting it on."

I ask if he remembers walking into this room and he frowns. "No. I wouldn't have come but you insisted."

"I'm glad you're here. It's about time for us to stop, so why don't we record the session next time and look at it then."

He smiles and nods his head. "I'll wear my Sunday best and you won't recognize me," he says with a grin. Then he tells me, "I'd like to go to church on Sunday."

"You do? Do you believe in God?"

"Yes sir. I do."

I find this interesting and would like to ask Jay for his feedback. So, with Jack's permission, I count from thirteen to ten and Jay opens his eyes. He asks what Jack had to say and I tell him about our plan to have him look at a video of our next session. I also tell him that Jack wants to go to church.

"Did he really tell you that?" Jay asks, and then tells me he knows about a small Protestant church on the other side of a nearby field.

I point out that Jack is interested in dressing up for church and for the videotaping next Friday.

"I don't pay any attention to what Jack wants because he isn't real. I only pay attention to James and make sure he stays in the body," he says. Then Jay changes the subject and says he wants to go to a picnic at Lake Shawnee this weekend.

CHAPTER 80

Shea returns after a two-year absence.

May 1, 1978

After Jay signs in he tells me that there have been more times when he's not been in the body. When I ask who comes into the body, he doesn't want to tell me because he wants them to speak for themselves. However, he agrees to let me summon one of the others. I decide to count to thirteen. When he opens his eyes, I ask who I'm talking to.

He looks at me and asks, "Who do you think?"

"Are you Shea?"

He smiles. "I guess that's what they called me."

"I haven't seen you for two years."

"I've been away that long? Where have I been?"

"You tell me."

"I don't know where I've been but I wanna go home. I haven't seen Betty or Pappy for two years. And another thing, why don't I have any money?"

"Jay has been taking care of the money. You'd better ask him."

"Who is that?"

"Jay takes care of James."

"Where are these people you call James and Jay?"

"They are sharing your body," I explain as I point at him.

"Aren't I always in this body?"

"No, you aren't. When you are not in the body one of the others is."

He frowns and throws up his hands to display his confusion. "So, if this is not my body where is my body?"

337

"This is your body when you're in it, and when James is in it, it's his body."

"That's just too deep!" Shea is exasperated.

"Why is that so hard to believe?"

"I'm not about to share this body with anybody."

"You give your body to James."

"If that's true then get me a new body."

"So, you don't want to have someone else use your body?"

"No. Not in that way."

"How do you feel if Jack uses your body?"

"I have no idea who you're referring to."

I point out that Jack is living in half of the apartment. Shea frowns and says she has a vague awareness of a dirty old man there.

"It's about time you get to know him because sometimes he uses your body," I point out.

She scowls. "I don't want some dirty old man anywhere around my body!"

"When I talked to you, over two years ago, I asked you not to have any kinds of sexual relationships. You can have loving feelings but no sex," I clarify.

"I'm quite capable of telling that dirty old man he's not having sex with me," Shea insists.

"Indeed, you should, but can you treat him in a loving way?" I ask.

Shea objects. "You're asking too much."

Our time is running out, so I make a request for Shea to return in two weeks. Before the session ends, I ask to talk with Jay. Shea reluctantly agrees and I quickly count to ten.

Jay appears and asks who I talked to. I tell him I talked with Shea, who has returned from a two-year absence. I explain that Shea appears to be a female, and I asked her to treat Jack with loving respect. Jay makes the announcement that he's going to have to vacate the body, but he'll wait until after I get back.

CHAPTER 81

Jay leaves the body to Shea and her
son Jimmy, and to Jack and his son Jim.

June 2, 1978

Jay comes to today's session and the first thing he says is "Are you ready?"

"Why should I be ready?" I ask.

"I'm going to leave the body," he declares, which surprises me. He closes his eyes and sits motionless in the chair.

After a few seconds his eyes open. I ask who I'm talking to, and it appears to be Shea. She says, "I had a busy day yesterday and couldn't leave the apartment.'

"How did you get here?"

"I don't know. I don't really remember coming. But I really need to talk to you. Jimmy was just hanging on to me all afternoon. I finally got him to lay down and take a nap. He should have been exhausted for all the crying he did."

I'm captivated by Shea's description and ask for more information.

"I tried to pick him up, but he wouldn't let me pick him up. He just cried but I'm not used to someone crying like that around me."

"Do you know why he's been crying?" I ask.

"No, I don't. But he finally fell asleep, and I let him sleep."

"Is he in the apartment now?" I ask.

"Yes. That's the reason I must get back."

"How do you like the apartment?" I ask.

"I don't like not being allowed to go into Jimmy's room. I've tried to get in, but the door is always locked. Sometimes the door is open a crack and I look in. But I still can't seem to get in there."

"If you went in there, what would you do?"

"So far, I've never had any reason to go in. But last night, I wanted to see what Jimmy was doing because I was concerned." Shea goes on to say that Jimmy was all curled up with a magazine in one hand and a teddy bear in the other and was asleep like a typical three-year-old.

I ask if she is able to go into the room, but Shea says the door wouldn't open any further.

"How did Jimmy get in?" I ask.

"I don't know. I never really saw him go in there."

"Were you happy that he left the door open?"

"Yes, but it's kind of scary though."

"For whom?"

"For me. What if something happens to him and I get blamed for it."

"I guess you'll just have to go in there and keep something bad from happening."

"But I can't get in there. I've never been in there."

"Do you think there's someone keeping you out?"

"Who else is in there?"

"Jay," I explain.

"What would he be doing in there?"

"He's been the protector. I wonder if he's been waiting for you to arrive to care for Jimmy."

"I've always wanted a child you know. Now that I've got one, I don't know what to do."

"Maybe Jay is waiting for you to learn."

"But I don't know how I'll be able to live and how the rent gets paid. I don't make any money you know."

"Why not ask Jay. He might have the answers."

"You keep saying Jay. Who is he?" Shea asks.

"If you don't know him now, you'll get to know him."

"I'm only thinking about that child," Shea says.

"Would you like someone to help you give the love and care Jimmy needs?"

"That's why I have wanted to come to see you. But I just couldn't leave him alone because he was crying so hard."

"I talked to Jack last week. Do you know him?"

"Should I know who that is?"

"He's a man and you'll get to know him."

"I don't need a man around. The only reason I had one around was so I could get pregnant and have a son. Do you know if I got pregnant during those two years you keep saying I wasn't here?" she asks.

"How could you get pregnant without knowing about it?"

"That's what I'm asking you. I don't even remember getting exposed," she smiles.

"If you don't like men and ..."

"I didn't say I didn't like men. I don't need a husband. I don't like husbands. I don't like wives either. I only like a man if I want to get pregnant."

I point out that I would like to talk to Jack now but Shea appears disappointed and tells me she must leave anyway. "I've got to get home and take care of Jimmy. He might wake up and be crying now," she sighs.

I explain that if she closes her eyes, I will proceed to count to fifteen. When I reach that number Jack opens his eyes and looks around. He finds a pair of glasses in his pocket and puts them on.

"How are you today?" I ask.

"Fine sir," he replies in his gravelly voice.

"I've been told that there is a child who's been crying in the apartment."

"I haven't heard anything," he replies.

"I also heard that the child's mother is there."

341

"I've never seen a female in that apartment. I've seen female things around, but I have no need for those things."

"It's strange that a man and woman living in the same apartment don't pay any attention to each other."

Then Jack tells me about Jim, the boy he's supposed to take care of, and the difficulty he has in the apartment. He says he's been told he only has two rooms he can use, and he has to avoid the woman and her son who also live there. But he's ignoring her because his only concern is Jim.

"I must think about Jim, sir. Not anything else."

"By the way, how old is Jim?"

"I think he's ..." He pauses and then raises his hand about four feet from the floor. "Six or seven, I think. All I know is that he's awful big for his age. He's a strapping young boy."

I ask what he's teaching Jim and Jack replies, "I teach him what I'm trying to learn."

"What's that?"

"I'm reading books about how to grow things in an apartment because I don't have any ground to plant seeds in."

I ask where he got the books, and he says he bought them in the grocery store. I ask if he can bring the books in for me to see next Friday. Then I ask about the shoes he's wearing, but he doesn't remember putting them on. He has nothing more he wants to talk about, so I count back to thirteen. Shea immediately removes the glasses, which I explain are Jack's. I tell her about my conversation with Jack and ask if she wants me to tell him anything.

"The only thing he needs to know is that I have a child now, and if he tries to take him away or wants me to do something I don't wanna do then I'm going to have to move out of there."

Since our time has ended, I ask her to tell me more on Monday. She quickly responds that she must get home and take care of Jimmy.

I explain that I will count to ten so Jay can come, and Shea half-heartedly agrees. At the count of ten Jay opens his eyes. When I tell him that Shea talked about her need to get home to take care of a crying baby, Jay grins. "She said that? There's no logic there at all. How can an imagination take care of an imagination? That's like the blind leading the blind, isn't it? There is no sense in it."

I agree that it's only logical to Shea. We spend a short time discussing the future of these different personalities. When I ask Jay how he views our ultimate goal, his response is very accurate: "Before we put them all together we need to separate them out. That's why it's important for Shea to be Shea, Jimmy to be Jimmy, and Jack to be Jack. Then as they become individuals, they'll be able to take the next step, to get together and become integrated into one person."

"I agree."

"But James must first know each one as themselves. That's the reason why I figured Shea should come back here. He has a very strong imagination, is very dominant too, and likable. Of course, Shea's a him though maybe he's a transexual[28] I think it's called. But perhaps it's best to call Shea she."

CHAPTER 82

*What have we been through
and where do we go from here?*

Book One covered the first sixteen months of psychotherapy, from March until June 30, 1976, during which the young James emerged from his "contamination" by unwanted alternate personalities and experienced a "rebirth." The essence of Book Two, which covers the following two years until May 1, 1978, describes a therapeutic process that helps a reborn James discover his identity as a real person and begin to grow up. As his therapist, I emphasized the significance of love in the therapeutic relationship, which was essential for him to continue his emotional development. However, I came to learn that the word love was emotionally distressing for James because the word had been sexualized by his alternate personality Shea, an exploitative homosexual as described in Book One.

To help James grow from a young child into a young adult, my relationship with him paralleled that of a parent-child relationship that soon moved into a more mature relationship characterized by a boy bonding with his father. This therapeutic effort was an attempt to counteract the personality split that occurred at age seven when James's father struck him and severed the father-son relationship.

During therapy, James's personality matured rapidly. Jay, who has been James's protector from the beginning, became insistent that James become independent and be able to leave the hospital. This was facilitated by Jay and his nephew, who rented an apartment for James to move into.

Eventually a new personality named Jack emerged and assumed many of father's characteristics. Then Shea returned after two years. Instead of being a gay male, Shea believed she was a female who had a son, Jimmy, and that she had to put up with Jack and his son, Jim.

In the forthcoming Book Three, Shea, who might be described as a transgender female, will raise her son and Jack will raise his. It will be very challenging for these two "parents" to get along with each other as they each share one half of the apartment that Jay and his nephew had originally rented for James. During this time, Shea's female characteristics will become a transference issue in the therapeutic relationship, and Jack's increasing age will be a factor during the brief time he remains.

James will struggle with emotional turmoil because different personalities frequently take over his body. He will have both Jay and Latot as protectors as he gets older, although Latot will eventually replace Jay and become the primary personality.

Endnotes

[1] An out-of-body experience (OBE) is characterized by seeing things, events, and one's self from a distance while outside his or her own physical body. One in ten people have experienced one or more OBEs, which can be induced by such things as traumatic brain injuries, neurological disorders, dissociative disorders, psychedelic drugs, sleep disorders, or training as has been promoted by programs such as The Monroe Institute. Many survivors of drownings, shootings, freezings, surgeries and other life threatening events have also reported OBEs, although they've usually been called near-death experiences (NDEs).

[2] A boy's relationships with other boys and girls is modeled from his father. I will find additional literature about the importance of fathering. For example, 82 percent of studies since 1980 found "significant associations between positive father involvement and offspring well-being." In an analysis of over 100 studies on parent-child relationships, it was found that having a loving and nurturing father was *as important* for a child's happiness, well-being, and social and academic success as having a loving and nurturing mother. Some studies even indicated father-love was a *stronger* contributor to some important positive child well-being outcomes. When a father is absent his son will hopefully find another strong male to learn how to behave and survive in the world. James looked to his older brother Clarence as a role model, and followed in his footsteps to enter the Air Force. Paul R. Amato and Fernando Rivera, "Paternal Involvement and Children's Behavior Problems," *Journal of Marriage and the Family* 61 (1999): 375-384. Ronald P. Rohner and A. Veneziano, "The Importance of Father Love: History and Contemporary Evidence," *Review of General Psychology* 5, no. 4 (2001). Kyle D. Pruett, *Fatherneed: Why Father Care is as Essential as Mother Care for Your Child* (New York: The Free Press, 2000).

[3] Each side of the body is connected to opposite sides of the brain. I have previously speculated that James embodied the left

side of the body—associated with right brain hemisphere functioning, and Jay embodied the right side of the body—associated with left hemisphere functioning. Jay and James came to be separated by a physiological boundary in the form of a band of white fibers connecting the two hemispheres called the corpus callosum. Perhaps the physiological boundary that blocked communication between the two hemispheres is now opening up.

As I study the function of the corpus callosum more closely I find that in normal adults it is the largest inter-hemispheric commissure that provides communication between the two sides of the brain. The corpus callosum consists of approximately 200 million fibers of varying diameters and degrees of myelination, and is divided into smaller groups of fibers or commissures that communicate with similar specialized areas between both hemispheres. In a normal infant the corpus callosum begins to develop at approximately eight weeks of gestation. The failure of the corpus callosum to form, although a rare occurrence, may be associated with a higher incidence of epilepsy, learning disability, and neurodevelopmental conditions such as autism spectrum disorder, attention deficit disorder, and schizophrenia. Adults with psychiatric and mood disorders frequently suffer from dysfunction within the corpus callosum.

Applicable to James's brain is primarily the information about the parts that affect identity, movement, intellect, and emotions. Anatomical and physiological studies have found that the fibers interconnecting the frontal lobes transfer motor information (body movements), while the anterior commissure connects the temporal lobes, which store the memories and images that help an individual to define his (or her) sense of identity. The temporal lobe in the dominant, or left brain, is involved with understanding and processing language, intermediate and long-term memory, emotional stability, and visual and auditory processing. The dominant temporal lobe also influences emotional responsiveness, while decreased or increased activity is associated with unpredictable moods and behaviors. The temporal lobe in the non-dominant, or right brain, is involved with recognizing facial expressions, decoding vocal intonation, music and tonality, visual learning, and spiritual experiences. According to research performed by Dr. D.G. Amen, decreased activity or increased activity in the temporal lobes is associated with fluctuating, inconsistent, or unpredictable moods and behaviors. Daniel G. Amen, *Change Your Brain Change Your Life* (New York: Harmony Books, 2015). Megumi M. Tanaka-Arakawa, Mie Matsui, Chiaki Tanaka, Akiko Uematsu, Satoshi Uda, Kayoko Miura, Tomoko Sakai, and Kyo Noguchi Yong Fan, Academic Editor, "Developmental Changes in the Corpus Callosum from Infancy to Early Adulthood: A Structural Magnetic Resonance Imaging Study," (March 19, 2015) doi: 10.1371/journal.pone. 0118760.

[4] Children who have been traumatized may refuse to speak. Soldiers who have survived lethal combat may stare hollow-eyed into a void because their terrifying memories are too difficult to articulate. Bessel van der Kolk, *The Body Keeps the Score, Brain, Mind, and Body in the Healing of Trauma* (New York: Penguin Books, 2014), Chapter 3.

[5] Kluft has written that fusion may be achieved when there have been three stable months of continuous personality existence, no evidence of a newly emerging alternate personality, a subjective sense of unity, and an absence of new personalities after re-exploration. Richard P. Kluft, "Treatment of Multiple Personality Disorder: a Study of 33 Cases," *Psychiatric Clinics of North America* 7, no.1 (1984): 9-29.

[6] Richard P. Kluft, "Treatment of Multiple Personality Disorder: a Study of 33 Cases," *Psychiatric Clinics of North America* 7, no.1 (1984): 9-29.

[7] Psychiatrist Bessel van der Kolk has published a widely read book in which he details a great deal of information about trauma and its effects on the mind, emotions, and body. He reports on research using new technology—positron emission tomography (PET scans) and functional magnetic resonance imaging (fMRI)—to discover that specific parts of the brain are activated when traumatized individuals experience flashbacks. "During flashbacks our subjects' brains lit up only on the right side .... Our scans clearly showed that images of past traumas activate the right hemisphere and deactivate the left." This research validates my understanding that the identity of James, the trauma victim, is linked closely with the right side of the brain. Bessel van der Kolk,

The Body Keeps the Score, Brain, Mind, and Body in the Healing of Trauma (New York: Penguin Books, 2014), 44.

[8] While most individuals exposed to extreme stress react with a fight or flight response, comprised by the sympathetic nervous system's rapid heart rate, the freeze response spreads throughout the body via the parasympathetic nervous system, causing a slowing of all physiological functions. This response is the first primal response against danger found in many species to avoid the attention of predators. Individuals exposed to trauma have symptoms that include heightened anxiety and sometimes a prolonged freeze response which resembles a state of catatonia including inhibition of muscle movement and speech.

James's physiological response to my request that he have an EEG was a cessation of movement which seems like catatonia, a condition I have encountered in occasional psychiatric patients during my career. What is unique about James's catatonia is that it is a likely physiological response to the memory of the time Dr. Baird gave him ECT. It may have occurred as a freeze response, which is characterized by a physical and emotional paralysis in response to the body's expectation that there is a life endangering threat. Karin Roelofs, "Freeze for Action: Neurobiological Mechanisms in Animal and Human Freezing," *Philosophical Transactions B, The Royal Society* 372, no. 1718 (April 19, 2017). Arthur Janov, *The Primal Scream: Primal Therapy, The Cure for Neurosis* (New York: Dell Publishing, 1970).

[9] Van der Kolk's research of qEEG (quantitative electro-encephalogram) patterns demonstrated that trauma victims displayed predominantly high frequency beta waves above 20 Hz in the right temporal lobe, the fear center of the brain. Many of these individuals were trained to use neurofeedback to modify their brain wave frequencies. They learned to reduce their high frequency beta waves from 20 Hz to slower alpha waves of 7 to 13 Hz, associated with relaxation and trance states. Bessel van der Kolk, *The Body Keeps the Score, Brain, Mind, and Body in the Healing of Trauma* (New York: Penguin Books, 2014), Chapter 3.

[10] A person's sense of self begins at about eighteen months of age, and goes through constant evaluation and adjustment throughout

the lifespan. By two years the young child becomes aware of his or her gender as a boy or a girl. At four, the child will describe himself or herself by physical features. By age six, he will understand emotions and personality traits. With increasing age, he will learn how others perceive him and gain more awareness of his own abilities. Throughout childhood and adolescence, the self-concept becomes more abstract and complex. Neuroimaging studies have shown that information about the self is stored in two areas of the brain—the medial prefrontal cortex and the medial posterior parietal cortex. The posterior cingulate cortex, the anterior cingulate cortex, and medial prefrontal cortex are thought to combine to provide humans with the ability to self-reflect. The insular cortex is also thought to be involved in the process of self-reference. J. H. Pfeifer, M. D. Lieberman, and M. Dapretto, "I Know You Are But What Am I?!: Neural bases of self- and social-knowledge retrieval in children and adults, *Journal of Cognitive Neuroscience* 19, no. 8 (2007): 1323-1337.

[11] There are reported stories from people, mainly children, who recalled an existence shortly before birth called the pre-birth experience. Those who described pre-birth experiences seemed to "remember" existing in the same or similar plane to near-death experiences (NDEs). They recalled being in a spirit world where they were given a preview of their life and future parents. Whether fetal memory exists has attracted interest for many thousands of years. This article draws on recent experimental evidence to consider two questions: does the fetus have a memory? And if so, what function(s) does it serve? Evidence from fetal learning paradigms of classical conditioning, habituation and exposure learning reveal that the fetus does have a memory. Possible functions discussed are: practice, recognition of and attachment to the mother, promotion of breastfeeding, and language acquisition. It is concluded that the fetus does possess a memory but that more attention to the functions of fetal memory will guide future studies of fetal memories abilities. Research data collected over twenty years found that many individuals reported that they believed their existence began prior to conception or birth. After studying his accounts of pre-birth experiences (PBEs) and comparing that data with other researchers of spiritual phenomena, the author identified typical traits, types, and characteristics, as well as when,

to whom, and where they occur. In a typical pre-birth experience, a preborn soul first appeared to communicate with someone on earth to announce his or her readiness to be born. According to a survey reported on Prebirth.com, 53 percent remembered a time when they first came into being occurred before they were conceived, and 47 percent remembered their existence began before birth. Stephen Wagner, *Life Before Birth,* Liveabout.com (April 20, 2018), https://www.liveabout.com/life-before-birth-2594548. P. G. Hepper, "Fetal Memory: Does it exist? What does it do?" *Acta Paediatrica* 416, supplement (1996):16-20.

[12] The significance of love in psychotherapy is not generally discussed in scientific journals. However, noted psychologist Eric Erickson described the empathic relationship between patient and therapist as a necessary precursor for loving and enduring close relationships. Object-relations theorist Gregory Hamilton described love as the binding element in the object relations unit between mother and child. He also emphasized the significance of the patient-therapist relationship as providing the 'holding' functions of therapy—defined as the empathic listening and responding to the patient's words and behaviors. Otto Kernberg emphasized the significance of the relationship between therapist and patient, referred to as transference, and emphasized transference interpretations within the therapeutic process. Transference Focused Psychotherapy (TFP) particularly helps patients who suffer from contradictory fragments of the self and identity confusion. Since James's symptoms met those characteristics, I incorporated the principles of TFP into my therapeutic approach. O. F. Kernberg, F. E. Yeomans, J. F. Clarkin, and K. N. Levy, "Transference Focused Psychotherapy: Overview and Update," *International Journal of Psychoanalysis* 89, no. 3 (2008). E.H. Erickson, *Childhood and Society* (New York: Norton, 1950). N. Gregory Hamilton, *Self and Others- Object Relations Theory in Practice* (New Jersey: Jason Aronson,1988).

[13] Smell and emotions are anatomically close to each other within the brain's limbic system. The brain's limbic system contains the amygdala (emotions) and hippocampus (memories), and encompasses the olfactory bulb. The sensation of smell develops fully within the olfactory center while the unborn child is growing

in the womb, and is the primary neuro-receptor until that child's sight takes over at age ten. During a child's early years the odors he perceives will be linked to either pleasant or unpleasant emotions he will remember for the rest of his life. Colleen Walsh, "What the Nose Knows," *The Harvard Gazette*, (February 27, 2020), https//news.harvard.edu/gazette/story/ 2020/02/how-scent-emotion-and-memory-are-intertwined-and-exploited/.

[14] Latot is described as James's guardian angel, who has been present in his life since before he was born. My research of this subject reveals that many persons have believed there are guardian angels. Native Americans call on the spirit world for knowledge and protection. In Shamanistic cultures, spirits empower shamans with special capacities that can help them during spiritual journeys or healings. In the Bible there are references to angels roughly 300 times from the first book of Genesis to the final book of Revelation. In the Bible, angels can't usually be seen by humans unless God reveals them (see Numbers 22:31, 2 Kings 6:17, Luke 2:13). However, from time to time angels took on a bodily form and appeared to various people in Scripture (Matthew 28:5; Hebrews 13:2). Angels in the Bible appear to have a rank and order. The angel hierarchy is supported by Jude 9, when the angel Michael is called an "archangel"—a title that indicates rule or authority over other angels. He's also called "one of the chief princes" in Daniel 10:13, and appears to lead God's angelic army in Revelation 12: "Now war arose in heaven, Michael and his angels fighting against the dragon; and the dragon and his angels fought, but they were defeated," (Revelation 12:7–8). Paul also tells us that the Lord will return from heaven "with the archangel's call" (1 Thessalonians 4:16). Scripture doesn't tell us if this refers to Michael, or if there are other archangels as well. The archangel Michael is mentioned in Jude 9, Revelation 12:7–8, and Daniel 10:13 and 21. David Etkin, Jelena Ivanova, Susan MacGregor, and Tali Serota, "Risk Perception and Belief in Guardian Spirits," *SAGE Publications* (July-September 2014), sgo.sagepub.com. *The Common English Bible*, (Nashville: E.T. Lowe Publishing), Wikipedia.org.

[15]Psychiatrist Bessel van der Kolk study's with fMRI brain imaging indicate that the right cerebral hemisphere is associated with telepathic messaging, but is not found in non-telepathic

individuals. Bessel van der Kolk, *The Body Keeps the Score, Brain, Mind, and Body in the Healing of Trauma* (New York: Penguin Books, 2014), Chapter 3.

[16] Because James said "I felt Latot's presence," I became interested in knowing if this subject has been researched. I investigated the subject of "felt presence" and found it means having a sense that someone, unheard or unseen, is present in the room. Although it's not a common experience for most people, it is more commonplace for those who have survived close calls with death and lost loved ones. Sixty percent of individuals suffering bereavement have experienced a "felt presence," particularly during the first month of bereavement. Fifty percent of them say they have actually "seen" the deceased individuals. These experiences have been reportedly found in one third of the population at some point in their lives. A "felt presence" has also been associated with sleep paralysis in some individuals. They may have felt someone or something in the room moving towards them, sometimes accompanied by a sense of dread or pressure upon the chest. Other common contexts for "felt presences" are psychiatric or neurological disorders such as Lewy body dementia, traumatic brain injury, and Parkinson's disease. One research study found that 50 percent of individuals with Parkinson's disease reported a "felt presence." Researchers studying this phenomenon hypothesize that this experience is similar to a NDE, or near-death survival experience, during which survivors see their bodies from a distance. Physiological studies have found a disruption to the internal mapping of the body which involves the insular cortex and the temporoparietal junction body (TPJ) in the brain, since a "felt presence" can be elicited by electrical stimulation to the TPJ. Ben Alderson-Day, "The Silent Companions," *The Psychologist* 29, no. 4 (April 2016): 272-275, The British Psychological Society, bps.org.uk.

[17] I had been taught psychotherapists should not accept gifts from their patients because that clouds the therapeutic relationship. I believe that a blanket rule of refusing all gifts is unnecessarily cold and inhuman for many patients. The matter should take a case-by-case consideration between accepting all gifts or unyielding refusal. Steven Reidbord, "Should Therapists Accept Holiday Gifts?

Gift-giving in the therapeutic relationship," *Psychology Today*, (December 24, 2010), https://www.psychology today.com /us/blog/sacramento-street-psychiatry/201012/should-therapists-accept-holiday-gifts.

[18] I received excellent consultative help from Dr. Donald Rinsley. His impeccable credentials included the following: Associate Chief for Education, Psychiatry Service, Topeka VA Hospital; senior faculty member for adult and child psychiatry, Menninger School of Psychiatry; and Spencer Foundation Fellow in Advanced Studies, Menninger School of Psychiatry. During this educational program Dr. Rinsley discussed an object-relations, psychodynamic understanding of this patient:

Of the patient's various personalities James is clearly the central or nuclear one. Able to experience only painful emotions his helplessness and ambivalence reflected a perceived terror of abandonment and loss which in turn indicated the presence of unresolved mother-infant symbiosis. Indeed James' identity as a boy appeared to be masculine and his features were based, in part, on the little boy's effort to internalize a protective paternal image both to ward off awareness of the father's rejecting actions and to defend against a regressive maternal symbiotic tie. Two sub-personalities, Jim, the little boy who sought love from his father and Jimmy, who felt unloved by his mother, were accordingly split-off from James who disappeared at age seven years when he was assaulted by the father. This trauma led to the emergence of Jay, the rational but superficial and intelligent personality, who was incapable of experiencing painful emotion. Jay's appearance during James's psychosocial period of early latency pointed to an attempt at a schizoid obsessional solution of the pre-oedipal problem of threatened abandonment by the mother and the sadistic assault by the father. Jay's presence during this stage of psychosocial development could also reflect a displacement from the ambivalently perceived maternal figure split into an abandoning and rejecting / attacking bad object.

(In order to grasp an understanding of normal psychosocial development, latency is the fourth stage and

spans the period of six years to puberty. During this stage the boy is able to repress his earliest traumatic or sexual memories and give up his oedipal fantasies of possessing mother and replacing father by focusing on achieving skills and peer activities with other boys. If trauma or abandonment issues prevent him from moving normally through these phases he may withdraw into a paranoid-schizoid position and remain interpersonally isolated.)

In the course of therapy Shea emerges as the personification of a seductive, hysteriform, effeminate part of the patient, reflective of his pathological identification with the mother. The latter, in turn, could be seen to comprise a very oral, primal identification with the exciting part of the introjected bad object and the later counter-phobic identification to ward off the bad-object's dangerousness. It is interesting that Shea is reported to have emerged during early adolescence with the upsurge of libidinal instinct and strong drive toward separation from the parental and internal imagos. The ultimate banishment of Jay and Shea during therapy allowed James to form a therapeutic alliance and to re-experience the feelings defended against the split-off Jay and Shea and to begin to integrate them via the therapeutic transference and to resolve the paranoid-schizoid position reflected in the conviction that love destroys. The application of insights derived from psychoanalytic object-relations theory in cases of multiple personality constitutes a significant new approach to the psychodynamic understanding of the etiology and treatment and eventual cure including the archaic splitting defense which lies at the root of their symptomatology.

[19] Why does Jay repeatedly say that time has no meaning to him? What part of the brain controls time perception? As I research the published literature pertaining to this subject, I find that there are many neuro pathways involved—frontal cortex (expressive language and higher level executive functions), parietal cortex (sensation-touch and pressure), basal ganglia (integration of voluntary behavior), hippocampus (learning and memory), cerebellum (coordination and movement), and are all associated

with receiving and interpreting information about the passage of time. The extent of involvement of these brain regions also involve the participation of memory, attention, and emotional states. On many occasions individuals' time estimates are affected by specific events. For instance, when persons are looking forward to an important event, such as going on vacation, time seems to pass more slowly than when the vacation is coming to an end. Time perception also depends on the interaction between the aspects of the brain linked to the internal clock and the specific task. In this respect, the frontal cortex has been widely associated with the perception of time information related to short and long-term memory. The role the frontal lobe plays in terms of time perception seems to differ according to the activities of the left and right hemisphere. Some authors support the theory that the activity of the right frontal lobe ceases when task duration is memorized, while frontal lobe activity helps to maintain attention until this point. The dorsolateral prefrontal right cortex is considered as the region most involved in time perception. Rhailana Fontes et al., "Time Perception Mechanisms at Central Nervous System," *Neurology International* 8, no. 1 (April 1, 2016): 5939, doi:10.4081/ni.2016.5939.

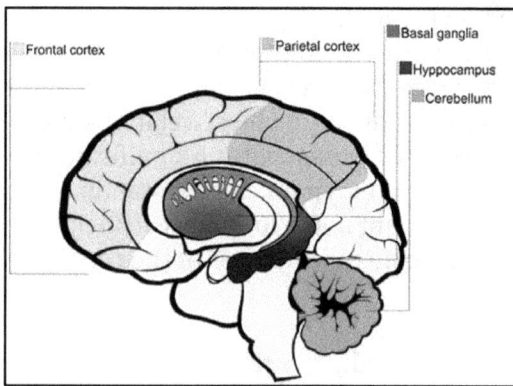

This diagram provides a visual image of the different cortical and subcortical areas involved in time perception.

[20] The Jayhawk Hotel is located at 700 SW Jackson Street in downtown Topeka, Kansas. The building was later renamed the Jayhawk Tower and is on the Register of Historic Places. There are two large signs of the University of Kansas Jayhawk mascot figure

on the rooftop, associated with the nationally acclaimed Jayhawk athletic programs located at KU in Lawrence, Kansas, a thirty minute drive east of Topeka.

[21] Catatonia is a psychomotor syndrome characterized by a state of verbal unresponsiveness that occurs in more than 10 percent of patients with an acute psychiatric illness. Once thought to be a subtype of schizophrenia, catatonia is now recognized to occur with a broad spectrum of medical and psychiatric illnesses, particularly depressive disorders. The neurophysiology associated with catatonia is not well understood, although abnormalities in gamma-aminobutyric acid and glutamate neurotransmitters have been discovered. The treating physician should proceed with one of the recommended therapies (benzodiazepines or ECT) to prevent worsening symptoms. Sean A Rasmussen, Michael F. Mazurek, and Patricia I. Rosebush, "Catatonia: Our Current Understanding of Its Diagnosis, Treatment and Pathophysiology," *World Journal of Psychiatry,* https://www.ncbi.nlm.nih.gov/pmc/articles/PMC5183991/6, no. 4 (December 22, 2016): 391-398, doi: 10.5498/ wjp.v6.i4.391.

[22] There have been many reported cases of misdiagnosed death. These have included a sixty-six-year-old man who woke up seventeen minutes after a cardiac arrest during surgery, and a seventy-eight old man in hospice who was found without a pulse and declared dead, but woke up in a body bag at the morgue hours later. This syndrome was first described in the medical literature in 1982 by researchers who reported eighty-two cases of mis-diagnosed death, though some researchers believe this phenomena is greatly under-reported. The name for these extraordinary cases is the Lazarus Syndrome, named after the story of Lazarus, who was resurrected by Christ four days after his death. Not all of these individuals were able to sustain life, although 45 percent of them experienced good neurological recovery. Jan Bondeson, *Buried Alive: The Terrifying History of Our Most Primal Fear* (New York: W.W. Norton and Company, 2002). Lindsay Dodgson, "There's a condition that makes people think you're dead when you're not – and it could explain why three doctors sent a living man to the morgue." Businessinsider.com, Jan 10, 2018. JG Bray, "The Lazarus Phenomenon Revisited," *Anesthesiology* 78, no. 5 (1993): 991.

Vedamurthy Adhiyaman, Sonja Adhiyaman, Radha Sundaram, "The Lazarus Phenomenon," *Journal of the Royal Society of Medicine* 100, no. 12 (December 2007): 552–557. Honor Whiteman, "The Lazarus Phenomenon: When the 'Dead' Come Back to Life," *Medical News Today*, May 26, 2017, https://www.medicalnews today.com/articles.

[23] The primary motor cortex on the left side of the brain controls movement of the right side of the body, and vice-versa; the right motor cortex controls movement of the left side of the body as shown on this brain map known as the homunculus.

[24] His left hand has a neurological link to his right brain, and his right hand links to the left brain. I have previously discussed my theory about James's brain and it's linkage to his body. I have also published a research study demonstrating these linkages using skin conduction as a measurement. J. O. Brende, "The Psycho-physiological Manifestations of Dissociation, Electrodermal Responses in a Multiple Personality Patient," *Psychiatric Clinics of North America* 7, No.1 (March, 1984): 41-50.

[25] Hypnotic suggestions are one effective way to help someone enhance his self-image according to research studies pertaining to the technique that some hypnotherapists have called self-image hypnosis. Ellen R. Coleman, "Hypnotherapy for Self Image," MindworksHypnotherapy.com.

[26] One of the first psychotherapists for patients with DID was psychiatrist Richard Kluft. Richard P. Kluft, "Clinical Presentations of Multiple Personality Disorder," *Psychiatric Clinics of North America* 14, no. 3 (September, 1991):605-629. Richard P. Kluft, "Treatment of Multiple Personality Disorder: a Study of 33 Cases," *Psychiatric Clinics of North America* 7, no.1 (1984): 9-29. Richard P. Kluft, "Personality Unification in Multiple Personality Disorder: a followup study," in *Treatment of Multiple Personality Disorder*, ed. B.C. Braun (Washington, DC: American Psychiatric Press, 1986) 29-60.

[27] Psychoanalytic theory describes a time during a young boy's life around age four when he competes with his father for mother's

attention. This has been called the oedipal conflict. In James's case I make the proposal that if his parents reconcile that would prevent him from thinking that his anger caused his parents to be in conflict with each other.

[28] In an unexpected twist, a newly emerged female personality named Shea, a transgender female who existed previously as a male homosexual, has appeared on the scene. I reviewed literature about this subject and found several reports of DID patients with histories of abuse who were found to have alternate personalities of a different sex. There was a case report of a man asking for hormonal treatment for gender dysphoria (GD) who had eight distinct personalities with different gender identities. I found a literature review of eleven patients who received the diagnoses of DID. In one interesting case a twenty-year-old transgender male patient was born as a female and sexually abused by the mother's boyfriend at age three, and was subsequently diagnosed with PTSD and depression during early adolescence. He was eventually found to be suffering from DID while receiving outpatient therapy for PTSD and depression.

While a female this patient received testosterone therapy to facilitate a gender transition, and during this time identified having six personalities, most of whom were the male gender. Monique Mun, Mohan Gautam, Renee Maan, and Bassem Krayem, "An Increased Presence of Male Personalities in Dissociative Identity Disorder after Initiating Testosterone Therapy," *Case Reports in Psychiatry* 2020, 8839984 (2020), published online October 5, 2023. Lorenzo Soldati et al., "Gender Dysphoria and Dissociative Identity Disorder: A Case Report and Review of Literature," *Sexual Medicine* 10, no. 5 (2022), 100553.doi: 10.1016/j.esxm.2022. 100553, epub August 20, 2022.

Acknowledgements

There are many individuals who have helped me with this project. In my first book, THE JAMES TAPES Book One, I acknowledged the camera and production work accomplished by the members of the audio-visual production team, Jim Wright, Dick Shackleford, and Karla Westmoreland at the Topeka VA Medical Center where James was a patient. I also acknowledged the assistance of Dr. Donald Rinsley, my consultant at the VA medical center and co-author of two papers about the case. After I left the Topeka VA MC there were a number of others who assisted me. Dr. Bernie Berkowitz, the Chief of Psychiatry at Bay Pines VA medical center, enabled me to obtain grant funds to buy back the videocassettes that were being held at the Topeka VA. Dr. Harold Voth, the Topeka VA Chief of Staff, subsequently facilitated the shipment of these cassettes to Bay Pines VA where I was a member of the medical staff. After I left the VA system my stepson Derek Kershner spent many hours using special viewing equipment over a period of two years to convert all 255 videocassettes to DVDs. I'm thankful to Patricia Chong, a talented graphic designer who helped design the cover of Book One as well as the cover of Book Two. My wife, Jackie has given me a great deal of support and read early versions of the manuscript before I sent it to my skilled editor Linda Ingerly. She has been enormously helpful with her creative ideas, attention to detail, and detailed work during final preparation and submission to the publishing company.

About the Author

Dr. Joel Osler Brende is a graduate of Luther College, Decorah, Iowa, the University of Minnesota Medical School, and the Karl Menninger School of Psychiatry in Topeka, Kansas. Prior to entering his chosen medical specialty of psychiatry, he practiced general medicine for six years initially in St. Croix Falls, Wisconsin and Littlefork /International Falls, Minnesota. Upon completing his residency training in psychiatry, Dr. Brende served our nation's veterans for eighteen years in the VA healthcare system and was an early pioneer in the diagnosis and treatment of Vietnam veterans with post-traumatic stress disorder.

He spent the last ten years of his lengthy professional career in academic medicine and retired as chairman of the Department of Psychiatry and Behavioral Sciences at Mercer University School of Medicine, Macon, Georgia in 2005. However, he later practiced hospital psychiatry part time for ten years, until he retired from Mosaic Health Care in St. Joseph, Missouri in January 2018.

Dr. Brende is a diplomate of the American Board of Psychiatry and Neurology and a Distinguished Fellow of the American Psychiatric Association. As a prolific scholar and researcher, he has a total of sixty-eight publications to his credit. He has authored or co-authored four books and two online books, eleven book chapters, twenty-one peer-reviewed journal articles, nine non-peer-reviewed articles, four electronic media articles and eighteen self-published recovery workbooks. Two of his books are *Vietnam Veterans, the Road to Recovery* and *The James Tapes*. Three of his book chapters are "A Case of Multiple Personality with Psychological Automatisms," "Physiological Manifestations of Dissociation," and "Dissociative Disorders in Vietnam Combat Veterans."

Music has always been an important in his life, originally playing the euphonium before switching to trombone in college. He resumed playing sixteen years ago and is now quite active musically as a member of a concert band and several local jazz groups.

www.ingramcontent.com/pod-product-compliance
Lightning Source LLC
Chambersburg PA
CBHW051710020426
42333CB00014B/918